HITTING ACROSS
THE LINE

HITTING ACROSS THE LINE

An Autobiography

VIV RICHARDS

BCA
LONDON · NEW YORK · SYDNEY · TORONTO

This edition published 1991
by BCA
by arrangement with
HEADLINE BOOK PUBLISHING PLC

CN 2928

First published in 1991
by HEADLINE BOOK PUBLISHING PLC

10 9 8 7 6 5 4 3 2 1

The publishers are grateful to Don Charles for his help in
tracing photographs and to the following sources for other
illustrations used in this book:
Allsport Photographic, Rex Features, Alain Lockyer,
Syndication International, David Munden, Patrick Eagar,
Eric Coombes of *The Somerset County Gazette*, *The Cricketer*.

Statistics provided by Richard Lockwood

Produced by Lennard Books
Mackerye End, Harpenden, Herts

Printed and bound in Great Britain by
Richard Clay Ltd, Bungay, Suffolk

CONTENTS

Acknowledgement

My thanks to Mick Middles who helped to record my thoughts and memories, adding his own observations along the way.
Many of the chapters are introduced with his descriptions of the settings within which this book was created.

PROLOGUE

6th March 1991 – Sabina Park, Jamaica
Although a day lost to rain has ruined any chance
of a result in this first Test against Australia, the
West Indian early-order batsmen have made amends
for a disappointing first innings. After an opening
stand of 114 between Gordon Greenidge and
Desmond Haynes, Richie Richardson continues to
restore West Indies pride. On the departure of Carl
Hooper, he is joined by his captain, Viv Richards,
who has earlier queried the wisdom of continuing a
'dead' game on a dangerous pitch.

The match may be dead but the crowd is alive
with excitement at the prospect of witnessing an
historic moment in West Indian cricket history. Viv
Richards needs 32 runs to pass Gary Sobers's record
aggregate in Test cricket. Reluctant to be out there
at all Viv starts cautiously with little regard for
record-breaking. As he nears the required total
Clive Lloyd, in the commentary box, prepares the
crowd for the great moment. Almost without seeming
to be aware that he is making history Viv Richards
passes the record.

The noise around the ground the reminds him
of the landmark that he has reached and somewhat
as an afterthought he raises his bat in
acknowledgement. To Viv the real satisfaction is
not as much in becoming the new recod-holder as in
having provided a reward for those who have stayed
to watch the match draw to its inevitable conclusion.

Viv Richards, master batsman, record-breaker
and cricketing entertainer has once again given the
crowd their money's worth and sent them home
happy, with a tale to tell.

WEST INDIES vs. AUSTRALIA (First Test)
at Sabina Park, Kingston on 1st, 2nd, 3rd, 5th, 6th March 1991
Toss: West Indies. Umpires: D. M. Archer and S. Bucknor
Match drawn

WEST INDIES

Batsman	Dismissal	Runs	Dismissal (2nd)	Runs (2nd)
C.G. Greenidge	c and b McDermott	27	c Healy b McDermott	35
D.L. Haynes	b McDermott	9	c Healy b McDermott	84
R.B. Richardson	c Healy b Hughes	15	not out	104
C.L. Hooper	c Marsh b Hughes	0	b McDermott	31
I.V.A. Richards*	c Hughes b McDermott	11	not out	52
A.L. Logie	not out	77		
P.J.L. Dujon+	c Marsh b Hughes	59		
M.D. Marshall	lbw b McDermott	0		
C.E.L. Ambrose	c and b Waugh	33		
C.A. Walsh	lbw b McDermott	10		
B.P. Patterson	b Hughes	4		
Extras	(lb 6,w 1,nb 13)	20	(b 15,lb 6,w 1,nb 6)	28
TOTAL		264	(for 3 wkts)	334

AUSTRALIA

Batsman	Dismissal	Runs
G.R. Marsh	c Dujon b Ambrose	69
M.A. Taylor	c Hooper b Patterson	58
D.C. Boon	not out	109
A.R. Border*	c Dujon b Ambrose	31
D.M. Jones	c and b Hooper	0
M.E. Waugh	lbw b Marshall	39
G.R.J. Matthews	c Dujon b Patterson	10
I.A. Healy+	lbw b Walsh	0
C.J. McDermott	b Patterson	1
M.G. Hughes	c Hooper b Patterson	0
M.R. Whitney	b Patterson	2
Extras	(b 4,lb 23,w 4,nb 21)	52
TOTAL		371

AUSTRALIA	O	M	R	W	O	M	R	W
McDermott	23	3	80	5	24	10	48	3
Whitney	21	4	58	0	17	3	55	0
Hughes	21.3	4	67	4	22	5	79	0
Matthews	11	2	28	0	25	2	90	0
Waugh	6	1	25	1	13	6	20	0
Border					9	2	21	0

WEST INDIES	O	M	R	W	O	M	R	W
Ambrose	30	3	94	2				
Patterson	24	1	83	5				
Walsh	23	4	73	1				
Marshall	22	3	57	1				
Hooper	21	7	37	1				

FALL OF WICKETS

	WI	AUS	WI	AUS
1st	33	139	118	
2nd	37	159	134	
3rd	57	227	216	
4th	68	228		
5th	75	329		
6th	75	357		
7th	144	358		
8th	166	365		
9th	234	365		
10th	264	371		

THE YOUNG
ANTIGUAN

November 1990. Darcy's Bar, St John's, Antigua. Feet embedded in large white trainers, torso proudly sporting a black Bob Marley T-shirt, the young Rastafarian swaggers along the shop-lined street. To naive tourists, who trickle continuously, if nervously, through the bustle of mid-day St John's, the Rastafarian might seem rather intimidating. But this is an illusion, be it intentional or otherwise. The Rastafarian is quite blind to tourism, immersed as he is, in the complexities of local society. The tourists, equally, seem rather blind to this web of life. True enough, they like to feel as though they are tasting the culture of the Caribbean, but more often than not they prefer to drift idly about the gift shops and café bars.

As they sit, drinking Red Stripe lager or ostentatious cocktails, Antiguan daylife pulsates all around them. But it is not within their vision, it is in the supermarket next door, or the dilapidated chemist's shop on the corner, or down in the market. However, although this divide seems, at all times, massive and unbridgable, it is a far from unhappy separation. On the contrary, both sides of the divide co-exist quite harmoniously. Whatever problems, financial, social or political, Antigua may face, the prevailing atmosphere is one of contentment. And if the tourists really do wish to step out of 'themed Antigua' to sample genuine local life they are welcomed with open arms.

This crossover is particularly successful if the tourist is prepared to spend endless hours chatting about sport. For sport is the lifeblood of Antigua, especially among the young or young at heart. It permeates everywhere – on street corners, in bars, in taxis. Sporting gossip can bring traffic to a standstill; it can make the participants very late for important meetings; it can cause shop tills to cease ringing. Sport is all important. It crashes through the barriers of race, religion, class and age. Amongst the locals, of course, sporting chat is delivered at great speed and they seem happy for it to remain completely unfathomable to the casual listener from foreign parts. However, this mysterious dialect can be dispensed with instantly if an outsider is to be welcomed into the conversation.

The Rastafarian wanders past the faded pinkness of Darcy's Bar. The bar is a silent oasis in the centre of this ever lively city. It is patrolled by lizards and seems to attract only those who are in the most desperate throes of thirst. But today this silence is savagely ripped apart by the sudden shriek of a transistor radio. An excitable, disembodied voice snaps through the atmosphere. The bar man shakes his head sadly, as the news from Pakistan begins to register. The West Indies cricket team, on tour in that most difficult of lands, seems to be in all kinds of trouble. Things will improve over the coming weeks but, for the moment, the sports crazy people of the Caribbean are united in thought with the despondent commentator:

'...and, as the Windies seem to be at their lowest ebb for a decade, it must be said that Viv Richards, who is at home in Antigua recovering from an operation, is more than a little conspicuous by his absence.'

Across the dusty street a Range Rover pulls to a careful halt. From inside, the face of Antigua's most famous sporting legend, Viv Richards, can be seen casting a reflective glance towards the bar. 'Man, when I used to work in there, that place was kickin',' he states, and his concentration is only broken by the constant car horns and demands for attention which punctuate his every public moment on the island. On noticing this scene, the Rastafarian spins around in delight. His hand rises in acknowledgement, and for once his profound dialect needs no decoding. "HEEY MAASTER BLAASTER!"

Viv Richards is in his natural habitat, happy to be away from the spotlight, if only for a month or so. After which he will reunite with a remarkable career path, heading, hopefully, towards a climactic final three years. But despite being, so many times, at the epicentre of a raging controversy, he has never really taken time out to explain his side of the story. Viv Richards has much to say.

I could not possibly begin this book without immediately talking about my parents. Today I can feel really proud in the knowledge that I had the kind of parents who had the foresight necessary to shape me and prepare me for what turned out to be an extremely unusual kind of lifestyle. They provided me with a very pure upbringing, which may not be all that fashionable today, but I now realise that they made it possible for me to build upon that family base. I owe everything to them.

I was very fortunate in having a mother and father who not only went to, and believed in, the Anglican church but were extremely involved in church activities like Sunday school. I am not saying that I was an angel, far from it in fact, but, in time, I did come to understand the importance of living in such a family. I even sang in the choir at one period.

I grew up very much under the influence of my father. He was a proud man, and a disciplinarian, and it was the sheer power of his presence that initially shaped my approach towards life. He was acting-Superintendent at the local prison in St John's. It was a tough job which required a good deal of self-control, and I think it is fair to say that he did bring a little of his attitude towards work home with him.

Looking back, I feel that I was extremely fortunate to be subjected to his discipline. I certainly did not lose out because of it even if I did not see it that way at the time. On many occasions I disliked having to buckle down to his way of thinking. I thought he was just too direct, but then I was blind to what he was trying to do.

I suppose, in my childish way, I resented the prison and the effect it had on our everyday life. I am not saying that he was a rough man, but he was an individual who was conditioned to living in a very military kind of way. There were all kinds of little things, details, which he impressed upon me and which I now think were very important. I always had to be tidy, my shoes immaculate, that kind of thing. I am certain that, had he not instilled that discipline in me, I would never have reached as far as I did in life. I will be eternally grateful for that. I think that my father understands and accepts my gratitude.

My mother, equally, was always a great believer in discipline, although she was quieter and always used a more subtle approach. But, in her own way, she was just as strong, just as influential.

We were brought up in a basic Antiguan wooden house. That might sound as if we were poor, but that was never the case. We were not, in any sense, poverty-stricken. My father always had a good job. To be a civil servant, as he was, in those days gave you some form of social standing and provided you with a feeling of security.

They were strange times in Antigua. In areas like ours, you would encounter so many different standards of living. Poverty and wealth seemed to co-exist quite happily. We lived in an area that was pretty much 'in town', right at the centre of everything. I can remember having a few fairly hard times, when my father would want to buy something for the house but would not be able to afford it on his civil servant's salary. But he always made sure that we had the essential things in life. We always had plenty of food – always had cornflakes in the morning. There was never any doubt that we would be able to eat and be comfortable. That might not sound like much, especially these days, but it meant that we had a higher quality of life than many of our neighbours.

I was not particularly successful at school, to say the least. At first I went to St John's Boys School, which was a basic, honest, open school – no different, really, from junior schools across the world. After that, I attended Antigua Grammar School.

I was only really interested in the sports side of things and, to my delight, my father encouraged me in this. Mind you, he was a sports fanatic himself. He was an excellent footballer and cricketer, and the happiest photographs of him seem to have been taken when he was playing cricket. He was the father of four sons – Mervyn, Donald, David and myself – and took great delight in playing cricket with us. And it *was* mostly cricket that we played, because our back yard was not big enough for football. All we had was this little strip of land, a yard which became a little cricket pitch of our own.

I think that I was no different from any other kid growing up in Antigua. Everyone of that age seemed to be heavily involved in sport. In a sense it was expected of them. As they grew older, most would draw away from sport and start trying to establish themselves in a career. But sport was where they learned to get along with other people and where they learned some kind of discipline.

I loved those knockabouts with my father. He was a sporting hero of mine. After all, he did play a lot of cricket for Antigua, which did make him something of a local star and he often brought home his bats for us to play with.

I remain very proud of my father's achievements in cricket. Mainly because I know that my own talent is something that has been passed down. I am always glad when I hear the guys talking who played or watched cricket in his era. What they see in me today, either batting or bowling, they saw in him long ago. It is fascinating to me because they pick out bits of my game which, apparently, are identical to the way my father played. It makes me feel good to know that people still think that highly of him.

He was an unusual character in many ways, and his approach to cricket reflected his individualism. He was an all-rounder, which was not so fashionable in those days, but for him it was natural. He wanted to work hard. He had this tremendous power within him, this massive self-confidence, and felt that he was capable of doing anything and everything. Most cricketers in his day wanted to specialise in one area, and then use the rest of the game to relax a little. But my father wanted to do it all.

At Antigua Grammar, I began to follow in my father's footsteps. Like him, I had a natural tendency to want to be involved in all aspects of the game. It was very fashionable, even in those days, for a boy to want to become a macho fast bowler, but I bowled slow off-breaks. I did receive a certain amount of criticism for my bowling which was not helped by the very uneven pitches we played on. Eventually I decided to devote more of my time to batting. This was not part of some great plan for the future. At that time, around the age of eleven, I saw myself as no more than an average young cricketer.

We never had any facilities that we could depend on. We had no groundsman. We had to do our own rolling. If we wanted a game, we had to go and prepare our own pitch. Sometimes we had to make one from nothing, the two teams helping out to clear away some patch of waste ground. It could be any piece of land, most of the time we never bothered to check out who the owner was. It was quite hard work, too, preparing a roughly playable cricket pitch in those temperatures.

The night before the game, we would wet the strip and just hope that the cows did not move in overnight. Quite often in the morning we had push them off with our own hands, then shovel up the cow dung and fill in the hoof marks. If we found hoof marks on the wicket, and we often did, we tried to roll them out, but the ball could still bounce anywhere – and I mean *anywhere*.

At the time we did not know it, but the total unpredictability of those pitches provided us with the best possible cricket training. For a start, we hardly had any protection at all. Much of the time we wore home-made pads, fashioned from cardboard or the like. Sometimes we had no proper bats, and wicket-keepers had to risk all kinds of injuries because they had so little protection.

It was madness in a way, and it was certainly some of the most dangerous cricket I have ever played, but it gave us a real sharpness. Wherever you were playing, you really could not afford to lose concentration for one second.

When I think of young English cricketers, all training on perfect, slow, springy pitches, they are learning a completely different game. We were learning to be sharp, to be attentive in order to survive. It was far more than just a quiet afternoon's game of cricket. Even in those days the competition was fierce and, as I have stated, the pitches only served to add to the volatile nature of our game.

The player in most danger was the the batsman. He just had to be able to see the ball at a very early stage. The ball would move all over the place. It was full of surprising bounces. It made the batsman instinctively want to go for the big hit, to get rid of the thing. Playing defensively was pretty pointless and just as dangerous, so the batsman might as well try to hit the ball into the surrounding undergrowth. The hook shot was a particular favourite. And there was no point in telling a batsman not to hit across the line, in fact that was the way everyone *had* to play.

It was not the most beautiful cricket ever played. Sometimes it was far too frantic, but it was certainly exciting. I can't imagine how a cricketer in, say, England could possibly have received such valuable training. Just think, not only were we playing against the unpredictable bounce but we also had very little protection. It helped us to develop a natural sense of judgment. It gave us an awareness. It made us streetwise and set us apart. If you compare our game with the English game where they cover a young cricketer in all kinds of padding and put him in to bat on a perfectly predictable pitch, there is no way he is going to develop the same degree of skill. We were given this sense of survival. It came from our relative poverty, and it provided us with something that no other young cricketers in the more developed world could possibly experience. It was, and continues to be, the basis of the West Indian cricketing philosophy.

We also played beach cricket, which was a different game altogether. The accent was on fun, and we played to a different set of rules using tennis balls or little sponge balls.

The beach was another great learning ground. The batsman could make the most perfect defensive stroke imaginable, but if the ball bounced once, and the fielder caught it, he was out. So he had to play really cautiously. He had to know just the right time to break his wrists, to stop it dead. Standing up close to him he had a mass of fielders. There were no limits to how many could play beach cricket, and there were times when twenty or more fielders would be hovering around the batsman.

I remember this scene well. It left you with two options. You had to be so cautious. Either you played an immaculate, uncatchable defensive stroke, or you really hit out. You had to make this decision very early in each delivery, and go for one shot or the other. A moment's hesitation and you were lost. Most times, when you hit out, you tried to hit the ball as far as possible into the surf. Then it was the task of the bowler, not the fielders, to swim out and retrieve it. The problem was that many bowlers just could not swim and the ball, if you really hit it, would be fifty or sixty yards out. More often than not the game would simply halt there and then and dissolve in one big argument. The bowler would scream, 'Can't swim!' To which would come the stinging reply, 'If you can't swim, don't play cricket.'

I became captain of the Antigua Grammar School team at around the age of sixteen. I think it is fair to say that I was a little bit wild, especially as a batsman. I did have a few huge innings, but quite often my recklessness would cause me to be needlessly caught. When I was at the crease I found I had this aggressive urge within me to hit out at everything. It was not easy to contain it. Some people would say that this urge has never left me, has never been fully disciplined. That may be so, but I do not feel it is necessarily a bad thing. At Antigua Grammar I was determined not to listen to the schoolmaster who told me, again and again, not to hit 'across the line'. I would like to have complied, but I just had to play my natural game.

I had no particularly high opinion of myself. At that time I thought my brother, Mervyn, was a more naturally gifted cricketer than I was. I could never get to play the shots quite as well as him. But he was not so single-minded about sport. He had a lot of different interests and liked to pursue them all.

At one time, for instance, he was representing Antigua at cricket and was also part of a singing group called The Mindreaders. Antigua were playing in Nevis in a Leeward Islands tournament and Mervyn actually wanted to travel home after a day's cricket so he could sing with the group in the evening then return to Nevis, and the cricket, the next day.

I could not understand how anyone could want to do that. I would never, in a million years, even dream of doing such a thing. I was worried about him wasting his talent and thought he should make his mind up, once and for all, about what he really wanted to do. After all, there were many truly dedicated people who would have given anything to have got a place in that Antiguan team.

Mervyn was also one of the best footballers around. But even though he played well, certainly better than me, he never really had that passion, that single-minded ambition. He wanted fun, and everybody loved him for it, but it meant he was never serious about anything. He was also involved in drama and would have made an excellent television comic. He loved to imitate people, and to this day he has kept his happy-go-lucky nature. He now works as a supervisor for Northern Telecom and still enjoys his life. He is much cleverer than me and much better at practical things. Even when we were boys, if the radio was not working, he would be there with his screwdriver. I was the opposite, I had no interest in such things at all. I was hopeless at them...and still am. While Mervyn can fix anything, I can't even set the video, or wire a plug. In this sense, there is only one way of saying it. I am bloody hopeless...DIY drives me nutty.

Like Mervyn I also played an awful lot of soccer. I loved the flow and pace of the game and, like most of the kids in Antigua, I quickly became a 'soccer expert'. Initially I played for the local team, The Ovals, but I did get to play quite seriously and even finished by playing for the Antigua national team in the qualifying rounds of the World Cup. For a while my sporting life was evenly divided between cricket and soccer. I had no idea which one to pursue. Many times I found myself having to pull out of a cricket match because I had a more important soccer game...and many times the opposite would happen. My loyalties were equally divided, and soon a day came when I had to make a big decision, probably the biggest decison of my life. I sat down with all my folks to talk it over.

It was my father who really made the decision. He stated, very simply, that he had never heard the West Indian football team on the radio. If there was a good deal of soccer talent in the Caribbean, which there obviously was, and still is, then something must be very wrong with the soccer system. What happens to all this talent? There are no local football heroes to match the likes of Gary Sobers or Everton Weekes.

I had to agree. There was another aspect to consider. As a kid, I had spent many years being totally mesmerised by the cricket commentaries on the radio. There was a certain magic about cricket that was lacking in soccer, not least because we were not a world force in soccer. I could listen, completely spellbound, to commentaries by John Arlott. As I sat in my room I could really feel the atmosphere and Arlott, through his knowledge and deep love of the game, managed to transmit the utter magic of Test cricket through to me. He was a massive influence. When he described the atmosphere from, say, Lord's, the

Mecca of cricket, it sounded like heaven. Looking back now, it might seem that there was no argument. It had to be cricket over soccer. However, at the time I was very confused.

The strange thing about this debate was that, although we all treated my decision as if it was a matter of the utmost urgency, we did not really see cricket as a future career. We talked about it, but in the family we had other priorities which had to be sorted out.

It was a very unsettled period at home. My father was not happy in the prison service. He was, at all times, a fairly outspoken man. He did not believe in tact. He was very straight and very honest too, but those qualities, however admirable, do not always help a man in his career. His refusal to toe the official line meant that he was moved around a lot. Although he knew more about prison security than anyone around, the authorities sent him off to do the book-keeping at the hospital, or work in the post office, things like that. He was constantly moved on and found this increasingly hard to take. Finally it made him decide to go to America.

It was a decision which I could feel him moving towards and, frankly, the prospect appalled me. Most of our relatives were living in America and he wanted me to go with him. He had this idea that I would be able to develop as an electrical engineer. I knew this was not for me and I was determined not to move. It led to arguments, and we fell out quite badly.

Although he had always encouraged my sport he could not see it as a career. I cannot say I blamed him for this. He, after all, had been a better cricketer than I ever thought I would be. So how could I make a go of it? He always said the same thing. I can hear him now.

'CRICKET BALLS CAN'T COOK! WHAT ARE YOU

GOING TO EAT?'

Although it was quite a sensible statement I thought he was being totally unreasonable. When my parents finally did leave, I stayed behind with my grandmother. I knew that going to America was never going to be my cup of tea. The prospect of living in a land so huge, so alien, terrified me. More importantly, I knew that they did not play cricket in the States.

So I had no doubts about making the decision to stay on the island. Cricket was becoming my life, even though I was not paid for playing. I felt emotionally tied to the sport and it would have broken my heart to leave it. I know it hurt my father, but I had to go with my passion.

There was one other reason for staying. My girlfriend, Miriam. We first met when I was just eight years old, then, as friends, we grew to know and rely upon each other more and more. She knew everything about sport. She grew up with it and had two brothers who were part of the same school soccer team as me. Whenever I went round to her house, the talk was always of sport. She came to the matches and was almost as obsessed and single-minded as we were.

Although I fell in love with Miriam at a very early age, how could I have realised how absolutely perfect she was for me? And how incredibly fortunate I was to have someone so close, someone with whom I could share an extraordinary life, from such an early age. Not only did she understand sport, she grew to understand the demands made on someone who chooses a sporting lifestyle. I could never be big-headed or 'showy' with her. There would never be any point. Miriam knew the basic Vivian.

Even though we did not get married until 1981, our relationship is almost lifelong. Throughout this story Miriam's presence remains a constant if often unmentioned force for good.

However, for a young Antiguan, an inspiring girlfriend and a desire to perform well in sport were not enough. Reluctantly, at the same time as my father was struggling with his own work, I began to try and earn some sort of living. My first job was at Darcy's Bar in St John's. It was a really lively little place and, with tips, I would bring home a full ten pounds a week. It made me proud to be able to contribute towards the family upkeep. But even that job had come about as a result of cricket. The owner was a keen cricket supporter and wanted to help me in my game. I think he thought it would benefit my game if I had this safe job where he could keep an eye on me.

I was not a particularly good barman. In fact I spent most of my days dreaming about some legendary innings or other – probably like every other young man in the West Indies. While I was serving cold beer, in my head I would be Gary Sobers. Back in tedious reality, I also toyed with the idea of becoming an apprentice mechanic. A cousin tried to convince me that if I spent time working on cars, I might one day be able to graduate into engineering. Frankly I think I would have made a pretty lousy engineer. I really was not much good at anything non-athletic. I would always be dreaming of cricket.

It is difficult for me now to remember just how far I saw myself going in cricket. Perhaps I thought that I might just be able to eclipse my father's achievements in the game. Meanwhile, as time went by, more and more people were saying that one day I would play for the Leeward Islands. The further prospect of playing for the West Indies was something which I did not dare to contemplate too seriously. Deep down, I think I really did believe that it could happen. But doesn't every young cricketer have similar thoughts? It is natural for all boys who play sport to develop a certain confidence in their abilities. Then they look ahead, and dream about taking it all the way. However, in their own little sporting circle, how can they possibly know how good they really are, or how close they might get to becoming an international sportsman.

It is strange to reflect on these things, on the fates of others and on my own future, then unknown. For myself, as I look back now, part of me thinks that it was all meant to happen. But then, I wonder, how many people there are who have the talent and the ambition, but don't make it because of some quirk of fate which is no fault of their own. When people charge me with arrogance, they do not really know me at all. Deep down I *know* that I have been lucky. I know how close I came to settling for a much more mundane kind of life. It could all have been so different.

In the days of my youth, Antigua was a sporting backwater. Nobody expected this little island to produce sportsmen of international standard. It was a dream that may have been in the heads of kids like myself but, other than that, nobody ever entertained such a notion.

At the start of the 1968 season, when I was just seventeen, I played in probably my most important cricket match to that date. It was important because it taught me one mighty lesson and helped to curb my arrogance, which I must admit was pretty rampant at the time. I had become the cricket wonder-boy of the island. Old men in bars would talk about my game, and I suppose I had attained the status of a very minor celebrity. Not because I particularly deserved to be talked about, but because the island was just bonkers about sport. It was the easiest way to make some kind of name for yourself. I was sharp but I was over-confident and felt I could compete against anybody.

Those Leeward Islands Tournament games were very well attended. Even the smaller, local matches drew crowds of about 4,000 and the atmosphere was really intense. We were playing the neighbouring island of St Kitts. The local-derby atmosphere went to my head and I began verbally attacking the St Kitts bowlers. I sauntered out at number three, feeling very cocky indeed. It was one of those moments which many cricketers dream about. I was living my own drama. But, on the very first ball, they appealed for a catch at short-leg. There was no way I had hit that ball, but the umpire gave me out.

I was outraged. For a while I just stared at the umpire. Then I stamped my foot and, very slowly, I thumped my bat on the turf. Then, before walking off, I remained for a few more moments at the crease, in some kind of enraged contemplation. By this time the crowd must have sensed that something was very wrong. After watching my reaction they leapt onto the field and began to demonstrate. Within minutes they were holding placards saying, 'NO VIV NO MATCH'.

It was a weird situation and all I could do was to keep looking up at the jail, which was next to the ground. I was looking for my father. I knew damn well that he would be there and would be very aware that something had gone wrong. Then something extraordinary happened. The authorities, instead of standing behind the umpire's decision and ordering the match to continue, as they should have done, asked me to go back in and bat again. In this way, they thought, peace would be restored to the ground.

Had I been a more experienced player, I think I would have refused to go back. But go back I did. Then, the real irony, I was out immediately without scoring. In the second innings, I scored yet another duck. I don't think there are many people who can boast three ducks in two innings.

After the match, I expected there would be some kind of punishment for me. After all, I had behaved very badly at the crease. On the other hand it was the authorities who had asked me to go back in to bat. What these same authorities did was to ban me for two years. I could not believe it. They did not even have the courtesy to tell me to my face. I heard about the ban on the local radio.

The incident became front-page news in Antigua. Almost immediately I was cast as a bad sportsman and people began to make nasty remarks, not just to me, in fact rarely to me, but to the rest of my family. It was an intense kind of hatred. People shouted abuse at our house from the street.

I went under for a while and refused go out. It was a truly horrible time but I think it explains something about the intensity of passion which is reserved for cricket in the West Indies. It is something that many people in England cannot understand.

I said that it was a very important match for me, and so it was because it helped to build my character. I knew that I had been treated very shoddily and I set out to prove the authorities wrong. I was determined to be seen as a good sportsman and a good cricketer. I was fired with a new-found enthusiasm which I am sure was more healthy than the blind youthful arrogance I had felt before that match. I had to fight to get back to the top. It was not easy to regain the support of the local crowd, but regain it I would. I had become a wiser person and would become a much better player.

DARK DAYS, COLD NIGHTS

B efore, as I saw it, blasting my way back into the spotlight of Antiguan cricket, I had to work out my two-year ban. I played basketball, boxed a little, played soccer and, needless to say, more than a little unofficial cricket, on a beach and elsewhere.

When the ban was over I set about getting back into cricket. I had a fierce appetite for the game and it was not long before the men in the bars were once again talking about Viv Richards. This time, as I will explain, I had really given them something to talk about.

In 1972 I went to England for the first time. A voluntary committee in Antigua decided to send me and Andy Roberts, another promising youngster, to a coaching school in England. Andy was a year older than me but we were good friends and had been playing together in the Leeward Islands team in the 1971-72 season. The build-up to this trip was a moving experience. The people of Antigua, who had obviously forgiven me, organised many functions such as barbecues and dances to raise the money to send us. This, in itself, helped to increase my determination. When such faith is placed in you, how can you possibly give less than one hundred per cent? And yet, even at this stage, it looked more likely that I would become an engineer, or at least something other than a cricketer. My parents still wanted me to go to New York.

I went to England full of optimism. I had been

WINDWARD ISLANDS vs. LEEWARD ISLANDS
at Roseau, Dominica on 15th, 16th, 17th January 1972
Leeward Islands won by 4 wickets

WINDWARD ISLANDS

D. Haynes	c Hector b Roberts	0	c Allen J.C. b Willett		36
L.C. Sebastien	c Hector b Allen G.R.	22	c Hector bWillett		6
I.T. Shillingford*	c Allen J.C. b Willett	20	c Greenaway b Gould		47
C. Browne	st Hector b Willett	0	st Hector b Gould		0
R. Polius	c Gould b Willett	0	st Hector b Willett		1
T.M. Findlay+	c Hector b Gould	22	lbw b Allen G.R.		57
M.L. Francis	b Carter	25	b Willett		16
N. Philip	not out	60	c Amory b Gould		11
G.C. Shillingford	lbw b Willett	0	c Gould b Carter		16
D. Defoe	b Willett	0	not out		34
J.G. Gibbs	c Hector bWillett	8	c Amory bAllen G.R.		0
Extras	(lb 2,nb 3)	5	(b 8,lb 7,w 5,nb 1)		21
TOTAL		163			265

LEEWARD ISLANDS

V.A. Amory	c Haynes b Gibbs	39	c Browne b Francis	31
S. Greenaway	b Defoe	2	b Shillingford G.C.	2
L.C. Sergeant	c Findlay b Gibbs	61	not out	37
I.V.A. Richards	st Findlay b Gibbs	20	c Shillingford I.T. b Francis	26
J.C. Allen	st Findlay b Gibbs	1	c Polius b Gibbs	82
G.R. Allen	run out	43	c Findlay b Shillingford G.C.	20
A. Hector*+	c Shillingford I.T. b Gibbs	8	b Francis	18
G. Gould	c Findlay b Gibbs	0		
E.T. Willett	st Findlay b Gibbs	12		
A.M.E. Roberts	c Findlay b Defoe	6	(8) not out	6
E. Carter	not out	0		
Extras	(lb 2,nb 2)	4	(b 1,lb 7,w 1,nb 2)	11
TOTAL		196	(for 6 wkts)	233

LEEWARDS	O	M	R	W	O	M	R	W
Roberts	12	6	13	1	7	3	12	0
Carter	20	8	43	1	9	2	23	1
Willett	30.1	7	72	6	44	13	106	4
Allen G.R.	12	8	7	1	21.2	12	27	2
Gould	3	0	23	1	26	6	67	3
Richards					1	0	9	0

WINDWARDS	O	M	R	W	O	M	R	W
Shillingford G.C.	13	5	28	0	18.1	5	41	2
Philip	13	2	26	0	11	3	26	0
Defoe	11.3	3	32	2	7	2	11	0
Francis	16	3	57	0	29	8	82	3
Gibbs	27	10	49	7	21	1	62	1

FALL OF WICKETS

	WI	LI	WI	LI
1st	4	16	24	10
2nd	42	68	26	55
3rd	42	116	72	132
4th	42	118	103	168
5th	58	127	126	172
6th	71	149	169	224
7th	106	149	192	
8th	107	185	226	
9th	114	196	241	
10th	163	196	265	

making lots of runs in Antigua, and to achieve a trip to the magical homeland of cricket was like seeing a dream come true, or so I thought.

Once I had arrived in England the dream soon faded. Suddenly I realised why everyone back home had given me all those clothes – overcoats, jackets and stuff. It was November and from the moment I stepped out of the airport, I could not believe the ferocity of the coldness. It was something that was totally alien to me. The sun had been present all my life and I had never even contemplated what it would be like without it.

I had never felt so depressed in my life. London was a nightmare to me. Everything seemed drab and grey. Midday seemed like midnight. During that six-week stay, I never really became more than partly acclimatised. I immediately lost all my pocket money and, to this day, I'll swear that the weather was responsible for that. I had my money stuffed in my back pocket but, because of the coldness of my hands, I just couldn't feel anything. I couldn't feel the paper as I fumbled for the notes and must have left several pounds on the pavement or the shop floor. It was more than a culture shock, it was like living on a whole new planet.

Andy and I stayed in a guest-house in Putney owned by a lady from New Zealand. At night, before we went to bed, we had to make sure that we had enough ten-pence pieces in order to keep the meter running all night. This was something that I could not understand. We paid our board and lodging and yet we still had to pay to keep warm. It seemed very unfair, and the fear of not having enough coins was a constant worry. I was convinced that here in London, without constant heat, we would die.

It may not have been as bad as my imagination told me, but it was still freezing. I did not dare get up to go to the toilet. I just lay there until morning. It affected my whole constitution and I felt ill just about all the time. It really was a nightmare for two young Antiguans, with no experience of the world. I had never been so miserable in my life. Many times I just wanted to pack up and go home. I could not envisage myself ever living in such a country, let alone playing a full cricket season there. Then, slowly, I came to realise that it was just one more thing that an individual has to get through. You either walk away from such situations or you decide to face them and get stuck in.

After a while things got better. Andy had a sister in Hackney and she took pity on us and invited us to stay at her place. We were much more comfortable there and, believe me, very grateful to be given some good hot Caribbean food. We also began to meet more of our own people and found that they had experienced the same kind of traumas. Suddenly everything did not seem so bad.

I still found it difficult to adapt to English social habits. Drinking was a particular problem. Some of the British we mixed with just seemed to live for the pub. Back in the Caribbean it was always the night-time that was reserved for drinking but some of the English guys would go to the pub, maybe at midday, and get stuck into pints of lager. I could not cope with that. It would destroy me for the rest of the day and yet these guys seemed to just carry on.

I did eventually get used to going to the pub, maybe to have a Ploughman's Lunch or something, and I began to drink Guinness. I had this notion that Guinness was good for you like the advertisements used to say. I thought to myself, well, if I've got to drink it might as well be a drink that helps me play. That was just another part of my naivety. I don't think it did an awful lot for my health. It was only good for my wobbly legs.

The main purpose of our visit was to attend the Alf Gover Cricket School. This was not at all what I had expected. Back in Antigua, I had been allowed to nurture my natural game. I was surprised to learn just how raw my cricket was. I accepted this but soon found myself rebelling against the coaching. In the West Indies, we had been lucky. The wickets over there are true and coaches did not really see the need to dismantle the natural flow of a player. In England it seemed that they placed far too much value on the text book. They did not seem to want to allow individuality to flourish.

Suddenly I had all these technical things to learn. Alf, to his credit, did help me with my stance. He saw that I was too open and he worked on tightening up my defensive game. It shook me to have to take so much advice. No one had ever told me how to hold a bat before and I began to resent it happening now.

During our stay Andy and I went to Surrey for a trial. The idea was for them to look at us to see if they thought we could do the business in county cricket. We played in front of one of the old wicket-keepers of that era, the late Arthur McIntyre. He watched us and, from the way he was moving his head from side to side, our prospects did not look too good. It was very disappointing. We had expected an enthusiastic response but we were left with our confidence in tatters.

It was, at last, beginning to dawn on me that the game of cricket was not all that easy. There were a lot of technical things to learn. I felt confused and, for the first time in my short cricket career, filled with self-doubt. To this day I do not know how I managed not to go running home to Antigua with my tail between my legs, hastily seeking a career in engineering. What kept me going was something within me, some instinct which told me not to take too much notice of the coaches. I had a feeling that my natural game was, apart from needing the odd refinement, basically correct.

It was dangerous thinking, all the same. Who was I, this inexperienced and untried lad, to challenge the experts? And yet, I think that if I had listened obediently to everything they told me, instead of being selective, my game might well have been stunted at that point. I was lucky to escape. Somehow I had this insight into the true value of coaching. It was important, I decided, but not all that important.

To back up this view, I could look at all the great players of the world. They always seemed so natural and it was obvious to me that they had not learned their craft by studying textbooks. I was strangely aware that I needed coaching to control my natural ability but I was determined not to let them take my basic feel away. Even to this day, I have the same opinion of coaches. They are only useful when they help a player to enhance his own game. They cannot teach the game.

This is one of the perversities of cricket. To play the game, you need a method. This, however, leads too many people into thinking that they can squeeze the essence of the game inside the pages of a textbook. They regard themselves as experts but, in reality, they are only really experts at their own personal game. Their rules do not necessarily apply to other players. I now know many people who have written such books and, when they see a new player who plays completely against their theories they cannot handle it.

It appeals to me that cricket is so indefinable. Coaching is important because it can shape your game, teach you where to improve and where to relax, but it must never be allowed to get out of control. I have never attempted to ridicule coaching. That is something that I have often been accused of, but that is not the case at all. I just feel that we need to be wary of it at the same time as we encourage it. A bad coach can kill a player's game, not just his technique but the joy he gets from playing. That is one thing. Another is that a great player needs a certain amount of freedom to develop if he is to add something unique to the game. By its very nature, coaching can restrict such uniqueness.

When I returned to Antigua after those six weeks in London, I had already started to sift out the important parts of the coaching. I would carry on with my own game. That was my decision. I also had to resist further pressure from my parents who still wanted me to move to New York. They had this idea that I could attend college at night, in New York, and work for a living during the day. But I was still adamant. I just wanted to play cricket.

At this point, and just in the nick of time, an extremely important development in my career took place. I was spotted by Somerset Vice-Chairman Len Creed. He came to Antigua with an international touring side, the Mendip Acorns. Apparently, he had noticed my name after seeing a comment by Colin Cowdrey in *The Cricketer*. At least,

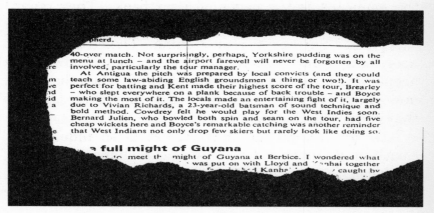

pherd.

40-over match. Not surprisingly, perhaps, Yorkshire pudding was on the menu at lunch — and the airport farewell will never be forgotten by all involved, particularly the tour manager.

At Antigua the pitch was prepared by local convicts (and they could teach some law-abiding English groundsmen a thing or two!). It was perfect for batting and Kent made their highest score of the tour, Brearley — who slept everywhere on a plank because of back trouble — and Boyce making the most of it. The locals made an entertaining fight of it, largely due to Vivian Richards, a 23-year-old batsman of sound technique and bold method. Cowdrey felt he would play for the West Indies soon. Bernard Julien, who bowled both spin and seam on the tour, had five cheap wickets here and Boyce's remarkable catching was another reminder that West Indians not only drop few skiers but rarely look like doing so.

a full might of Guyana

to meet th might of Guyana at Berbice. I wondered what
was put on with Lloyd and hhai together
d Kanha caught by

that is the story that was going round at the time, although I have no idea how Cowdrey might have known about me. I had a meeting with Len at the Blue Waters Hotel on the north side of the island. I was a little nervous because I had heard that Len tended to 'discover' rather too many cricketers. I must admit that, although I could respect him as a person, it seemed to me that he knew very little about cricket. He talked a good game and obviously he had seen a lot of good cricket. But I quickly became convinced that he knew nothing about the refined areas of the game. He could only see part of the chess match that is cricket and so, although he knew a lot about the individual skills of players, he was unable to place them in the full context of a game. That's just my opinion, of course.

What he did have, as a professional bookmaker, was a certain gambler's skill. He decided to take a gamble with me and, as it happens, it paid off. But I don't honestly think he really foresaw my future. He didn't discover *me* so much as 'a young player'.   In other words he was determined to discover someone and if it had not been me it would have been someone else. So, although I will be forever thankful to him, I still feel that he just got lucky.

I remember several funny incidents from the game he came to see. It was a strange game and, as I said, I was feeling a little nervous. I wanted so much to impress him with my batting that, of course, the inevitable happened. I was stumped off Underwood. I remember going forward to drive at a delivery which was far quicker than I had anticipated. The ball spun away and, like an amateur, I was well and truly stranded. To my utter amazement the umpire did not call me out. He knew, and so did the crowd, about this English guy coming to see me. So he gave me a reprieve. However, I was so tense that the shots would not flow at all. I struggled to reach 24, but it wasn't a particularly elegant innings. After it I felt as though I had let down not only myself but the whole of Antigua. They had given me every chance to prove myself and I had failed.

Later, after thinking that I had blown it, I began to relax a little and I did great things in the field. My self-confidence seemed to have returned and, most notably, I remember catching the ball and flicking it back to the stumps in one flowing movement, in the true West Indian way. I began to play really well and ran a few people out. I was still sure that I had blown it but Len Creed obviously felt differently. He decided to book my passage back to England.

I had clearly arrived at a crossroads in my life, and it worried me. On the one hand my parents still wanted me to go to New York. Although I had no real desire to go, I did have a fear that I might regret not doing so. On the other hand, after that bad experience with the English climate no amount of persuasion would convince me that in summer things would be much warmer. To make matters worse, I had really been enjoying life in Antigua. I felt happy amongst my friends and, more importantly, I was close to my girlfriend, Miriam. Although I had always dreamed of going to England to play professional cricket, when the reality came into view, I was not sure that I liked the idea.

There was another complication. I had already had discussions about going to play for Oldham in the Lancashire League. Len, however, was persistent. After he left Antigua, and went on to tour the other islands, he kept in touch. He more or less convinced me that I had no choice but to go with him. He put me well and truly off the idea of Oldham. He told me how grey and wet and smoky it was in the north of England. He told me about the mills and the grim living conditions of the locals. Obviously he was exaggerating, but the one thing that really convinced me was when he said, 'The sun never shines up there...it rains all the time.' That really got to me and I decided to give the Oldham idea a miss.

Slowly I was persuaded to go to the West Country. The plan was for me to begin playing with the Lansdown Cricket Club in Bath. This was where I was expected to settle into the routine of the English game. I knew that playing on English wickets would be very different from playing in the West Indies but I did have a certain confidence in myself. I knew I could bat and, whatever else the world might throw at me, I knew how good I was.

It was never going to be easy, all the same. On my flight out to England I felt really anxious and, when I was stopped at Heathrow for not having a work permit, I began to feel very miserable indeed. Thankfully, Len Creed managed to sort the situation out.

Adapting to life in Bath was really difficult. I missed Miriam, of course, and just about everything I loved in Antiguan life. I missed my friends and all that sporting gossip I would get caught up in on every street corner, I missed playing beach cricket and soccer and, of course, I missed the sun. On the plus side, I soon began to love the countryside around Bath and, to this day, I am still fond of the area. Bath itself was a completely new experience. The Georgian crescents, the architecture...I wandered around with my head in the air, amazed that buildings could be so beautiful. There were even times, though not many, when I began to forget about the cold.

There were other pleasures. Jazz music in the pubs, the nightclubs where I would see the pretty local girls and the country inns, a couple of which soon became my favourites. Here, as in Antigua, I discovered that it was possible to get to know people just by talking about cricket. Socially, as well as professionally, cricket was providing the key, or so it seemed.

Still I had to adapt to England in the cricket sense. When I had been over to the Alf Gover School, we had mostly played indoors and we had little chance to play on English wickets. This time, I was straight out onto the turf and immediately faced with all sorts of problems. For a start, I could not feel my hands because of the cold. I had to wash under a hot tap to try and get the blood circulating. As for my feet, it may sound silly, but my feet never felt quite right. One way or another I had all kinds of fitness problems.

This was a new situation for me. I came from a very fit background. All my life I had trained and I was used to feeling really sharp. But I no longer felt like an athlete. I had lost that state of feeling on top of the world, capable of anything. Even when running, I could not seem to flow properly. It was like having a constant mild dose of 'flu.

A really strange thing was that I could not sweat. Back in Antigua, when I played hard, I would soon start to perspire and this was all part of getting the adrenalin going. But at Lansdown I could not sweat. For months I never perspired at all. Because of this I could not tell when I was getting hot nor could I ever feel good about myself.

These experiences gave me enormous respect for all the West Indian cricketers who had preceded me to England. They were already my heroes, but now they became gods. I could not believe how they had managed to overcome so many obstacles.

On top of the fitness problems, we had to play on a wet wicket. It was only as I began to play for Lansdown that I realised the value of some of the things that Alf

Gover had taught me. That six-week course suddenly became immensely valuable to me as I came to terms with the hard truth that my cricket was, whether I was acclimatised or not, very raw indeed.

There was another problem. When I first arrived in Bath I was sent, for obvious reasons, to lodge with a guy from Barbados. All he had to offer, unfortunately, was one tiny room and a smaller, adjoining room where I was supposed to sleep. This was also where he kept his steel drums. Sleep was impossible in that house. All the time he was coming back from late-night parties and dragging his steel drums into the room where I was trying to sleep. I put up with this for a long time but it hardly helped me put my cricket game together.

Finally, I was moved to a more suitable place, the home of Mrs Joan Oliver and her family. They were pleasant people and soon became my friends. At last I was beginning to relax. I also spoke to other people who were going through a similar phase in their lives. I began to see that my misfortunes were partly my fault because I did not prepare myself properly for the day ahead. I was a young lad and, of course, I did not eat very well. Because of this my whole system became tired and the cold made me even worse. I did cook, but not very well. However, slowly but surely, I began to notice that things were getting better. I thought about Antigua in a slightly less painful way. I took time to listen to the older players at Lansdown and I began to adapt.

I remember, in particular, Les Angel who was one of the openers. He had a very quiet, reserved manner and his cautiousness proved to be a good counter to my impulsive nature. He had played for Somerset and his knowledge of the county game was immense. It has been said that Somerset asked him to keep an eye on me, perhaps even groom me for county cricket. If this was true, then it certainly worked. He proved to be an excellent guiding influence.

In time my physical power improved and fairly soon after that I started to earn a reputation with my batting. Obviously I could not earn a living playing club cricket, so Len Creed arranged for me to work as assistant groundsman at Lansdown. I was very grateful for that – I really was – but I probably did not show it. All I wanted to do was play cricket and I suppose it was always obvious that I did not enjoy pushing a heavy roller down the wicket. Looking back, I would say that working as assistant groundsman probably helped me to understand the English wickets a little better. I might have been paid only £1 a day but I was learning all the time, both about the ground and the weather.

As for the future, I still did not know if I stood much of a chance of making it or not. For all I knew, there could have been hundreds of hopefuls like me, possibly far better than me, and very few of them would succeed. I felt insecure and scared. But my game had improved as I came to terms with the damp pitches. Also, I found myself playing against occasional county players and I was encouraged to find that I could hold my own in their company.

The team spirit at Lansdown was excellent. After every Saturday match, home or away, we would meet in the pavilion. There were three teams operating from that base and we would all swap the stories of the day and share each other's successes and failures. I made some great friends during that first year in Bath, among them Shandy Perera, an all-rounder from Ceylon, and a gentleman known as Ian Botham. I liked Ian from the moment we first met, he was so warm and open, just the kind of person

I needed at that point. True enough, and I will come to this later, many English cricketers do tend to be a little cold, but not Ian. We played several matches together that summer and they became the base of a lifelong friendship. I think I knew at the time that it would be a very special kind of relationship.

This all helped me to rebuild my confidence and I began to feel that I had a chance of getting somewhere. I remember, in particular, a couple of innings against Trowbridge, a good team with a sophisticated cricketing attitude. On their ground I hit a century in 76 minutes and back at Lansdown I smashed my way to 146 not out. I hit a number of sixes on that day and, once again, it began to feel like the good old days back in Antigua. I thought I had the measure of club cricket. A local journalist, Gerry Goodman, who had supported me from the beginning at Lansdown, gave me a glowing report which hinted that I might be ready to step up from club cricket.

Things improved, even more, when I played for Somerset Under-25s against Gloucestershire at Bristol. I managed an impressive 71 not out in very quick time. I knew that Somerset officials were watching me and that favourable reports would be going to Taunton. I also knew, after that match, that Gloucester might also be interested. I secretly hoped that there might be a little rivalry between the two and that Somerset might sign me, if only to prevent someone else taking me on.

For a time nothing happened, which was a little frustrating. Why were they taking their time? Well, I think they were also looking at other overseas players at the time including an Australian named Graeme Watson who, to be honest, had a much bigger reputation than me. Would they take him instead of me? Time dragged on.

There was one more thing – a silly thing – which

throughout my first season in England I found difficult to come to terms with. That was playing cricket in the evenings. Over in the Caribbean it gets dark very quickly at about 6 pm, and cricket matches never extend past that time. It was funny, writing to my friends and telling them that I had been playing until eight or nine the previous evening. They thought it must be floodlit cricket because in Antigua they play floodlit basketball at night.

Meanwhile I still nurtured pie-in-the-sky dreams about playing professional soccer. They were only half serious but, after a push from my Lansdown team mates, I did attend a hugely unsuccessful trial for Bath City. It was probably for the best. Soccer success would certainly have complicated the situation.

At the end of the season I finally received the news. I was to be offered a two-year contract with Somerset. Suddenly all the anxiety of the previous seven months seemed to fly out of the window. I could not believe it. It was a notably modest contract, but who cared? I was going to be a county cricketer. After that news, I flew home to Antigua and even my father seemed pleased. There was a little talk, still, of the possibility of my getting a 'proper' job, but I was not listening. I relaxed in Antigua, with Miriam by my side, and dreamed of future glory.

DAYS AND NIGHTS OF SPORTING BONHOMIE

At Taunton, it had been arranged for me to stay in the club flat which adjoined the cricket ground. Maybe they wanted to keep an eye on me, I don't know. I was to share the flat with two other lads, Dennis Breakwell and my friend from the previous season, Ian Botham. We had a good time, that year. Ian was from the Somerset town of Yeovil and often took me out to pubs in the area to meet his friends.

Ian was always a lively person to be with. Even then he was a very charismatic character. People were naturally drawn to him. Remember, he was not a 'star' at that point, in fact he was not even an established member of the Somerset side, he was just a noisy kid, fresh from the Lord's groundstaff. But he did have a huge power within him, he simply gushed with confidence. I found him then, as I still find him now, a tremendously inspiring character.

It is true to say that we were up late most nights. Dennis Breakwell, who had just come out of a marriage and seemed to be fully enjoying a second bachelorhood, was, if anything, even worse than Ian and me. I'm not sure that this arrangement was entirely good for my cricket and, to be honest, alarm bells did begin to ring. Perhaps wisely, I moved into a quieter place with my friends Terry and Trissie Smith. It was domestic, warm and, if only for a short while, helped me to keep my head intact.

My first game for Somerset was against Glamorgan at Swansea and it was, I think, a Benson & Hedges game. Needless to say, I was terrified. I knew that in many respects it would be the most important game of my career. Although I was sure that the Somerset authorities were beginning to be fully aware of my capabilities and that even if I performed badly they would give me space to become properly acquainted with county cricket, I desperately needed the boost of performing well on my début. And I did play well. I relaxed, I concentrated hard and ended up winning the Man of the Match. I scored 81 not out. Wandering back into the pavilion was an extremely emotional moment for me. All the Somerset team were standing at the bottom of the pavilion steps, applauding – and Len Creed, I remember, was in tears. His gamble had paid off.

At that moment, all the trauma of moving to England

GLAMORGAN vs. SOMERSET
at Swansea on 27th April 1974
Toss : Somerset.   Umpires : J.F. Crapp and D.L. Evans
Somerset won by 6 wickets

GLAMORGAN

A. Jones	c and b Jones	65
R.C. Davis	b Clapp	24
Majid J. Khan*	lbw b Burgess	29
A.R. Lewis	c Clapp b Moseley	32
M.J. Llewellyn	not out	16
M.A. Nash	b Moseley	1
E.W. Jones+	not out	8
G.P. Ellis		
J.W. Solanky		
D.L. Williams		
R.D.L. Dudley-Jones		
Extras	(b 2,lb 13,,nb 4)	19
TOTAL	(for 5 wkts)(55 overs)	194

SOMERSET

S.G. Wilkinson	b Nash	3
D.B. Close*	c Davis b Dudley-Jones	31
P.W. Denning	c Jones E.W. b Dudley-Jones	40
I.V.A. Richards	not out	81
J.M. Parks	c Jones E.W. b Williams	16
G.I. Burgess	not out	18
T.W. Cartwright		
D.J.S. Taylor+		
H.R. Moseley		
A.A. Jones		
R.J. Clapp		
Extras	(lb 6,nb 3)	9
TOTAL	(for 4 wkts)(41.4 overs)	198

SOMERSET	O	M	R	W	FALL OF WICKETS		
						GLA	SOM
Jones	11	2	38	1	1st	81	14
Moseley	11	2	45	2	2nd	112	50
Clapp	11	1	29	1	3rd	139	110
Burgess	11	2	41	2	4th	179	167
Cartwright	11	5	22	0	5th	182	
					6th		
GLAMORGAN	O	M	R	W	7th		
Nash	7	1	29	1	8th		
Williams	9	2	40	1	9th		
Dudley-Jones	7	0	31	2	10th		
Solanky	6	1	40	0			
Ellis	8.4	1	37	0			
Davis	4	0	12	0			

and all the uncertainty suddenly seemed worthwhile. Just a few days earlier I had been harbouring grave doubts about my ability, but here, after my first game, was the proof that I could cut it at this level. It instilled tremendous confidence in me. I had no doubts that I could, and damn well would, accomplish much in county cricket. For the first time since leaving Antigua, I felt a wave of happiness.

TEST INITIATION

Almost immediately I began to relax into the role of a county cricketer. Following my début at Swansea I scored 71 in the match against Gloucestershire and, again, I won the Man of the Match award. These were the two games that effectively kicked my career into gear.

Already, and to my mind unfairly, I was becoming known as a big hitter. I never really went out there with that kind of macho attitude. I just wanted to play well and I was more than willing to learn the subtleties of the county game.

Contrary to what may have been said elsewhere, I was always aware that this would be a slow learning process. Perhaps my flamboyance gave people the wrong idea. They seemed to think that I could not see deeper into the game than just getting out there and blasting away. It was never true, and anyway, how could I have got away with such a style playing under Brian Close? Brian taught me so much, and was never afraid to dish out the odd verbal lashing. His attitude towards captaincy may have been controversial, but I valued his sense of discipline. I needed it. I had to be bashed into shape and Close was probably the perfect captain to play under at that time.

I was a little in awe of him. I had often heard his name on the radio back home in Antigua. Everyone respected Brian Close in the West Indies. This was the man who refused to be intimidated by the likes of Wes Hall

– the man we always feared would ruin our dreams of a historic West Indies victory.

Now here he was, trying to improve and sharpen me as a player. At times my concentration would lapse on the field and Closey soon put a stop to that. I think it's fair to say that, even though he more than justified my initial awe of him, I never played under him when he was at his peak. He too had his problems at Somerset. I know he did not like a couple of the officials. I was probably too young and too naive to understand the internal politics of a club like Somerset. But he was still a hell of a good captain, even in the most bizarre circumstances. Once, when we were on our way back from Scarborough, and Closey was driving – and driving really fast – I noticed that he had fallen asleep at the wheel. After I woke him he immediately regained his composure and, after giving me a 'You dare mention this' look, resumed his authoritative manner.

There were some good players in the Somerset team. It was wonderful for me to be playing alongside people like Close, Botham, Peter Roebuck, Vic Marks, Colin Dredge, Nigel Popplewell and Hallam Moseley. Slowly I become a more complete cricketer. Reputations, however, are often made, not by consistent play but by the odd innings, or even the odd hits, that capture people's imagination. I remember, in one game, hitting two sixes in the first over I faced. It was said that these hits gave us the psychological edge needed to win the game, and I am sure there was some truth in that. It is strange in a way but people remember little instances like that, rather than a player's progress throughout the whole season. Which is just as well because I did have some very lean periods that year.

I remember one day very well. We were playing against Yorkshire at Bath, when someone came to me with a telegram saying that I should make myself available to join the West Indies squad to tour India under Clive Lloyd. This came as a total surprise to me. To say it was a shock would be an understatement. I had only just got over the initial exhilaration of playing well at county level and now, before I knew I was ready, the ultimate challenge was thrust upon me. Let's face it, I had barely made my mark, and suddenly I would be sharing the same dressing room as Clive Lloyd.

At first I just felt unready. I thought I would be totally out of place. Although I had started to achieve things at county level, there still seemed to be many bridges to cross. It had all happened with such speed. True enough, not only had I made my mark in county cricket, I had performed well in the Shell Shield Tournament back in the West Indies. I think that was really why I was selected.

I was anxious before the tour began but it turned out to be a great pleasure to go to India and discover how well they treated cricketers. It was easy for me in a way. Nobody took much notice of me. I was just creeping into the team through the back door and had yet to make any kind of impression, let alone begin to carry the burden of reputation. So, in those first few days in India, I would sneak around and remain shyly in the background. Of course, it was Clive Lloyd and the senior members of the party who took all the heat from the press and the public. I was filled with admiration and awe at the way Clive handled himself.

I was beginning to learn that to play cricket at that level one had to adopt a certain day-to-day discipline, not just on the field or on the training ground, but for more or less every minute of the day. As for giving interviews, I was happy to be a minor figure, a late picking for the journalists who would, naturally, only come to me after pumping all they could from the stars. The pressure of playing in my first Test series seemed to pale into insignificance compared with what the senior players had to contend with. I began to enjoy my anonymity and concentrated on my game.

As a country, India made a strong impression on me. Coming from a small island, I was amazed to see people living so close to breaking point and to realise that, however bad things might get in Antigua, they would never be that bad. What I saw in India opened my eyes so much. For the first time I saw how privileged I had been, growing up in the comfort of Antigua. I saw millions starving and suffering – *millions*. It was very humbling and made me question the value of my life compared with what these people were going through. They were openly fighting to survive, they owned nothing and had no real prospect of ever owning anything. Despite their hopeless position they still carried with them a passion for cricket, which I found extraordinary. Perhaps they used it as a form of escapism or even a way of reclaiming a little dignity.

I always look back upon that tour to India when young players come to me for guidance or express a wish to give up because times seem so hard. I can tell them what hard times are really all about. I had felt immensely moved by what I saw over there.

The people were full of warmth and, if anything, I felt a little embarrassed by their enthusiasm for the game. I thought they were being a little too generous to us, just a few visiting sportsmen. Even though they were the opposing crowd, I felt as if I just had to go out and entertain them.

Coming to terms with the Indian cricket team was no

less of an awesome experience. I had never played against such a display of spin bowling. I remember watching the Indians throwing the ball about. I had never seen people do things like that to a cricket ball, it was more than an education, I was mesmerised. These guys, I thought, are incredible.

Once again, I knew that I would have to play with great patience if I was to come to terms with such remarkable bowling. I remember that the off-spinner, Prasanna, seemed to be able to control the ball even after he had delivered it. It was a weird experience. He would make you play for the off-break and then, as if by magic, the ball would continue straight and just nick the side of your bat. I found that I had to alter my sense of timing in mid-stroke, because the ball would seem to 'slow' in flight.

Then there was the unforgettable Chandrasekhar. It took me a long, long time to come to terms with 'Chandra'. He was the most teasing bowler I ever had to face, and I never quite knew whether I was in charge or not. That was his greatness. His ability to lure opponents into a false sense of security was deadly. How is a batsman supposed to dominate such a man? How can he build his own confidence when he does not know whether the bowler is faking or not?

Bishen Bedi, the left-armer, also had a formidable mastery over variation. He was almost impossible to read. Talk about being thrown in at the deep end. All these great spinners in my first Test. It was the luck of the draw, of course, but I could not help wishing we were in Australia, say, rather than India, where I could have started against a pace attack. At least I would have understood what I was doing!

As it was I got off to a good start in India. We played against West Zone in Poona and I managed to score a century. That certainly felt wonderful and my confidence, with the first Test looming ahead, was soaring. I was looking forward to playing a similar innings, against India, at Bangalore.

It was to be a strange Test, mainly because of the unexpected rain which occurred the night before. We were all worried about how it might help the already formidable line-up of Indian spinners. Clive won the toss and decided that we should bat. On the first day Gordon Greenidge, who was also making his Test début, scored a superb 93 and his success only served to increase my confidence. But, on the second day, after another downpour, the Indian spinners seemed to tear us apart. Alvin Kallicharran scored what, in relative terms, was a magnificent 60 but there were seven other batsmen, myself included, who failed to amass more than 17 between us.

I played a stupid shot and was out for four. I felt devastated but still, there would be another innings to come. The second time out I fell foul of Chandra. He totally outfoxed me and I was caught for three. I walked off the field knowing that I was suffering a nightmare Test début. I thought, most of all, of Antigua. I thought of all my friends, with their ears pressed to their transistor radios. The success of the West Indies team meant everything to them and here I was, walking off the field, having taken two innings to score just seven runs. It was a shattering experience. I knew the wicket had been appalling but that was no excuse. I had flunked at the first opportunity and I seriously doubted if I would ever be good enough to compete with the likes of Chandra. Was that what Test cricket was all about? This bowler had terrified me.

What I did not know at the time was that

Chandrasekhar did not represent a true measure of Test standard bowling. In fact, to this day, he probably remains the one bowler for whom I have the most respect. He could do things with the ball that seemed supernatural.

Needless to say, the period between the first and second Tests was a tense one. I thought long and hard. Had I been thrown into the top league too soon? Had my arrogance pushed me into a situation which I could not control? I was dejected and, although I was pleased for Gordon Greenidge, who had scored 93 and 107 in his first two innings, his success seemed to make my efforts look all the more futile. What would the people of Antigua think? Mind you, I did take some heart from the spirit of the team. Despite that second day collapse, we had won the Test to go one up in the series.

My feel against the spinners did improve a little and I scored 103 in one of the interim matches. This helped me to get my confidence back but then, as the second Test got under way in Delhi, all my apprehension returned. Once again I would have to face the Indian spinners and, in particular, Chandra. Although I was worried, deep down I knew that if I really was going to proceed any further in Test cricket, if I was going to make any kind of mark at all, then I would simply have to do it against bowling of this quality. There would be no excuses, either you can cut it or you can't.

I do not know what would have happened to my confidence had I failed in that second Test. It remains, probably, the most important match of my career. I did not begin at all well, and in fact I was nearly out after scoring a very nervous ten or twelve. It was an extremely close incident. To this day I know that the ball had not nipped my bat although the Indians all appealed with such sincerity that I began to doubt my own instincts. But

Clive Lloyd, at the other end, walked over to reassure me.

Clive was playing superbly, he just exuded confidence and I seemed to pick it up from him. I learned an enormous amount during that innings, especially from the way Clive handled Chandra. Soon I began to relax and, once past my fifty, I felt invincible. Now even those spinners could not contain me. It was during that innings that I realised the true possibilities of my game. I began to hit the ball so hard and, I suppose, not without a certain look of arrogance. But that was because it felt so glorious out there, partly because I knew that I had truly arrived at Test level, and also because I could not help but think of those guys in Antigua. I could almost hear them cheering every stroke. When I passed 150, I knew that I had really achieved something special. The people of Antigua would, once again, be totally behind me. I made 192 and was still not out at the end of the innings. I suppose some people would feel frustrated with such a score, with it being so close to a double century, but that did not bother me in the least. I was part of the West Indian team and that felt good – man, that felt good.

My euphoria was short-lived. One of the beautiful aspects of cricket lies in its unpredictability. You can be part of the finest team in the world and all of a sudden you find yourself on a slippery slope to defeat. You should never be too confident. Perhaps, after that second Test, we began to underestimate the Indians. It was stupid of us, really, after we had so clearly seen the danger in their bowling. We were well and truly beaten in the third Test at Calcutta. Personally, I had to be content with 15 and 47. The fourth Test followed a similar pattern. Although I got a fifty in the first innings, we were once again torn apart by the spinners. All of which seemed to pave the way for a particularly memorable fifth Test at Bombay.

INDIA vs. WEST INDIES (SecondTest)
at Delhi on 11th, 12th, 14th, 15th December 1974
Toss : India.   Umpires : M.V. Gothoskar and B Satyaji Rao
West Indies won by an innings and 17 runs

INDIA

S.S. Naik	lbw b Boyce	48	b Julien	6
F.M. Engineer+	b Julien	17	b Gibbs	75
H.S. Kanitkar	lbw b Roberts	8	b Gibbs	20
G.R. Viswanath	c Murray b Julien	32	c Lloyd b Gibbs	39
P. Sharma	c Julien b Willett	54	run out	49
B.P. Patel	c Kallicharran b Wilett	11	c and b Roberts	29
E.D. Solkar	c Lloyd b Gibbs	1	c Kalliacharran b Gibbs	8
S. Abid Ali	c Boyce b Gibbs	8	run out	4
S. Venkataraghavan*	c Greenidge b Roberts	13	c Richards b Gibbs	5
E.A.S. Prasanna	not out	8	not out	0
B.S. Bedi	b Roberts	0	c Greenidge b Gibbs	0
Extras	(b1,lb 3,nb 16)	20	(b 5,lb 8,w 1,nb 7)	21
TOTAL		220		256

WEST INDIES

C.G. Greenidge	c Engineer b Prasanna	31
D.L. Murray+	c Patel b Solkar	0
E.T. Willett	b Prasanna	26
A.I. Kallicharran	c Patel b Bedi	44
I.V.A. Richards	not out	192
C. H. Lloyd*	lbw b Solkar	71
R.C. Fredericks	c Engineer b Venkat'avan	5
B.D. Julien	c Bedi b Prasanna	45
K.D. Boyce	c Patel b Prasanna	68
L.R. Gibbs	run out	6
A.M.E. Roberts	run out	2
Extras	(b 2,lb 1)	3
TOTAL		493

WEST INDIES	O	M	R	W	O	M	R	W	FALL OF WICKETS				
										IND	WI	IND	WI
Roberts	17.3	3	51	3	16	6	43	1					
Boyce	11	2	41	1	3	0	10	0	1st	36	2	9	
Julien	16	3	38	2	9	2	33	1	2nd	51	50	81	
Gibbs	29	17	40	2	40.5	17	76	6	3rd	104	73	103	
Willett	13	3	30	2	26	9	61	0	4th	132	123	204	
Fredericks					2	0	12	0	5th	164	243	214	
									6th	173	248	246	
INDIA	O	M	R	W					7th	189	320	249	
Abid Ali	7	0	47	0					8th	196	444	252	
Solkar	13	3	43	2					9th	220	467	256	
Bedi	53	13	146	1					10th	220	493	256	
Prasanna	34	7	147	4									
Venkataraghavan	34	6	107	1									

I remember this Test for two reasons, neither of them to do with my own performance which was somewhat less than satisfactory. It was marvellous to watch Clive Lloyd forge his way to 242 not out and virtually wrestle the game, and the series, away from the Indians, even though they were still playing dangerously well. When Clive reached his double century, some of the crowd invaded the pitch, more out of sheer enthusiasm than anything else. Unfortunately the police reacted a little too harshly and there was a small riot. This was a shame because it marred the climax to a fantastic series between two very different but evenly matched teams. I could not have hoped for a more fascinating start to my Test career.

FEAR AND LOATHING IN AUSTRALIA

Antigua, by night, is ringed by pockets of floodlit paradise. Pass over by plane, and you will see these softly lit havens of fantasy, glimmering sweetly and, apparently, adrift in a sea of intense blackness.

These are Antigua's world-famous beach hotels and they awake, around 8 pm, to greet the guests as they drift from room to restaurant and, later, from restaurant to dance floor. Unlike many similar islands, this activity remains, by and large, refreshingly reserved. The island prefers to offer itself to the tourist world as a place of charm and it is not for nothing that the current catchphrase 'ANTIGUA NICE' seems to carry with it the mildest possible warning to those wishing use their visit as one long, noisy hedonistic binge.

Antigua is not like that. Picture now, a typical beach hotel. Unthreatening waiters weave politely around a scattering of pre-dinner guests who are reflecting over their day spent lazily on the beach or, more demandingly, aboard one of the many sailing ships which cruise around this small island on a daily basis. One or two of the guests, those of greater financial stature, might have taken a plane hop to St Kitts or Montserrat and back. Some of them may have enjoyed wine and barbecues on the island's most popular beauty spot, Shirley Heights. Tomorrow's activities will, almost certainly, creep into the conversations and the waiters will take great delight in being probed for suggestions and advice. Unlike the waiters of many similar resorts, their enthusiasm will not be fired merely by the possibility of financial gain. These waiters are openly proud of their island and, although most of them will have a secret life – that of a great sportsman – they remain professional enough to adopt an attitude of servile contentment.

A band, an ungainly looking gaggle of local part-time musicians, locks into a muffled calypso groove. The music is, at least initially, mild. Later in the evening, as a few more of the holidaying couples are tempted onto the dance floor, the music will harden into reggae. The Rastafarian bass player, in particular, will break free from the constraints of the cabaret norm. During Bob Marley's Stir It Up, *the liberated bass will find its true power and, all of a sudden, all the chairs in the Beach Bar will be reverberating to the roots 'rockers' sound. It is a significant moment. For the first time in the evening the young culture of the West Indies is allowed to penetrate this fantasy. The bass player smiles with satisfaction.*

Unnoticed, the Range Rover driven by Viv Richards crackles to a halt in the gravel car park. Two minutes later the man himself is being greeted by a succession of waiters. Once again, an atmosphere of sporting bonhomie proliferates and the sounds of the indecipherable dialect cut through the, until now, predominantly English chatter.

Viv Richards is here to talk about his career but, before he will allow himself to relax into any kind of reflective mood, he takes great pains to seek out and talk to the hotel's chef, who happens to be a star player in the local football team run by Richards.

Ten minutes later, Richards selects a floodlit seat by the side of a deserted swimming pool. Hidden from the band and its pleasantly intoxicated audience, one would expect him to be able to talk in uninterrupted isolation. This proves to be impossible. His talk, although at times extremely passionate, is regularly punctuated by interruptions from passing Europeans:

'Oh, hello Viv, sorry to barge in like this but you have been my hero for many years. Would you mind signing this please? I own a hotel over in Andover, if you are ever over there would you like to...' etc., ad infinitum.

From behind a large Banana Cocktail, and backed by the now rampant bass of the Rastafarian, Viv Richards begins to talk about his first Australian tour.

I had not been entirely content with my performances in India and, to be honest, the prospect of being selected for the Australian tour was by no means a foregone conclusion. At one point I convinced myself that I would not be included. Had I known exactly what was to come, maybe I would have welcomed being passed over.

In many ways it would prove to be just about the most important cricket tour in the history of West Indian sport. On a personal level, that tour hardened me up. I think it hardened a lot of other players too. It was a period when Australia were causing havoc. England had been over there the year before and had taken a real smacking, not just by losing matches, but by being physically bruised as well. Obviously, I had had a certain amount of prior warning about what it was going to be like but nothing, *nothing*, could have fully prepared any of us for what we were to experience.

Without doubt, it was to be the hardest, meanest cricket tour that I have ever been involved in and it changed my whole concept of Test cricket. Until then I had believed, however naively, that Test cricket was the ultimate sport of gentlemen. The Australians smashed that view wide open. Forewarned or not, it came as a total surprise to me to come up against a team that contained so many openly aggressive people. It was a kind of nastiness that I had never encountered previously, not just in cricket but in life in general. The force of their hostility was nothing short of frightening.

We had to take so much. The verbal abuse, in particular, left our team completely stunned. West Indian people are, in general, mild, good-natured folk and we had anticipated an atmosphere of friendly rivalry. But as soon as we wandered out on that field, we had to face their taunts. It did not prove easy to concentrate when someone was snarling at you and saying, 'You f**k off, you black bastard!'

In cricketing terms, too, we took a terrible smacking. I felt like an amateur, as though I had never before been let loose in a 'real' cricket arena. That tour produced in me the complete opposite of the elation I felt when settling into the county cricket routine in England.

We were beaten 5-1 in a six-Test series, which is a hiding in any terms. Their bowling was furious. I had never faced bowling like that before. Guys would bump you in a way which verged on pure violence. There was no other way to describe it. They gave cricket an entirely different feel.

The Australians had found a way of using their natural aggression to shift cricket onto a new axis. They had, and still have, this way of just being very, very physical. Not just in their playing, but in every aspect of their attitude. We took so much stick. In every conceivable way, we were utterly savaged on that tour. The Australians did not seem to have any code of practice. They would take every opportunity to humiliate and ridicule us.

I quickly learned to put some of it down to gamesmanship. A lot of what they said was probably just spur-of-the-moment antagonism and I can forgive a man for that. Sometimes, when you are competing, and competing hard, things like that do come out of your mouth. It can happen and I know that Australians are just as aggressive towards the English as they were towards us. In that sense, I would say that they probably were not racist, although this is a theme that I will return to a number of times in this book, because racism is rife in cricket circles.

The Aussies tried every trick in the book. When I am faced with such hostility, I try to reserve a certain amount of doubt about the motives, nevertheless when you are black you never really know what is inside another man's heart. In Australia, and on that particular tour, we seemed to face nothing but sheer hatred.

Things began to go horribly wrong in the first Test at Brisbane. I hate to make excuses, but the wicket was astonishingly fast. Looking back, I blame my inexperience for my own failure. I allowed the Australians' aggression to overwhelm me. After that I never stood a chance and that probably goes for the rest of the West Indian batsmen. If only we had replied to the aggression of Lillee and Thomson. If we had responded in a positive manner, and really gone for them, the end result might easily have been so different. But we did not. Our batting was lousy and we were well and truly crushed.

In the first innings, I played a lazy shot and, much to my embarrassment, I was out for a duck. It was no consolation to realise that most of the team were playing just as badly. We fell apart. The atmosphere in the West Indies dressing-room was one of deathly quiet, almost as if we were resigned to our fate. To this day, I do not think I have been in a West Indian dressing room that was so quiet. Traditionally they are inspiring places to be. This is one team which feeds off the enthusiasm of all its members. If one player is feeling down the rest will help lift him. But, on this day, something was obviously missing. There was no magic.

After the match, I remember being annoyed at the way the Australian press attacked Clive Lloyd's captaincy. It did not seem fair, but I was still to learn that there are very few areas of the cricket media that can be considered fair, in any sense.

Clive, as always, seemed to take it in his stride. He was the master and, time and again, I found myself looking towards him in admiration, looking and learning. I could not have had a finer tutor.

One of the problems was that, after we had beaten the Australians in the World Cup the previous summer in England (more of which later) too much was expected from our team. In many ways we were inexperienced. In the end, I think we salvaged a bit of pride from the tour. For myself, I did at least manage a few high scores, and I shall never forget the feeling of satisfaction which came with hitting Thomson straight back over his head, or from hooking Dennis Lillee, surely one of the most dangerous shots in cricket history.

This was the first time I had come up against such a high standard of fast bowling and I was determined, from day one, not to let it frighten me. I think I was given a certain amount of courage while playing alongside Brian Close at Somerset. He always showed tremendous bravery and no fast bowler, even if he managed to bruise him, would ever be allowed to dominate. There had been times, at Somerset, where I had been hurt but I would never let it show, especially to Brian Close. I took this attitude with me to Australia. I had also, long since, reached the decision that I would not wear a protective helmet.

Some people thought that I was crazy to face Lillee and Thomson without a helmet, but this, I felt, and still feel, is an important part of my cricketing philosophy. I

AUSTRALIA vs. WEST INDIES (First Test)
at Brisbane on 28th, 29th, 30th November, 2nd December 1975
Toss : West Indies.   Umpires : R.C. Bailache and T.W. Brooks
Australia won by 8 wickets

WEST INDIES

R. C. Fredericks	c Marsh b Gilmour	46	c Marsh b Gilmour	7
C.G. Greenidge	lbw b Lillee	0	c McCosker b Gilmour	0
L.G. Rowe	run out	28	(4) c Chappell I.M. b Jenner	107
A.I. Kallicharran	c Turner b Lillee	4	(5) b Mallett	101
I.V.A. Richards	c Gilmour b Lillee	0	(7) run out	12
C.H. Lloyd*	c Marsh b Gilmour	7	c Redpath b Jenner	0
D.L. Murray+	c Mallett b Gilmour	66	(8) c and b Mallett	55
M.A. Holding	c Chappell G.S. b Gilmour	34	(3) c Turner b Lillee	19
Inshan Ali	c Redpath b Thomson	12	b Lillee	24
A.M.E. Roberts	c Chappell I.M. b Mallett	3	lbw b Lillee	3
L.R. Gibbs	not out	11	not out	4
Extras	(lb 1,nb 2)	3	(b 4,lb 15,w 5,nb 14)	38
TOTAL		214		370

AUSTRALIA

I.R. Redpath	run out	39		
A. Turner	b Roberts	81	b Gibbs	26
I.M. Chappell	lbw b Gibbs	41	not out	74
G.S. Chappell*	c Greenidge b Roberts	123	not out	109
R.B. McCosker	c Kallicharran b Ali	1	(1) c Murray b Roberts	2
G.J. Gilmour	c Lloyd b Gibbs	13		
T.J. Jenner	not out	6		
D.K. Lillee	b Roberts	1		
J.R. Thomson	lbw b Gibbs	4		
A.A. Mallett	c Fredericks b Gibbs	0		
Extras	(lb 5,nb 4)	9	(b 5,lb 2,nb 1)	8
TOTAL		366	(for 2 wkts)	219

AUSTRALIA	O	M	R	W	O	M	R	W
Lillee	11	0	84	3	16	3	72	3
Thomson	10	0	69	1	18	3	89	0
Gilmour	12	1	42	4	11	4	26	2
Jenner	4	1	15	0	20	2	75	2
Mallett	0.5	0	1	1	21.4	6	70	2

WEST INDIES	O	M	R	W	O	M	R	W
Roberts	25	2	85	3	14	2	47	1
Holding	20	4	81	0	10	0	46	0
Gibbs	38	7	102	5	20	8	48	1
Ali	17	1	67	1	10	0	57	0
Lloyd	6	1	22	0				
Fredericks					2	0	12	0
Kallicharran					0.2	0	1	0

FALL OF WICKETS

	WI	AUS	WI	AUS
1st	3	99	6	7
2nd	63	142	12	60
3rd	70	178	50	
4th	70	195	248	
5th	81	317	248	
6th	99	350	269	
7th	171	354	275	
8th	199	361	346	
9th	199	366	348	
10th	214	366	370	

think it extends back to my young days in Antigua. I learned to have faith in my natural senses. Back there, on those awful, hard pitches, the ball could bounce anywhere and I learned to respond in an instinctive way. Without a doubt that increased my natural awareness as well as instilling in me a certain respect for the fundamentals of the game. It provided an outward appearance of courage but, to be honest, it also made me feel more comfortable both mentally and physically. With the helmet on, I could never feel at ease. I could never feel in total control and that, more than the bowling of Lillee and Thomson, would frighten me. But I can only speak for myself. I am not saying that it is wrong for people to wear helmets or any other type of protection. Every man has a right to look after himself, but I think it is equally essential for a batsman to feel comfortable and at ease at the crease.

I do not think that helmets have done anything to improve the game of cricket. They make it possible to play top-class cricket without fear and, with the removal of that fear, a certain amount of excitement has also gone. There are some players, now international players, who would not be in cricket at all if it was not for the helmet. They would not have the stomach, the bottle.

The psychology of cricket has changed. Fast bowlers can still intimidate, but a slice of tension has now been removed and the batsman is allowed to feel braver than he naturally is. In some ways this is a good thing, but it has shifted the axis of top-class cricket. I look back to Bradman, who never needed such equipment to face Larwood because he had total belief in his own ability. He would have been a lesser player had he used a helmet. I decided that, for better or worse, I would be on my own out there. I would not hide behind anything. No bowler would make me do that.

I actually did relish the challenge of Lillee and Thomson. I love the drama of facing a fast bowler. I love the way such a bowler will try to bully you, by shouting, snarling, glaring...any method of intimidation he can think of. It is all an attempt to unsettle the mind of a batsman and dent that all-important confidence. Given confidence, even a batsman of average skill can play the most beautiful innings, and the reverse is also true – great batsmen can be ruined by average bowlers. Not, of course, that there was anything average about Lillee and Thomson. That was murder but, although we were bumped all over the place and we lost the series 5-1, I still enjoyed it, mainly because we all learned so much.

As this particular series was something of a turning point in West Indian cricket, I would like to seize this opportunity to point out a few home truths. Everybody, even today, is quick to complain about our fast bowlers. I do not really want to discuss the accusation that the West Indians are brutal; in fact this subject has long since become a tedious issue. What few of our critics seem to remember are the conditions we endured on that Australian tour. The fact is, we started to play with four quick bowlers because *we* had this done to us.

I would like each and every one of those persons who have knocked us to remember the kind of savagery we faced on that Australian tour. We are basically very calm, very peaceful people. I do not know know of any West Indian cricketer who swears at the opposition in the way that those Aussies did. We came up against extreme savagery in that series, what many people would call extreme racism. Now what is a West Indian bouncer compared to that?

The Australians taught us and we took notice of

them. We decided that, if we really were going to survive in this game, something similar would have to be done. It makes me laugh to hear people complaining, especially in England, about our bowling and the next minute reminiscing fondly about the likes of Fred Trueman. What kind of hypocrisy is that? They did not call him Fiery Fred for nothing. But the cricket world is full of such hypocrites and racists. These are the people, and I know who they are, who want to ruin our beautiful team.

I hope they read this and understand why I want them to keep out of our business and allow us to get on with our style of cricket. They have got conveniently short memories. I can and will accuse them of wanting to see this particular race of people, from the West Indies, being put down. Now that we have our bowling, at least we have a deterrent. We have something within our armoury to say, 'All right, big brother, you have got some big guns...well, so have we.' We have managed to develop this particular talent and my message to the cricket establishment is simple, '*LAY OFF OUR BOWLERS!*'

The forces who are behind the current debates about shorter run-ups and over rates, I don't give a damn who they are, they have no justification in changing the rules. I'm not saying that there are not times when the run-ups are too long and do not really benefit the bowling, and maybe sometimes there is a bit of intimidation involved, but this is no reason for them to destroy something of great athletic beauty.

Just look at Michael Holding running up to bowl – one of the greatest sights in cricket. And they want to destroy it with all these snivelling, cynical little changes they come up with. If they were thinking about the welfare of cricket then, yes, I would help them. But they are not. They do not really care about cricket, all they want to do is cripple the West Indies. I know damn well that there are people at the top of the cricketing establishment who feel that the West Indies have been doing too well for too long. I can genuinely feel that force and it hurts. I will continue to fight for the things I feel are our basic rights.

There are, undoubtedly, some very genuine people running the game, but there is also far too much racism in the game. The racists are people with a perverse kind of pride, who think we have no right to be competing on the same stage as them. My pride, for the record, is as big as that of any other man!

Some people think that cricket is a game that only Englishmen can really play. I still hear that, even now. 'Oh, you only have to bowl outside the off stump and they hit across the line...they can never play properly in England...' All that crap. I still come across it. These guys still believe in their country's innate superiority...it is pathetic. They think they are strong but they are not. They are weak, fatally weak.

To feel strong you have to know that your heart and mind are in the right place. I try to remain perfectly healthy in mind and body and as long as I maintain that, the only thing I am looking to do is to move forward. Not going backwards, not negatively trying to crush the natural playing styles of other nations, but competing in a positive manner. I will never lose that sense of being strong. If I do lose that will to compete, I shall be finished. People still say, 'Oh, Windies will crumble soon.' No. They will not. What matters, is not what idiots say at the top of the establishment, or in the media, or even in the dressing rooms. What matters is what happens on that field.

I may get beaten in the media, at dinner, in the dressing room, but when I get on that field and look in the eyes of the guy opposite and suss out whether he has it or not...that is what the game is really about. That is cricket.

All these feelings come to the fore whenever I think back to that first tour of Australia because, all of a sudden, the game took on a new dimension for me. I realised how important cricket is and how it is not some irrelevant, eccentric sport played by a handful of countries, but a game that gets right to the root of the societies involved. During that tour I think I went through the whole spectrum of emotion – from elation when I performed a particularly good shot against Thomson, to humiliation at the final outcome.

And didn't the media just love to rub salt in our wounds? Ask them now about it and they refuse to remember what happened over there. I have not forgotten. They called us wimps. They called us cowards and worms. Do you remember the phrase 'Happy Hookers'? That's what they threw at us. Nobody accused the Australians of throwing down too many bumpers. Nobody attacked Lillee and Thomson and called them unfair.

More importantly, and this is where I feel proud, no West Indian started to try to change the rules so that our team would not have to face such bowlers again. Oh no. We had more courage than that. We accepted and learned from the situation. But the people who are trying to destroy us, they know what went on in Australia. They know why the West Indies decided to rebuild their approach and they know exactly what lay behind Clive Lloyd's decision to bring in the four pace bowlers. I will return to this later in the book. For the moment, I want to warn those people to stop their racism. I want them to *leave West Indian cricket alone.*

There was another positive aspect to that Australian tour – although some people may find my subject surprising.

I am referring to Jeff Thomson. I have already stated that it was, let us say, an education to come up against him on the field. Perhaps more importantly, it was a *pleasure* to begin a friendship with the man.

Everyone had warned me about him. They had told me about his unbridled aggression and many thought of him as nothing more than a brute. That was his world image, he was known as the guy who would deliberately bruise people up – a typical natural Aussie.

But, in truth, and despite the hostilities of that series – and, yes, he did play his part – I soon found him to be one of the nicest guys I have ever played against, certainly one of the nicest Aussies. He was not really a brute, he was just a hard trier and I soon came to relate to the way he played the game. Whenever he cursed, on a cricket pitch, which was often, he was basically cursing himself for not doing as well as he knew he could. His cursing, in fact his entire macho stance, was just a way of psyching himself up.

I thought in advance that the view of Jeff Thomson as nothing more than a thug, was a pretty shallow one. I may not have been entirely enamoured with many of the Aussies on that tour, but there was always something I respected about him. I never felt that he was, in any real way, a nasty person. Later in life we did some coaching together when I went over to play in Queensland and Perth. We were also employed by the same radio station, Station 4IP, and we soon became great friends. He would drive a great powerhouse car, a Ferrari, and I would accompany him on adventures across Queensland. It would be a whole new world of discovery for me.

Jeff showed me Australia in a very special way. I went fishing with him. I met his friends and became part of their circle. Over a period we sank many, many XXXX's together. It was a very relaxing time. I even went to his stag night.   We had a warm friendship, maybe it was helped along by the viciousness of our first meeting.

Jeff Thomson, the thug cricketer, was a product of media hype.   Jeff used this image to help his cricket, but, in reality he never lived the part.   He was not a bit nasty, just a real fun guy.   I still keep in touch with him.   It is good to see him now, fully immersed in his landscaping business.   Today everyone can see the real Jeff Thomson.

IRONIC TWIST

Immediately following our trouncing in Australia came the most ironic twist of fortunes.   India were to tour the Caribbean and were, I think, rather nervous about facing our two emerging pace bowling talents, my fellow Antiguan Andy Roberts and Michael Holding.   It was also to be the series when at last I felt like I was nearing my peak. Centuries seemed to fly from me and, I think it's fair to say that the rest of the team were uplifted by my performances. It was also a great time for me socially.   I was finally playing at home, seeing all my friends and feeling perfectly relaxed.   It was a wonderful feeling to conquer the Indian spinners in front of my home crowd, although, needless to say, Chandra did cause me a few problems.

Although we lost the third Test by six wickets due to a truly fantastic performance by the Indians – we did eventually win the series.   Unfortunately, it was not a series that would be remembered for much of the actual play, or indeed for the good feeling which had generally prevailed.   Instead it was the Kingston Test, which saw the Indians' historic protest against our bowling when they called an end to their innings at 97 for five with five batsmen retired hurt.

The spirit of the series dissolved with Indian captain Bedi's protest and I was sad to see this happen in the West

WEST INDIES vs. INDIA (Fifth Test)

at Sabina Park, Kingston on 21st, 22nd, 24th, 25th April 1976
Toss : West Indies. Umpires : R. Gosein and D. Sang Hue
West Indies won by 10 wickets

INDIA

S.M. Gavaskar	b Holding	66	c Julien b Holding	2
A.D. Gaekwad	retired hurt	81	absent hurt	-
M. Amarnath	c Julien b Holding	39	st Murray b Jumadeen	60
G.R. Viswanath	c Julien b Holding	8	absent hurt	-
D.B. Vengsarkar	b Holding	39	(2) lbw b Jumadeen	21
B.P. Patel	retired hurt	14	absent hurt	-
Madan Lal	lbw b Daniel	5	(4) b Holding	8
S. Venkataraghavan	lbw b Daniel	9	(5) b Holding	0
S.M.H. Kirmani+	not out	0	(6) not out	0
B.S. Bedi*			absent hurt	-
B.S. Chandrasekhar			absent hurt	-
Extras	(b 6,lb 6,w 12,nb 21)	45	(nb 6)	6
TOTAL	(for 6 wkts dec)	306		97

WEST INDIES

R.C. Fredericks	run out	82	not out	6
L.G. Rowe	st Kirmani b Bedi	47	not out	6
I.V.A. Richards	b Chandrasekhar	64		
A.I. Kallicharran	b Chandrasekhar	12		
C.H. Lloyd*	c and b Chandrasekhar	0		
D.L. Murray+	c sub b Chandrasekhar	71		
B.D. Julien	b Chandrasekhar	5		
M.A. Holding	c sub b Bedi	55		
V.A. Holder	not out	36		
R.R. Jumadeen	c Gavaskar b Venkat'avan	3		
W.W. Daniel	c Amarnath b Venkat'avan	11		
Extras	(b 1,lb 2,nb 2)	5	(nb 1)	1
TOTAL		391	(for 0 wkts)	13

WEST INDIES	O	M	R	W	O	M	R	W
Holding	28	7	82	4	7.2	0	35	3
Daniel	20.2	7	52	2	3	0	12	0
Julien	23	10	53	0	3	0	13	0
Holder	27	4	58	0	6	2	12	0
Jumadeen	3	1	8	0	7	3	19	2
Fredericks	3	1	8	0				

INDIA	O	M	R	W	O	M	R	W
Madan Lal	7	1	25	0	1	0	5	0
Amarnath	8	1	28	0				
Chandrasekhar	42	7	153	5				
Bedi	32	10	68	2				
Venkataraghavan	51.3	12	112	2				
Vengsarkar					0.5	0	7	0

FALL OF WICKETS

	IND	WI	IND	WI
1st	136	105	5	
2nd	205	186	68	
3rd	216	197	97	
4th	280	206	97	
5th	306	209	97	
6th	306	217		
7th		324		
8th		345		
9th		352		
10th		391		

Indies. To this day I insist on defending our position. Holding was not bowling in an evil manner but the wicket was not good.   There was a ridge which certainly caused tremendous problems for the Indian batsmen. Holding was certainly fired up, after all he was young and he was bowling in front of his home crowd. It was the sort of situation that Test batsmen have to contend with. Although I did sympathise with the Indians' feelings to some extent, I could not help but think back to the recent Australian tour and how we had taken all that hostility and were never heard to protest.

Personally, perhaps even selfishly, I felt disappointed because I thought I might never bat so well again, and was afraid that some of my best innings would be lost in the wake of the controversy.

THE
FOOTBALL MATCH

In Antigua, a 'road' is something which is not to be treated lightly. Unlike many parts of the civilised world, where a road is merely a stretch of tarmac along which automobiles and pushbikes, if not pedestrians and animals, will travel effortlessly, Antiguan roads cannot claim to fulfil such a simple role. Antiguan roads are not to be merely travelled along, they are to be 'negotiated'. In essence, they have a topographical quality all of their own. Their endless holes and lumps, hills and twists, often seem to have little in common with the surrounding landscape.

The best way to enjoy the experience of Antiguan travel is to place yourself in the hands of a master - a taxi driver. Initially, you will face true terror as the taxi bounces from side to side and recovers from seemingly hopeless angles where, in a less mysterious environment, it would surely have rolled off the road. When he sees your expression, the taxi driver will laugh, as if safe in the knowledge that some supernatural force is cementing that vehicle to the idiosyncratic surface. And, if you study the taxi driver, you will soon realise that he brings to the art of driving an uncanny degree of skill. He does not, for instance, drive over the potholes, he drives through them. He incorporates them into his general approach. It is a very strange skill indeed and one that, to all intents and purposes, would seem to be peculiarly Caribbean, if not peculiarly Antiguan.

Viv Richards is no exception to this rule. Watch him now as he glides his Range Rover (newly shipped over from Cardiff) down from the foothills which surround St John's. He drives with the fearless ease of one who is more than well acquainted with each and every pointless indentation, and maybe he is. His concentration remains, amazingly, unhindered by the other all-too-obvious distraction which accompanies his every journey.

Every other car which flashes past dangerously close on the other side of the road seems to contain a driver who is personally acquainted with him. The familiar greeting, a tooting of a horn followed by a swift exchange of 'Hey Mon' is certain to follow. Every Antiguan journey made by Viv Richards is punctuated in such a way. Which, incidentally, says as much about Antigua as it does about his enormous fame. The island is small and richly spiced with camaraderie; everyone seems to know everyone else. As far as Viv is concerned, although practically no living (or dead) Antiguan could possibly command a more universal admiration, his admirers seem to know him on a personal level, rather than merely 'of' him, from afar.

Today, as all days, Viv Richards is in a hurry. Business dealings have caused him to miss the first half of an all-important national football match, a local derby, between Antigua and neighbouring St Kitts. Strangely, this revered event is taking place, not in the usual venue, the Recreation Ground in St John's, but at a local police-owned sports field. As he drives Viv Richards talks fondly about football. The numerous distractions of road travel seem not to interrupt his flow. Fired by the oncoming prospect of the football, he touches upon one of his favourite subjects, Liverpool Football Club.

I went to watch Liverpool once, at Anfield. It was a game against Manchester United and what I saw terrified me.

I, being an Antiguan, had gone along simply to watch and perhaps comment upon a good football match. To me this seemed like a very simple and natural thing to do. I go to watch sport all the time...I'm going now, to watch a match. Anyway, I situated myself directly behind one of the goals and, when the United supporters arrived, I had never heard so much noise in all my life. It was, to a Caribbean person like myself, a profoundly unnerving experience. I had never seen sporting passion displayed so openly and fiercely. I couldn't understand it at all. And the hostility was so blatant.

People reading this book, perhaps in Britain, may think that I am over-reacting here, but this, to my mind, was very weird indeed. Then something happened on the pitch. I think the referee disallowed a goal for offside. All around me, well, everything just exploded. I found myself lifted off the ground and hurled forward. Until that moment, I had absolutely no idea that this was what happened at English football matches. I seriously thought that a riot had broken out. I thought people were going to get killed. Because I was not prepared for it, it was very, very frightening. I could not understand what was wrong with all those people.

I knew then that I had made the right decision not to go into football. I was happy to be playing in a sport which, most of the time, was watched by people of a more genteel nature. Nonetheless, I was a Liverpool supporter on that day and I remain a devoted follower. They have such a good thing going there – such an aura of absolutely unshakable professionalism – that they have managed to rise above the normal pressures of top-class football teams, that fear of failure which affects Manchester United, Spurs, Arsenal and the other clubs. Somehow, they have built an indestructible sense of self-belief. Even if they have a bad season, which is extremely rare, they seem to know that they will soon be back on top. And they do bounce back, like tigers.

I like to compare this with the attitude of the West Indies cricket team. This is the philosophy which we have built and I am sure it will stick with us. We expect to win. And we always expect to perform with dignity, professionalism and dedication. These are our key words. I like to think of that parallel between the West Indies and Liverpool. That winning habit – that is what I would like to share with them. It is as much do do with pride as anything else. I am not saying that the other clubs do not have a sense of pride, of course they do, and it must be a wonderful feeling to play for a club such as Manchester United, but Liverpool have taken it a step further. They have managed to instil that pride in every single Liverpool player...and, of course, the crowd are a part of it. That is what reminds me of the West Indies. I can see Liverpool still being at the top of football in twenty years' time – let's hope that we can do likewise.

We are driving, now, to see the second half of an Antiguan football match and I would, of course, love to see West Indian soccer take off like the cricket has done. That would be something wonderful because, quite clearly, there is sufficient talent. But we really need a good, strong, influential controlling body.

It was inspiring to see that Trinidad came so close to qualifying for the World Cup. That was a sign, I think, that greater things are imminent. One only has to look at the African nations who must, by now, be making the European and South American teams very nervous indeed, to see what is possible. Maybe we have the same strength in the Caribbean. Why not? We also play in that open, flowing manner which is, perhaps, a little too open at the moment. But I think the young footballers of the Caribbean have a lot to offer the world. What we achieved in cricket, we can do in football or, for that matter, basketball, athletics or netball.

You only have to look around this island. It is a mass of sporting activity, and great talent. Success, however, does not have a lot to do with how much talent you have, what matters is how you manage to collect and nurture that talent. You can have the finest potential sportsmen in the world, but if you do not catch them and train them while they are young, all that talent will be wasted. This is one of the problems with the West Indies.

The way we are scattered geographically makes us disparate by nature. Politically we are still in a mess. Sport in the West Indies will continue to suffer because of its mixed-up politics. Every island has its own little flag and every island hangs greedily on to whatever commodities it might have. Barbados has tourism, for instance, and Trinidad has some oil. All the large islands seem to prosper in some way and do not really care how or even whether the smaller islands can manage to struggle through. And often it really is a struggle. Our sport gets lost in this mess.

Cricket is perhaps the exception. The game has been something of a uniting force, possibly the only one around. When a Test match is being played, that is the only time that the people of the Caribbean come together as a cohesive whole. That is why, to a West Indian, a Test match is so special. It is the only time that the true power of the islands comes to the fore. To see this makes me proud, but it also saddens me, once a Test series finishes, to watch this power evaporate.

There is too much island nationalism. When the West Indies have accomplished a victory, each West Indian looks towards his own flag. What I long to see is one flag. Sometimes I get very embarrassed when someone asks me what is the colour of my flag. You look up and see all those different colours, all those different flags from all the Caribbean nations displaying to the world the nature of our problem.

Our political leaders must take the burden of the blame. We are simply too small as islands not to have come together as one particular unit or force. If only we had one common currency, so that one dollar would mean the same all around the Caribbean. If only we could get, for example, from Trinidad to Jamaica without going through all the immigration hassles. We should have a common passport, so we could travel freely throughout the islands.

That may sound simplistic – it *is* simplistic, but it is the only true solution to our problems. We have to find a way. Cricket, I believe, has managed to show people what can be achieved from a united West Indies. The rest of sport will follow. Together, we can be world champions. When we are separate, we are nothing. It is as simple as that. When I play for the West Indies, I represent *all* the islands, not just Antigua. When Andy Roberts and I came to that team, it was like two youngsters from Manchester playing for England. We had earned the right to represent the West Indies as a whole. Deep down, I am saddened that we did not sort this mess out long ago. It is a tragedy really, and the longer it continues, the worse it becomes. We are in a position of stalemate at present. We did once try to create an umbrella federation but it did not happen. There were always greedy individuals who felt differently, who wanted to keep hold of the lion's share.

Maybe that is just human nature, but would it not be wonderful to see, when one island goes through a bad time, the richer islands lending a helping hand? Would that not, in the long run, be mutually beneficial? It *can* be achieved. I will always believe that. Not until it happens can we challenge and compete economically in other parts of the world.

We need the strength of unity in order to negotiate, to get the right bargain for ourselves. Without it, we have lost out in so many areas where we could have been a much stronger force in the marketplace. There are all sorts of natural commodities that are peculiar to each island. But we have failed to capitalise on our resources in a united way. As a result some areas of the Caribbean have not prospered. America, as always, will continue to play the role of big father. Attitudes have changed a little recently because some of the stronger forces, the bigger islands, have been feeling the pinch a little harder than some of the smaller ones. But the situation has not really improved.

If only we could work together...if only. I see sport as being part of the overall answer. In sport our pride in the West Indies binds us together. Perhaps sport should be the model for all life.

The football match is nearing half-time. Although competition is fierce, and could hardly be fiercer, the supporters of Antigua mix freely with those who have made the short hop over from St Kitts.

Tactical arguments, most of them extremely knowledgeable, rage at all times. But whatever disagreements there may be, they are only about football. The prospect of causing an affray never occurs to even the most intoxicated elements of the crowd. Red Stripe lager is in plentiful supply and yet appears only to contribute to the further enjoyment of the afternoon's spectacle. Upon viewing this scene, British football-watchers might feel confused, if not thoroughly ashamed. Why is it that the good people of Antigua and St Kitts are capable of creating an enjoyably partisan atmosphere at a football match? How can it be that, within yards of the action, mothers watch over children who are engaged in tiny duplicates of the main event?

This entire scenario seems to be presided over by no more than four policemen, and rather bored policemen at that. Not that the event is dulled by any prevailing sense of apathy, far from it, the spectators at St John's are as passionate about their sport as even the most fervent Koppite or Stretford Ender. But, for some reason this passion never spills over into ugliness. Native Britons could learn a great deal from the good people of Antigua, most of whom, it must be noted, are hovering dangerously close to the poverty line.

The Range Rover belonging to, and containing, Viv Richards, is not merely allowed to pass freely through the turnstile area, it is beckoned inside with mighty enthusiasm. As it trundles to a spot adjacent to the half-way line, rows of heads turn away from the game and flash wide smiles of acknowledgement. As Viv Richards steps from the vehicle, young boys, their faces glowing with curious adoration, encircle him silently. The older members of the crowd, however, are far from silent. Viv wanders slowly around the ground, moving from heartfelt greeting to heartfelt greeting. Towering Rastafarians approach him, arms flailing madly in a dramatic declaration of friendship. Wise old men, pencil thin and ragged, cast nods of tempered enthusiasm and young girls, slinky and fine, drift past and note the presence of Richards with an enigmatic flick of a finger.

At the stroke of half-time, with Antigua leading 2-0, the crowd flows from the perimeter to engulf the multitude of beer sellers. The gossip flows, fast, furious and indecipherable to European ears. Then, long before the second half kicks into action, the spectators are back in position, poised, alert, passionate. One man, a local character of note, spent the entire match wandering around the inner perimeter of the pitch, often interfering with the play, and telling the crowd in no uncertain terms how he felt. 'That's all he ever does,' laughs Richards. 'He just tells everyone how he is feeling...crazy, but lovely.'

During the next 45 minutes of flowing football, Viv Richards melts into the character of a particularly vociferous member of the crowd. At the onset of every Antiguan attack, he lunges forward excitedly, uttering a stream of typical Antiguan soccer-speak. 'Gooo on, maaan...go on...nice...nice...oooooohhhh nnnnaaaa...what ye doin', maan...'

At the close of play, with Antigua holding on to their two goal win, the tension snaps and most of the crowd begin to drift cheerfully out of the ground. A sizeable number, however, including Viv Richards, remain inside the ground to engage in what must be regarded as some kind of unofficial seminar on the previous 90 minutes. Players, supporters, officials, beer sellers, policemen from both islands, all basking in post-match drama. Once again, a European could only look upon this peculiar and touching scene with a sense of envy, if not wonder. Not that partisan feelings have evaporated entirely. Half an hour later, as the bus containing the St Kitts team trundles away from the ground, a familiar figure is seen gesticulating wildly and attracting bemused glances from those at the rear of the departing bus.

'Two nil,' the figure chants. 'Two nil, two nil, two nil, two nil...' until the bus disappears into the enveloping gloom of St John's at early evening. The figure finally turns and, laughing heartily, begins a slow, proud – some would say arrogant – stride back towards his waiting Range Rover.

GROVEL!

Test cricket is a complex game, and not just on the field, where it has more in common with a game of chess than it has with any other bat and ball game. Each Test series seems to evoke all kinds of different pressures, tensions and prejudices. Playing against India, for example, would have a completely different feel to playing against Australia and it is only with experience that you begin to come to terms with that. Whatever the opposition you go out there and play as hard as you can, and, as a West Indian, you take pride in representing a body of people with such widely differing cultural and historical backgrounds.

Most West Indians would probably agree that playing against England is always something which seems to bring out the most passionate and united support from our people. When the West Indies are competing against England, the whole mood of the people changes dramatically with the fortunes of the game. I do not think that any other country apart from, perhaps, India, experiences a situation which is comparable to this. As popular as cricket is in England and Australia, it is not big enough to touch the very heart of the general public. But in the Caribbean, it seems like a matter of life and death...and especially against England.

Of course, the kind of pressure this situation inflicts on our players is enormous. Having listened passionately to Test matches against England all my life, I was more than aware of this as we approached the 1976 West Indies tour of England. Although it was a terrifying prospect – to perform badly against England would be unbearable – I did feel pretty good about myself. I knew that I was beginning to near my peak and I had begun to enjoy my cricket in a way that, with all the anxiety of my first steps into county and then Test cricket, I had not experienced since my latter days in Antigua. In short, I was pretty damn confident about myself and some people, I guess, saw this confidence as arrogance. I understand that, but in no way would I apologise for it. I was merely following my natural game...and pride and confidence play a large part in my basic philosophy about professional sport.

I had actually played against England, in the UK, before this series, as a part of the West Indian team which won the first World Cup tournament in 1975. That had been a different kind of tension and one which I will talk about in a later chapter. For the moment I will concentrate on the 1976 Test series, not least because I feel it was the series in which my true abilities began to reach fruition.

The series began very strangely when England captain Tony Greig stated publicly that the English team would make the West Indies 'grovel'. In later years I got to like Tony Greig. He was a 'go for it' guy and, after getting to know him a bit better, and indeed playing alongside him when he was captain of the Rest of the World team, I realised that he had a similar kind of personality to my own.

However when he said that word, 'grovel', I know that it gave strength to a lot of the West Indian players. I will never forget that day. Andy Roberts, Wayne Daniel and myself were sitting in a room waiting for a team meeting to begin. We had the television on but, I think,

Above The Antigua football team in 1971. I am second from the right at the back, brother Mervyn is four from the right and Miriam's brother is third from the left in the front.
Right Our local football team The Ovals. I am second from the left in the front row.
Below Leeward Islands, 1972. I am fourth from the left at the back.

Right Photocall portrait at
the beginning of my first
season with Somerset, 1974.
Below The Somerset team
which lost to Leicestershire
in the semi-final of the
Benson & Hedges Cup in 1974.
Back row (left to right):
D.Breakwell, I.T.Botham,
R.J.Clapp, A.A.Jones,
H.R.Moseley, D.J.S.Taylor,
I.V.A.Richards, P.W.Denning.
Front row: G.I.Burgess,
T.W.Cartwright, D.B.Close,
M.J. Kitchen, J.M.Parks.

Above On my first tour with the West Indies in 1974. I am six from the left in the patterned shirt. **Left** Two young men from Antigua, Andy Roberts and myself, arrive in England for the World Cup in 1975. **Below** One of my three run outs in the 1975 World Cup final. A direct hit dismisses Alan Turner.

Facing page I only got to 12 in this innings in the second Test against Australia at Perth in 1975 before being caught by Gary Gilmour off Jeff Thomson. But we did win the match to level the series at 1-1. **Left** On my way to a double-century at Trent Bridge in my first Test Match in England in 1976. **Below** Well satisfied with 291 in the fifth Test at The Oval at the end of the same series.

Above Wash-out at Lord's in the Gillette Cup semi-final against Middlesex in 1977. We eventually lost a reduced-overs game and I had to wait until the following year for my first one-day final with Somerset.
Right Although we lost the 1978 Gillette Cup final to Sussex we beat Northants the following year. After winning the Man of the Match award I posed for the cameras with our captain, Brian Rose.

Above left The winning hit – a six off Mike Hendrick wins the World Cup final of 1979.
Above The joy of hooking Dennis Lillee! This was in a one-day international at Melbourne later in 1979.
Left I was made Man of the Series in that three-way series in Australia which also included England. Geoff Boycott was on hand to put the presentation goblets to good use.

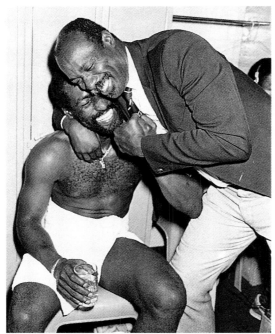

Left Celebrations with Wes Hall after winning the Frank Worrell Trophy in Australia in January, 1980. **Below** David Bairstow and Ian Botham visit the West Indies dressing room after we had won the third Test in Barbados in 1981. Clive Lloyd is busy autographing a bat.

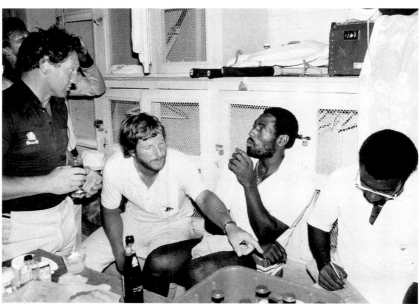

Above Miriam and myself after our wedding
ceremony in St John's in 1981.
Right That same week I was delighted to celebrate
the first Test ever to be played in Antigua with a
century in front of my home crowd.

We eventually got to 272 for 9 by the end of the 55th over in the Texaco Trophy match at Old Trafford in 1984

Above I had to call for a drink during my innings in the first Test at Edgbaston in 1984 but recovered to make 117. Larry Gomes, second from the left, made 143 and we shared a third-wicket partnership of 206. **Left** I was obviously feeling much better when David Gower was out for 12 in England's second innings.

Facing page Back home in Antigua with Miriam. Left The family came with me to England in 1983 for the World Cup and my daughter Matara was at Worcester to watch our game against Zimbabwe. Below Enjoying an English summer in our garden in Taunton.

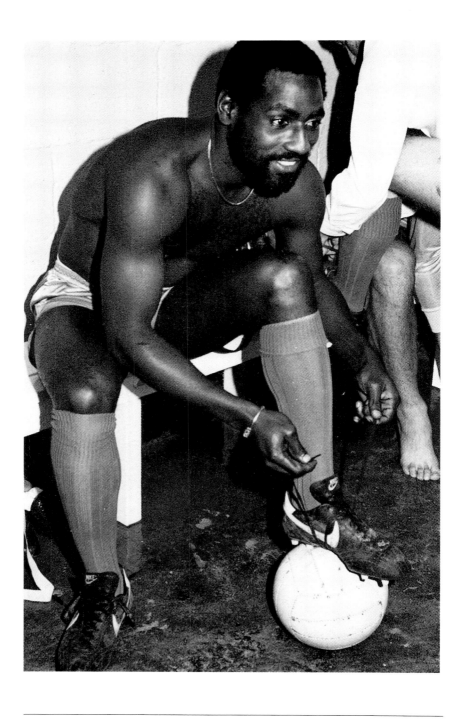

Happy days at Somerset. **Facing page** Preparing for one of our end-of-season football matches against Taunton. **Above left** Welcoming Greg Chappell back to Somerset during Australia's 1980 visit to England. **Above right** With Len Creed at the Bath Festival in 1981 **Below** With my great friend Pete 'Jock' McCoombe.

Left With my mother and father outside their house in Antigua.
Below My father, Malcolm Richards, in the Windward/Leeward team of 1946. He is second from the right in the back row.
Bottom Matara and Mali with their grandparents

ENGLAND vs.WEST INDIES (First Test)
at Trent Bridge on 3rd, 4th, 5th, 7th, 8th June 1976
Toss : West Indies.   Umpires : H.D. Bird and T.W. Spencer
Match drawn

WEST INDIES

Batsman		Runs		Runs
R.C. Fredericks	c Hendrick b Greig	42	b Snow	15
C.G. Greenidge	c Edrich b Hendrick	22	c and b Old	23
I.V.A. Richards	c Greig b Underwood	232	lbw b Snow	63
A.I. Kallicharran	c Steele b Underwood	97	(6) not out	29
C.H. Lloyd*	c Hendrick b Underwood	16	(4) c Brearley b Snow	21
B.D. Julien	c Knott b Old	21	(5) c Hendrick b Snow	13
H.A. Gomes	c Close b Underwood	0		
D.L. Murray+	c Close b Snow	19		
V.A. Holder	not out	19		
A.M.E. Roberts	b Old	1		
W.W. Daniel	c Knott b Old	4		
Extras	(lb 12,w 1,nb 8)	21	(lb 6,w 2,nb 4)	12
TOTAL		494	(for 5 wkts dec)	176

ENGLAND

Batsman		Runs		Runs
J.H. Edrich	c Murray b Daniel	37	not out	76
J.M. Brearley	c Richards b Julien	0	c Murray b Holder	17
D.S. Steele	c Roberts b Daniel	106	c Julien b Roberts	6
D.B. Close	c Murray b Daniel	2	not out	36
R.A. Woolmer	lbw b Julien	82		
A.W. Greig*	b Roberts	0		
A.P.E. Knott+	c sub b Holder	9		
C.M. Old	b Daniel	33		
J.A. Snow	not out	20		
D.L. Underwood	c Murray b Holder	0		
M. Hendrick	c Daniel b Fredericks	5		
Extras	(b 5,lb 1,w 3,nb 29)	38	(b 9,w 2,nb 10)	21
TOTAL		332	(for 2 wkts)	156

ENGLAND	O	M	R	W	O	M	R	W
Snow	31	5	123	1	11	2	53	4
Hendrick	24	7	59	1	7	2	22	0
Old	34.3	7	80	3	10	0	64	1
Greig	27	4	82	1	1	0	16	0
Woolmer	10	2	47	0				
Underwood	27	8	82	4	7	3	9	0

WEST INDIES	O	M	R	W	O	M	R	W
Roberts	34	15	53	1	9	3	20	1
Julien	34	9	75	2	16	8	19	0
Holder	25	5	66	2	12	6	12	1
Daniel	23	8	53	4	10	2	20	0
Fredericks	8.4	2	24	1	9	1	21	0
Richards	3	1	8	0	3	1	7	0
Gomes	4	1	8	0	9	1	18	0
Lloyd	3	1	7	0				
Kallicharran					10	3	18	0

FALL OF WICKETS

	WI	ENG	WI	ENG
1st	36	0	33	38
2nd	105	98	77	55
3rd	408	105	109	
4th	423	226	124	
5th	432	229	176	
6th	432	255		
7th	458	278		
8th	481	279		
9th	488	318		
10th	494	332		

only in the background. Suddenly the news came on about the 'grovel' remark. It simply stunned us. I do not know to this day whether someone was deliberately trying to stir up trouble – strange things like that do happen in Test cricket – but somebody told us that the word 'grovel' was often used to put down the blacks in South Africa. Of course, Greig was a South African so that only served to add fuel to our anger.

Even if Greig had not been having a racist dig at us, his remark really worked wonders for us. We were suddenly so fired up, it was as if he had unintentionally handed us the ammunition we needed to win the series. And that is what happened. The first Test began in extremely tense circumstances at Trent Bridge. I felt more than good, I felt pretty invincible out there. The 'grovel' remark remained in my head as I made 232 runs in something like 7 hours, helped by Alvin Kallicharran who made a very intelligent 97. However, despite being personally very satisfied by this performance and the fact that Tony Greig had been out for a duck, as a team we were far from happy when the match concluded in a draw.

I was unable to play in the second Test, which was disappointing for me, especially because it was at Lord's – and playing well in a Lord's Test has to be the ultimate dream of every cricketer. Again, the result was a frustrating draw. Then we won at Old Trafford, and again at Leeds which meant that we had the series won before the tour reached The Oval. Nevertheless this proved to be the match that many people remember from the tour, mainly because of my score of 291, which was not so far behind Gary Sobers's record Test innings of 365.

There was some controversy about the celebratory party which took place in my room at the Waldorf Hotel in London after the first day's play. I was on 130 not out and

ENGLAND vs. WEST INDIES (Fifth Test)

at Kennington Oval on 12th, 13th, 14th, 16th, 17th August 1976
Toss : West Indies.   Umpires : W.E. Alley and H.D. Bird
West Indies won by 231 runs

WEST INDIES

R.C. Fredericks	c Balderstone b Miller	71	not out	86
C.G Greenidge	lbw b Willis	0	not out	85
I.V.A. Richards	b Greig	291		
L.G. Rowe	st Knott b Underwood	70		
C.H. Lloyd*	c Knott b Greig	84		
C.L. King	c Selvey b Balderstone	63		
D.L. Murray+	c and b Underwood	36		
V.A. Holder	not out	13		
M.A. Holding	b Underwood	32		
A.M.E. Roberts				
W.W. Daniel				
Extras	(b 1,lb 17,nb 9)	27	(b 4,lb 1,w 1,nb 5)	11
TOTAL	(for 8 wkts dec)	687	(for 0 wkts dec)	182

ENGLAND

R.A Woolmer	lbw b Holding	8	c Murray b Holding	30
D.L. Amiss	b Holding	203	c Greenidge b Holding	16
D.S. Steele	lbw b Holding	44	c Murray b Holder	42
J.C. Balderstone	b Holding	0	b Holding	0
P. Willey	c Fredericks b King	33	c Greenidge b Holder	1
A.W. Greig*	b Holding	12	b Holding	1
D.L. Underwood	b Holding	4	(9) c Lloyd b Roberts	2
A.P.E. Knott+	b Holding	50	(7) b Holding	57
G. Miller	c sub b Holder	36	(8) b Richards	24
M.W.W. Selvey	b Holding	0	not out	4
R.G.D. Willis	not out	5	lbw b Holding	0
Extras	(b 8,lb 11,nb 21)	40	(b 15,lb 3,w 8)	26
TOTAL		435		203

INDIA	O	M	R	W	O	M	R	W
Willis	15	3	73	1	7	0	48	0
Selvey	15	0	67	0	9	1	44	0
Underwood	60.5	15	165	3	9	2	38	0
Woolmer	9	0	44	0	5	0	30	0
Miller	27	4	106	1				
Balderstone	16	0	80	1				
Greig	34	5	96	2	2	0	11	0
Willey	3	0	11	0				
Steele	3	0	18	0				

WEST INDIES	O	M	R	W	O	M	R	W
Roberts	27	4	102	0	13	4	37	1
Holding	33	9	92	8	20.4	6	57	6
Holder	27.5	7	75	1	14	5	29	2
Daniel	10	1	30	0				
Fredericks	11	2	36	0	12	5	33	0
Richards	14	4	30	0	11	6	11	1
King	7	3	30	1	6	2	9	0
Lloyd					2	1	1	0

FALL OF WICKETS

	WI	ENG	WI	ENG
1st	5	47		49
2nd	159	147		54
3rd	350	151		64
4th	524	279		77
5th	547	303		78
6th	640	323		148
7th	642	342		196
8th	687	411		196
9th		411		202
10th		435		203

many people seemed to think that it was somewhat inappropriate for me to be involved in such a party when I was not just in the middle of a Test match but, possibly, in the middle of an innings which might go on to break some kind of record. I know for a fact that there was a particular Somerset official who just could not believe that West Indian people, many of them my friends and relations, would keep me up partying until late.

But West Indian people are like that. In many ways we are made to feel small, perhaps insignificant, in this world. So when we manage to achieve something special like beating England at cricket, the people of the Caribbean just want to celebrate and nothing at all can be done to halt that celebration. It would have been very selfish of me not to have allowed that celebration to continue. After all, those people were celebrating *my* achievement. I felt that I owed it to them. In any case, the extent of the partying was exaggerated. I went to bed not too much later than at other times. The next day I went on to 291 and some people felt that, had I not been involved in the party, I might not have been out with such a lazy shot at that point. But that was at the end of an extremely long innings.

What is more important is that I remain very proud of that innings. I never did care for breaking records. Quite honestly, cracking the Sobers record was hardly uppermost in my mind. Although it was good nonetheless to break another of his records – for most runs by a West Indian in Test cricket– almost fifteen years later. We had beaten England in my first Test series against them and I felt that my individual performances were more than satisfactory. I felt on top of the world. Who cares about batting records, when you are feeling like that?

EARLY DAYS IN SOMERSET

I had many of my greatest moments at Somerset, no doubt about that. I still love the area as a place to live. I always felt totally relaxed there. I could do what I wanted to do in a nice, peaceful manner and, at least in the good days, there was always a healthy aura of optimism about the club. Outside of cricket, however, I soon realised that I did not really know anyone at all – not in England. It was like living in a cocoon.

The local cinema was one place I could go. I did feel a bit conspicuous because I don't think many people in England go out alone, but for a guy from the Caribbean, feeling very lonely and very chilly too, the cinema seemed like some kind of refuge. A place where I could lose myself in fantasy and not feel so isolated. One night, down there in that cinema, I chanced upon this Scotsman call Pete McCoombe (widely known as 'Jock').

It was an odd meeting. Almost immediately we seemed to strike up a conversation. I knew nothing about Scotland, I am not sure if I had ever met a Scotsman before, but it was such a relief to find someone who was on the same wavelength. We clicked. Soon we were spending many days together. I think he was on the dole at the time, although I never really knew. We went to the coffee shops in Bath, relaxed and talked and then walked around the town. He taught me so much about British life. In cricket circles players tend to live to one side of the mainstream.

Pete showed me the real England. At one time he had worked for Manchester United. He knew Best, Law and Charlton...they were just names to me until then, and so I began to understand just what the Manchester United legend was all about. On and on, he would tell me about the great days of the Sixties in Manchester and Liverpool.

Over the years we became very close friends. His wife became a close friend of my wife too, and he often came out to Antigua. Sadly, it was on one of these visits that he died about six years ago. It was a pretty heartbreaking time. I missed a one-day international – the Australians were touring here and were playing in St Lucia – but I went back to England with him. I felt that I owed it to him to go.

If this was a perfect world, the 1975 county season would have seen Somerset romping away with the Championship. It was their centenary year and it would have been so wonderful to have won something for the county – and the fans. We did not get our perfect ending, but as a season it was full of incident. One, in particular, stands out in my memory. It occurred when we went to Harrogate to play Yorkshire in midsummer.

Brian Close had a thing about playing against his native county and we all had to concentrate extra hard. It was obviously a very important fixture. It was a good batting wicket and Yorkshire, going in first, put together 387-9. When we went in Closey got his head down and battled away to reach 91. I too became determined to create a big score and did so. In the first innings I powered away to 217 not out. I was really flowing out there, loving every minute and, I am sure, getting on the nerves of the entire population of Yorkshire. Somebody later told me that this was only the third double century scored against

YORKSHIRE vs. SOMERSET
at Harrogate on 28th, 30th June, 1st July 1975
Toss : Yorkshire.   Umpires : H.D. Bird and D.L. Evans
Match drawn

YORKSHIRE

G. Boycott*	c Taylor b Burgess	25	c Taylor b Botham	14
R.G. Lumb	c Richards b Jones	31	lbw b Burgess	52
B. Leadbeater	b Burgess	2	c Close b Jones	15
J.H. Hampshire	c Moseley b Jones	115	b Burgess	18
C.M. Old	c Close b Burgess	7	c Rose b Close	86
D.L. Bairstow+	c and b Jones	37	not out	72
P. Carrick	c and b Jones	41	lbw b Jones	41
G.B. Stevenson	c Richards b Breakwell	53	c Jennings b Breakwell	5
H.P. Cooper	c Richards b Breakwell	5	not out	7
G.A. Cope	not out	2		
A.L. Robinson	not out	24		
Extras	(b 9,lb 16,w 3,nb 17)	45	(b 10,lb 3,w 6,nb 6)	25
TOTAL	(for 9 wkts dec)	387	(for 7 wkts dec)	335

SOMERSET

D.J.S. Taylor+	b Old	11	c Cooper b Carrick	41
B.C. Rose	c Leadbeater b Robinson	9	lbw b Old	1
P.A. Slocombe	c Bairstow b Cooper	24	c Boycott b Cope	46
K.F. Jennings	b Cooper	35	c Old b Cope	0
I.V.A. Richards	not out	217	run out	1
D.B. Close*	c Leadbeater b Cooper	91	st Bairstow b Cope	1
G.I. Burgess	c Stevenson b Robinson	19	c Boycott b Cope	4
I.T. Botham	c and b Stevenson	5	c Bairstow b Carrick	0
D. Breakwell	not out	3	not out	0
H.R. Moseley			c Robinson b Cope	0
A.A. Jones			not out	0
Extras	(lb 6,w 2,nb 1)	9	(b 18,lb 3,nb 1)	22
TOTAL	(for 7 wkts dec)	423	(for 9 wkts)	116

SOMERSET	O	M	R	W	O	M	R	W
Jones	21	7	48	4	20	3	49	2
Moseley	14	4	32	0				
Burgess	28	7	93	3	18	4	60	2
Botham	13	1	55	0	15	6	46	1
Jennings	11.2	3	44	0	6	2	18	0
Breakwell	9	1	45	2	15	3	83	1
Richards	3	0	25	0	2	0	11	0
Close					7	0	43	1

YORKSHIRE	O	M	R	W	O	M	R	W
Robinson	22	4	82	2	6	1	8	0
Cooper	21	6	57	3	4	2	3	0
Stevenson	14	2	74	1				
Old	19	3	63	1	5	3	3	1
Carrick	12	2	79	0	25	16	55	2
Cope	12	2	59	0	23	15	25	5

FALL OF WICKETS

	YOR	SOM	YOR	SOM
1st	53	14	47	8
2nd	55	49	79	63
3rd	82	49	112	65
4th	102	136	114	87
5th	249	363	229	99
6th	254	399	317	116
7th	346	411	326	116
8th	358			116
9th	358			116
10th				

Yorkshire since the war.

We reached 423-7 and were pretty confident. But Yorkshire were still in form with the bat and scored 335-7 in their second innings. This left us with an awful lot to do. If the truth be known, we were pretty well demoralised. After all, we thought that we had the edge on them after that first innings, and now here we were chasing a big fourth-innings total. The worst thing happened. We collapsed to 116-9 and we were fortunate to manage that.

My batting was hampered by an injured ankle. I knew that I was not really fit to chase after quick singles. My partner out there was wicket-keeper Derek Taylor and we had agreed to shape our innings to suit my ankle problems. Suddenly, he just touched the ball and called for a 'quickie'. I had no choice but to set off on what I knew would end in disaster and, true enough, I was run out. I was furious. I know I should not have let it get to me – in cricket you have to accept things like that. But you do not think on such reasonable lines when it actually happens. I began to limp away from the wicket, very slowly, lost in frustration and anger. It was probably made worse for me because I felt that I had soured my excellent first innings. Anyway, the Yorkshire crowd are never ones to shirk from showing their feelings and one of them, probably more out of a desire to wind me up than anything genuinely racist – although you never know – called out: 'Hurry up, you black bastard.'

That was too much for me. I looked up and dashed towards the group of spectators and, holding my bat aloft, shouted, 'Whoever said that, stand up.'

Needless to say, nobody did. It cannot have been a pleasant sight, seeing me standing there, eyes flashing with anger. I honestly don't know what I would have done. I was very, very angry.

This anger had not subsided when I stormed into the dressing room. Although I do not regret losing my temper – to an extent it was justified – I am not too proud of the fact that I smashed the door down with my bat.

That is my strongest memory from 1975 and not a particularly happy one. To counter it, I can recall a 126 not out I made against Gloucestershire when they were dramatically beaten in the last over. That was a good win and, all in all, it was not a bad season. However, in their centenary year, I felt that Somerset deserved better.

The following year, 1976, I had Test commitments and did not play for the county at all. It was in the 1977 season that I really made my mark in county cricket. Somerset's trophy-winning history had been, let's face it, non-existent. Although this particular season did not bring us a trophy, we could feel at least that great times were more than a mere possibility. There was a prevailing atmosphere of optimism and I felt that it was exactly the right club to be playing for at that particular time. County cricket is like that, you can spot the dominant teams of the future as they are emerging, sometimes two or three years before they finally reap the benefits of success. Well, that is how it was at Somerset in 1977.

The county became a delightful place to live in and, at last, I felt a sense of belonging. If I walked into a pub or coffee bar and fell into a cricket conversation, I could feel the hope in people's voices. This added to our sense of responsibility, but I was used to that. I felt empathy with the people of the area.

That season my batting reached something of a peak and I was relishing every opportunity to face new, untried bowlers. All I can really remember is a mass of different innings all merged together in my memory. However, at the end of the season I had managed an average in the mid-

80s which obviously signalled a very satisfying period for me.

I suppose my favourite memory must be the time we played against Gloucestershire at Bristol. We had not, as a team, been playing so well on that occasion, but I felt terrific and batted to an undefeated 241. I think that was the game in which I finally realised that I was a valuable asset to Somerset. But, to be honest, I hate to talk in that way and I hate it when people place too much importance on my individual performances. Somerset were certainly not a one-man team. Together we had the beginnings of something great and an awful lot of people made extremely valuable contributions during the season. It was a proud time for me. Finally I felt I had conquered the tensions of county cricket.

> And for the record, as Viv Richards is forever reluctant to wallow in self-congratulation, here is a run-down of his Somerset successes of 1977:
> 241 against Gloucestershire
> 204 against Surrey
> 204 against Sussex
> 189 against Lancashire
> 118 against Warwickshire
> 104 against Leicestershire
> 104 against Derbyshire (John Player League)
> 101 against Warwickshire

KERRY PACKER
AND
OTHER ECCENTRICS

I like innovative people. I like colourful people. I like people who have something to say, a contribution to make. Cricket is the strangest sport in the world because it is largely governed by grey men who seem to want it to remain as drab and uninteresting as possible.

For me cricket is the one sport which above all others is so full of hidden excitement. Any moves to highlight that excitement, that intensity, have to be good moves. I do not want this game to fade away into the mists of nostalgia. I want it to be brash and exciting – a game for the Nineties.

During the course of my career, I have encountered a number of people who have wanted to add a touch of colour to this lovely game, some literally so. Most notable of these was Kerry Packer, to whom I will turn in a minute. First I want to mention briefly my old friend, Tim Hudson, who suffered so much because he had a vision that was too great, too exciting for the dullards who run this sport to comprehend.

Tim Hudson came to the 1990 Test against England at the Recreation Ground in St John's, Antigua. He instantly fell in love with that little ground. I think he simply fell for the profound sense of occasion, the colour of the event and how musical the whole thing was. In the Caribbean we have never had any problem about bringing music and cricket together. The two co-exist quite happily.

We are a rhythmic people and this is how we build an atmosphere.

Tim has always had this feeling about music and cricket gelling together. Some people find this an appalling prospect but I think it makes very good sense. I have spoken to Tim on many occasions and, yes, I know that he talks a lot, but he has such fantastic enthusiasm for life – and fantastic enthusiasm for cricket. He really loves the game and could offer so much, if only people would listen to him. But people dismiss him, I guess, because he wears a pony tail and has a very unconventional manner. A great shame because he has some wonderful ideas.

He put them into practice at his own little ground, at Birtles in Cheshire. He did it on a very small scale, but he managed to create a unique kind of fun cricket. I always enjoyed playing there, even if the pitch was not so wonderful. It was just very refreshing to see somebody try to do things in a different manner.

However, what chance does a guy like Hudson stand against some of the strait-laced, humourless guys of the cricket fraternity? They think that everyone involved in cricket, and in most other walks of life, should be just like themselves. And just look at them. They are some of the dullest people on the face of this earth. How can they hope to attract big crowds to a game when they keep it under a blanket of pomposity?

It makes me laugh, and also cry, to think that people can hold such beliefs and still be granted a position of power. They think they are so strong. They did the same thing to Tim, obviously on a much smaller scale, that they tried with Packer. In the end though, Packer had the power to take them on and they finished up eating off his plate, which was glorious to see.

Tim had many knockers. People would pretend to

listen to him but it would go in one ear and out the other. They never wanted him to get any kind of foothold in serious cricket and they did everything possible to ridicule him. But all he ever really wanted to do was brighten up this lovely game. He wanted to shine a light on the drama. He wanted people who have been unmoved by cricket to become fascinated by it, to become involved.

My main hope for the future is that cricket is not allowed to remain in the control of guys who are living in the past. Cricket is not about the past. It is not masses of statisticians and long, rambling, pompous conversations about days gone by. There is some magic in reminiscing for older folk amongst themselves. Tim saw that. He was closer to the true heart of the sport than most of the so-called experts.

Cricket is about skill and athleticism, passion and pain. The drama of winning and losing. If we are not careful, cricket will die a slow death. We need to work at making cricket a more universal form of entertainment.

For example I am sure the authorities could do more to entertain people before big matches, in the lunch and tea intervals, or even after some games. I also feel strongly that the intensely loyal supporters of cricket should be treated better. Some spectator facilities are very poor. Supporters suffer all kinds of treatment just to watch a match. They, however, are the ones who fund the game, who pay people like me to indulge in the sport, so I think they should be treated with courtesy and consideration at all times.

If the cricket authorities really do want to retain their most loyal supporters and attract new ones then they are going to have to start attracting people with ideas who want to brighten up the sport. Cricket is a fascinating game, but we have to get people involved who are passionately concerned about the future.

There is a massive potential audience out there but we need to draw it towards the heart of cricket. We must make cricket as attractive as possible to other than traditional cricket audiences. People are interested in America and Canada and perhaps they could be in Japan. We must think of how we can reach them and hold them.

In American sport people are entertained throughout any event they attend. They have bright modern stadiums. The public would never accept anything less, and why should they? I have watched baseball matches and admired the way the crowds leave in a relaxed, satisfied state of mind, happy in the knowledge that they have been thoroughly entertained. I am sure the hooliganism in English sport would be reduced with better facilities and more entertainment whether it is marching bands, cheer-leaders or community singing. Tim Hudson loves cricket and wants to try new ideas to find out what appeals to the cricket audience. For example he wanted to put a band on during the tea interval. People thought this was preposterous. I thought it was a great idea providing the music appealed to the crowd.

If cricket is presented in a better, more lively way with the help of forward-minded people such as Kerry Packer, then I am sure it could be sold to other countries. Cricket already has a following in almost all the Commonwealth countries. It was marvellous to play in Canada and to realise how many people were really interested. Sure, they have their basketball and baseball but they are still prepared to support their cricket. Even in New York, where there is a cultural mix, cricket already has a following. And look at the teams entered in the World Cup – who would associate cricket with Holland and Denmark? I would love to see someone build on that, but it would have to be done with a little panache. It is more likely to come from an Australian or an American rather than an Englishman. With great respect nobody wants to listen any more to stuffy, pompous Englishmen.

THE KERRY PACKER CRICKET CIRCUS

I have absolutely no regrets about signing and playing for Kerry Packer in the late Seventies. Firstly there was the obvious reason that it paid well and I see no reason to apologise for this. A cricketer's life, even at the very top, is by no means secure and he has a duty, to himself and his family, to try to make the best of his talent. That was the first reason why people went to Packer and, as they were treated rather badly in many other areas of cricket, then I thought it was fair enough.

I remember how the circus came about. I was over in Trinidad playing in a Test against Pakistan. This guy from the Packer set-up approached a few of us (Michael Holding, Clive Lloyd and Andy Roberts were the others). It was a strange occasion. My mind was full of the thoughts of the Test match, and I found it difficult to take in the importance of what was being said. However, one thing did get through to me. When I realised that, by playing for Packer, I could net £75,000 my heart started to pound a little.

I knew there would be a lot of protest, but I also knew there would be an awful lot of hypocrisy. This was going to be a great chance for me so why should I let a lot of jealous guys spoil it for me? And there was a good deal of jealousy. Very few cricketers anywhere would have refused that offer. It was generous. It was a chance of a lifetime and I know that, had I refused through some misplaced sense of ethics, I would have regretted it for ever.

I shall never forget when the Packer representative, who had spelt out the deal very simply, and very honestly as it turned out, left Clive, Andy, Michael and me to chat things over. We all looked at Clive and he smiled. I knew then that we were making the correct decision.

My only reservation was the effect this decision might have over in England. I knew that Len Creed, and many more at Somerset, would be extremely concerned. I told him that it should not harm my playing for Somerset in any way, but I knew he was not convinced.

When I returned to England it was a difficult time. Everybody wished me well, in fact there was no ill feeling at all. Players offered me advice and I think they were genuinely concerned that I might be walking into some kind of cul-de-sac. 'It may all sound fine on the surface but be careful Vivian,' they said. 'Be careful.'

As the time to leave for Australia drew close, my nervousness increased – and for all kinds of reasons. Firstly would I be stepping outside the world cricket establishment? I felt the Packer project was right, but it still required us to walk into the unknown. This was not, for me, like going to England for the first time, where I would become part of a respected and established scheme of things. This was different. I had also heard disturbing reports of the Packer wickets, and how unnatural it felt to stand there under floodlights. Would I be able to cope as a batsman? Would I be able to spot the ball quickly enough? These were questions that, really, no one could answer but me – when I got there. There was only one thing for it.

Although I have never played cricket specifically in order to acquire money, Packer's financial inducement was important in that it gave the players a degree of reassurance. It settled us down while we looked forward to the main business in hand – to compete against the very best cricketers in the world. It was a matter of pride. If you considered yourself to be among the cream, then you naturally wanted to be part of the action.

When our little party from the West Indies flew out to Australia we were all clearly very nervous. I think we felt a strange sense of loss, of being cut off. Were we really mercenaries, selfish men flying to an uncertain and probably nasty end?

When we arrived many of our fears were soon dispelled. I immediately liked Packer. I saw in him a fighting spirit. By then I had plenty of evidence of just how awkward the cricketing establishment can be, and I felt a lot of sympathy for Packer, the man who had challenged them. Amongst the players a sense of comradeship soon built up. When Christmas approached, and Packer invited all the girlfriends and wives for a huge Christmas dinner, it felt like a happy place to be. It was a significant occasion because it helped us to feel we were in the right place at the right time. It forged a pioneering spirit. And, of course, there was the cricket itself.

It proved to be some of the hardest, meanest cricket that I have ever played in. With all those great players on the park it was impossible to relax for a second. The competition was as fierce as any Test match, fiercer if the truth be told. I think all the players were really fired up. Everyone wanted to make sure that they had their act together because it was a world stage. Cricketers were not used to being in such a spotlight and, given the added sense that it was something new, something bold and exciting, the cricket definitely had an edge to it.

I learned a lot from that period. It helped me to become a real professional. All the teams had trainers and physios. There was no loafing around, it was all hard toil.

I remember Packer and his aides giving us lengthy talks, very intense talks, explaining the nature of professionalism. It was hard and businesslike. Those guys did not mess around. Although it was described as the 'Packer Circus' all those stories about games being rigged were untrue. There was none of that. It was raw, hard-nosed cricket.

Packer was a businessman. He had no time for sentimentality, for resting on old reputations. He expected results. His aim was to assemble the best cricketers in the world in one arena and to provide the spectators with some of the finest and most competitive cricket that has ever taken place. I certainly cannot think of a tougher time in my cricketing career.

There were many mistakes. The way they experimented with the colours, at least at first with those outrageous colours, the so-called pyjamas, was ridiculous, but then, when you are trying something for the first time you are going to have a few hiccups. I do not think those colours actually helped the PR of the whole affair. The press jumped upon this aspect and used it to rubbish the whole concept. However, if you are out there facing a fearsome bowler like Lenny Pascoe, it does not matter if he is throwing a white ball at you instead of a red one. It still comes at the same pace. It is still capable of knocking your head off.

If anything, it seemed harder, more intense in the Packer Circus. Every bowler wanted to intimidate you. It was gladiatorial cricket at its finest. And the organisation was superb, the best I have ever played with. This, also, provided the players with something to live up to. Forget the press stories, it was far from shoddy. It was top-class, dangerous, intense, beautiful cricket. Today's cricket authorities could learn an awful lot from the Packer people. They were really sharp.

I remember that the Australian cricket authorities, who were less than impressed, forced Packer to stage some of the games in venues which had never been meant for cricket. They had to make 'instant wickets' and this attracted a good deal of criticism. But, as far as I was concerned, those wickets were superb – easily up to Test match standard.

It was a really exciting time for all of us. Just imagine what it was like, suddenly to be playing top-class cricket at night. I even got to like the colours. We all felt as though we were pioneering, doing something to change the face of cricket and to bring it up to date. I know many people objected but innovative measures are often controversial. They *need* to be if changes are to be introduced. Nothing would ever happen if we just sat around listening to those dull old guys.

On the whole, I was very satisfied with my own performances. My initial worries about the wickets and about my own ability to adapt to playing in such arenas, proved to be unfounded. I really enjoyed myself and, if I remember correctly, I did at one stage have an average of more than 90. Perhaps some of the criticism we got helped to inspire me, gave me something to prove. I wanted to show the world just how beautiful the game could be, even when linked to a new, hard-selling commercial set-up. Cricket tradition is fine, but it is not the be-all and end-all – not, anyway, for me.

Unfortunately, the Packer affair did little to help my relationship with the West Indies Cricket Board of Control, which had been uneasy from the beginning. Our problems began when we walked out of the West Indies team on the eve of the Test against Australia at Georgetown, Guyana

in March 1978. This was a terrible moment. Clive Lloyd, who was distraught when Des Haynes, Richard Austin and Derryck Murray had been dropped because of their involvement with Packer, resigned on a matter of principle. I believed, too, that Lloyd was deserving of our support. After we pulled out, the West Indian Cricket Board's president, Jeffrey Stollmeyer, made this statement:
'In view of the decision of the World Series Cricket contracted players to withdraw from representing the West Indies in a Test Match, the Board, in the interest of the future of West Indies cricket, has decided that these players will take no further part in the current series...'

This meant that the international careers of players such as Gordon Greenidge, Colin Croft and Joel Garner were in jeopardy. It was a very sad state of affairs. Around this time, there were many rumours circulating about my alleged dissatisfaction with the Packer project and that I was somehow turning my back on the whole affair. I was not. The confusion arose because I was managed by David Lord, not a Packer enthusiast, who also looked after Alvin Kallicharran and Jeff Thomson. They both pulled out of the Packer affair, and I think it was generally assumed that I would follow suit. Especially as I shared an involvement with Jeff in the Australian radio station, 4IP.

Anyway, there was a lot of nonsense talked and printed. It was a mess. I grew sick and tired of it. I just wanted to play cricket. I could not understand why people made such a big deal out of Packer's plans. He had a new angle, that was all, and wanted to give it a try. Sometimes I think that people are not happy unless they are causing aggro. Perhaps they lead very empty lives.

I know that many people longed to see Packer fail. And, during that first year, he nearly did. The cricket may have been beautiful but some of the crowds were disappointing. Mind you, true to form, the press made the most of the vast scale of some of the stadiums. They were not as empty as some of the newspaper photographs made them seem. On the plus side, I will always remember playing in front of a huge crowd of 25,000 in Melbourne. There, if anything, the floodlights helped to increase the atmosphere in the stadium.

I returned to England for the 1978 county season, and again found no ill-feeling at Somerset. In fact, the reverse was true. Most of the English players were fascinated to hear our first-hand accounts. People on the fringes of cricket could argue all they wanted but my fellow-cricketers all seemed to be genuinely excited by the possibilities posed by Packer. And I am sure, also, that the vast majority of fans felt the same way, although some people would no doubt disagree.

ADVERTISING AND ALL THAT

Cricket must move with the times. It needs sponsorship but I think the authorities must give more consideration to reasonable requests from sponsors. It is difficult to understand why the outfield of a Test Match ground can be branded with the logo of the series sponsor yet players cannot wear the logos of their sponsors when representing their country.

In almost every other professional sport players are allowed to display their sponsor's name and to wear products they endorse. Yet in cricket we still have to cover up sponsors' names when television cameras are present. Pay for professional cricketers is already low; I feel that the authorities should also give more consideration to players (as well as sponsors) and make sure that they have the same rights as other professional sportsmen. Thank

God for Kerry Packer! He really did try to advance the commercial interests of cricket and bring the game up to date. He certainly raised players wages.

If a cricketer wants to wear, say, a Reebok shoe, why the hell not? What right has anyone got to prevent him from doing so? Sponsorship can only benefit the sport and, perhaps more importantly, the individual players. They used to grumble about Kerry Packer, about not wanting to get involved with this man who was attempting to bring the game up to date. Thank God that Packer did try, that is all I can say. It is because of Packer that cricketers' wages have at least gone up a little. They should be much higher.

Packer had a great idea. Cricket, at that time, was even more in a cocoon than it is now. But if we are not careful, it will still die a slow death. You only have to look at other sports, like snooker which has totally eclipsed cricket in the earning power of the top performers – and should not have done. Snooker is a skilled game, but it is not as exciting as soccer or as intricate as cricket. Even darts sometimes seems to grab more attention than cricket in England. There are all sorts of possibilities in the broadcasting of cricket, it could make such a great package for a television company. But the game is being left behind, overtaken by inferior sports. The blame for this lies firmly with a few unimaginative guys at the top.

ALL THIS,
AND
CRICKET TOO

Vivian Richards guides the Range Rover around the small family of basking cattle which are spread, awkwardly, across the thin strip of Antiguan tarmac.   Then he glides the vehicle through the gears and, taking advantage of a relatively clear stretch of straight road, assumes a speed not normally associated with roads in the vicinity.   Window open, his arm hanging casually out, Suzanne Vega's voice floating soothingly from the stereo.

'I like this girl, man,' he states, flashing a broad smile, 'I feel that I can relax to her music...it just makes me feel nice and, at times, begin to think a little.'

The Range Rover, having slowed considerably, eases its way through the outskirts of St John's.   More than once, Suzanne Vega's voice is drowned by the sound of reggae bass lines pumping from unlikely looking buildings which are adorned with signs depicting, 'BURNING FLAMES TAPES SOLD HERE'.

'That's our local band,' exclaims Richards, 'The Burning Flames...they were at the Notting Hill Carnival last year...very good, too.'

Before long, the crammed buildings which flank St John's are replaced by the larger, more salubrious middle-class dwellings – and more cattle, which once again block the way, as Viv Richards chats about his initial thoughts and dealings with the British press.

I can honestly say that I have had, over the years, some great relationships with numerous people from the press. At different times I have worked with Chris Lander for both the *Sun* and the *Daily Mirror*, Pat Gibson on the *Sunday Express*, Peter Hayter on the *Mail on Sunday* and Colin Bateman on the *Star*. Sometimes they can get very close to you. Sometimes I have found myself forming a friendship with someone who, if I was to follow other people's advice, I should be extremely wary of.

I have never underestimated the importance of the press but I am not sure that I enjoy being written about. It is gratifying to read about a good personal or team performance or indeed considered criticism of a match or the game. However, the two aspects I deplore are first, the tendency for the journalist (or his editor) to make things up to suit the paper's interest and secondly, the concentration in certain tabloids on personalities rather than the cricket. Mike Gatting was a hero when he won the Ashes but Fat Gatt! when he was not so successful.

I am usually pleased to chat to reporters but there are times when you are wrapped up in trying to work out a particular game and you do not want to be disturbed. But I like chatting. The trouble is I put complete confidence in the guy I am talking to; this leads to some good discussion which I enjoy.

But then I read the article and find the guy has altered absolutely everything and has used the discussion to make up some story – some angle that never even came into the conversation. This still amazes me after all these years. English guys laugh at me for being so naive but you must remember that, growing up in the Caribbean, I never come across press like that at all. I had always believed that when a story actually makes it into print, in black and white, then that was a confirmation that an event or conversation had taken place.

So, in England, when it finally dawned on me that much of this stuff was totally made up, I was astonished. I found it to be absolutely unbelievable. To begin with I would confront the pressman concerned and he would always put the blame on his editor. I came to understand that the guy had his job to do and that this job, especially in England, consists of searching out non-cricket stories and fabricating them into something that is frankly nothing more than a story. Although I did come to accept the system, I never got fully out of the habit of befriending members of the press, even after all that was written. I will still put my confidence in a professional journalist.

But in the end I have learned to be very selective about those members of the press I would talk to. There are some very brilliant journalists, even in England, and I think I have developed the ability to suss out the good ones. People like John Woodcock, David Foot, Richard Streeton and quite a few more. These guys are always interested for the right reasons. They know how and when to approach me. I do admit that there have been times when I have been a little sharp, but that is when I feel that I have been violated, either by a poor line in questioning or by lousy timing.

I remember throwing one guy out of the dressing room even though his paper had an exclusive contract with me. He was a good journalist but he failed to understand that a cricketer does not want to be bothered just before a game – whatever his paper's deadlines. He was sniffing around for a non-cricket story just as we were about to go on the field. I was concentrating on my team. I felt his questions – his line of enquiry – were wholly inappropriate and he could not see that I needed peace and quiet. But normally I am very approachable as serious cricket correspondents know.

If 1977 had seen me relaxing a little, finding my feet and even building a reputation in county cricket, then 1978 was to be the cruellest kind of anti-climax. There was a glorious mood of optimism about the Somerset camp. During 1977, we all felt that we were laying the groundwork for great things to come. It was with this spirit in mind that we did not really mind finishing that season without a trophy. The county had been waiting an awful long time, so one more year would not be too unbearable. Perhaps this was a mistake.

Perhaps we entered into the new season feeling just too optimistic, I don't really know. We were a good team and we knew it. This year, we all thought (the team, the authorities and, most importantly, the spectators) would be the big one. History now tells us that it was not to be. I think I could have handled it better had we been totally knocked back and failed miserably, but that wasn't the case. In almost every area of cricket, 1978 would see us coming so close...and yet missing everything. It was not a classic season for me. Something was lacking with my game throughout the year. I don't really know what it was. Loss of form, for no apparent reason, is just one of those unpredictable things which help to add a bit of magic to the game – but it is very infuriating when it comes along.

Not that we did badly. We did, after all, finish a

respectable fifth in the Championship. Many of the larger counties would dearly have liked to swap places with us during the year. But if fifth position sounds frustratingly near to success, it was our two near misses that gave us the most agonising finish to the season. We lost two competitions in the space of forty-eight hours. How are passionate, competitive men supposed to cope with that?

We lost the final of the Gillette Cup, at Lord's, against Sussex, and then, immediately afterwards, we lost to Essex by two runs in our final match in the John Player League, which allowed Hampshire to take the title. The people of Somerset will never forget that terrible weekend.

Looking back on it, I think we were on too much of a high. Being a relatively small county, who were not accustomed to success, we in the team were happy to have got as far as we had. It was like a novelty to us and we did not then have the professionalism needed to carry it through to the finish. It was odd that, although we had this confidence, there was not really any depth to it. We had never been in such situations before and it affected our performances.

I personally felt very tense. I did not know how to relax and play my normal game under such pressure. I lost my aggressive edge and became a very careful player. I think I was too aware that the rest of the team were relying on my batting. They saw me as their strong point, someone to fall back on. I should, of course, have relaxed in a professional way and played as if these two games were just normal county matches. But I did not have the experience. Also, I knew the Somerset fans were relying heavily on me.

If it was bad enough at Lord's, it was even worse at Taunton. How are you supposed to re-motivate yourself

SUSSEX vs. SOMERSET
at Lord's on 2nd September 1978
Toss : Sussex . Umpires : H.D. Bird and B.J. Meyer
Sussex won by 5 wickets
Man of the Match: P.W.G. Parker

SOMERSET
B.C. Rose*	c Long b Cheatle	30
P.W. Denning	b Imran	0
I.V.A. Richards	c Arnold b Barclay	44
P.M. Roebuck	c Mendis b Cheatle	9
I.T. Botham	b Imran	80
V.J. Marks	c Arnold b Barclay	4
G.I. Burgess	run out	3
D.J.S. Taylor+	not out	13
J. Garner	not out	8
K.F. Jennings		
C.H. Dredge		
Extras	(lb10,nb 6)	16
TOTAL	(60 overs)(for 7 wkts)	207

SUSSEX
J.R.T. Barclay	c Roebuck b Botham	44
G.D. Mendis	c Marks b Burgess	44
P.W.G. Parker	not out	62
Javed Miandad	c Taylor b Garner	0
Imran Khan	c and b Botham	3
C.P. Phillipson	c Taylor b Dredge	32
S.J. Storey	not out	0
A.A. Long*+		
J. Spencer		
G.G. Arnold		
R.G.L. Cheatle		
Extras	(b 1,lb 9,w 7,nb 9)	26
TOTAL	(53.1 overs)(for 5 wkts)	211

SUSSEX	O	M	R	W	FALL OF WICKETS		
Imran	12	1	50	2		SOM	SUS
Arnold	12	2	43	0	1st	22	93
Spencer	12	3	27	0	2nd	53	106
Cheatle	12	3	50	2	3rd	73	106
Barclay	12	3	21	2	4th	115	110
					5th	151	207
SOMERSET	O	M	R	W	6th	157	
Garner	12	3	34	1	7th	194	
Dredge	10	2	26	1	8th		
Botham	12	1	65	2	9th		
Jennings	9	1	29	0	10th		
Burgess	10	2	27	1			
Denning	0.1	0	4	0			

after defeat in a Lord's final? We were still reeling from the anti-climax of it all and, suddenly, we had to walk out, once again, in front of the home crowd. All the optimism, all the enthusiasm of the previous years seemed to be working against us.

Travelling back, from London to Taunton, had been hell. I was aware that the fans were feeling as dejected as the players. Had we won at Lord's, then I am sure we would have won gloriously at Taunton and that it would have been a fantastic season. There was so much weight on our shoulders after Lord's that we just could not handle the pressure.

When we got to the Taunton ground the scene was unbelievable. The place was buzzing, the crowd all fired up. It stirred such a weird mixture of emotions in us. There we were, completely gutted by the defeat being inspired by the fantastic support at the ground. How could we possibly lose in front of those fabulous fans? But we did lose and it was unbelievably painful.

I felt as though I had just let the whole county down. It was not like losing back in Antigua, it was not like anything I had experienced before in my life. One minute we had absolutely everything going for us and the entire county singing our praises, and then, just like that, we had thrown everything away. I know it was not quite like that and, on reflection, we had still had the finest season in the history of the club. But then, you should have seen the Somerset dressing room at the end of the Taunton game. It was full of tears. It was just horrible. Then a truly remarkable thing happened.

I had assumed, especially after my Antiguan experiences, that the Somerset people would all slink home and ignore me in the streets, things like that. But the supporters gathered around the front of our dressing

SOMERSET vs. ESSEX

at Taunton on 3rd September 1978
Toss: Somerset. Umpires: W.E. Alley and D.J. Halfyard
Essex won by 2 runs

ESSEX

A.W. Lilley	c Denning b Burgess	13
G.A. Gooch	c Burgess b Botham	7
K.S. McEwan	b Moseley	2
K.W.R. Fletcher*	not out	76
K.R. Pont	b Dredge	35
B.R. Hardie	b Botham	38
N. Philip		
S. Turner		
R.E. East		
N. Smith+		
J.K. Lever		
Extras	(lb 16,nb 3)	19
TOTAL		190

SOMERSET

B.C. Rose*	b Lever	9
P.W. Denning	c Smith b Philip	8
I.V.A. Richards	c Hardie b Gooch	26
P.M. Roebuck	b East	30
I.T. Botham	c McEwan b Philip	45
P.A. Slocombe	b Lever	20
G.I. Burgess	c and b Turner	0
K.F. Jennings	not out	14
C.H. Dredge	b Lever	14
D.J.S. Taylor+	run out	4
H.R. Moseley	run out	0
Extras	(b 2,lb 12,w 1,nb 3)	18
TOTAL		188

SOMERSET	O	M	R	W	FALL OF WICKETS		
Botham	8	0	38	2		ESS	SOM
Moseley	8	0	20	1	1st	16	18
Burgess	8	0	20	1	2nd	25	18
Jennings	8	0	38	0	3rd	39	69
Dredge	8	0	55	1	4th	92	87
					5th	190	139
ESSEX	O	M	R	W	6th		140
Lever	8	0	38	3	7th		157
Philip	8	0	35	2	8th		177
Gooch	8	0	31	1	9th		185
Turner	8	0	32	1	10th		188
East	8	0	34	1			

room and began chanting our names, individually. I'll never forget that I wandered out to face them and a massive cheer went up. I broke down.

The fans taught us that day that we had not lost anything. We were still a happening team. We were still the team of the future and had everything to play for. So it would take another year, so what? We had competed with the finest in the land, beaten them on many occasions and only just failed at the final hurdle. All the same, we still had much to offer. The fans recognised the true situation before we did. Had they gone home, quiet and saddened by the defeats, then the confidence of the team would never have fully recovered as it did. The fans gave us a high. Next season, we thought, we would repay them.

In 1979, despite an almost cripplingly heavy schedule, we did win both the Gillette Cup and the John Player League. That was when we put Somerset well and truly on the cricket map; it was the beginning of a legendary era. It was also, of course, the beginning of the most tumultuous part of my career. Suddenly we were in the full glare of the press, especially Ian Botham and myself. It was not, I suppose, a completely natural situation – and maybe it was inevitable that, in the end, something would go wrong. I don't really know. But what I do know is that, for about three years, we were really kickin' at that club. We owned the world, we commanded attention and respect from every corner of cricket. We turned the spotlight well and truly on that beautiful little county.

I really felt that I was from Somerset. When we had a motorcade through town and went on to a civic reception at County Hall after winning our first title, it was the most fantastic feeling on earth. All that passion, that hope, that loyalty that the fans had shown back in 1978 – it all came flooding back to me at that reception. It felt as though we

SOMERSET vs. NORTHAMPTONSHIRE
at Lord's on 8th September 1979
Toss : Nothamptonshire. Umpires : D.J. Constant and J.G. Langridge
Somerset won by 45 runs
Man of the Match: I.V.A. Richards

SOMERSET

B.C. Rose*	b Watts	41
P.W. Denning	c Sharp b Sarfraz	19
I.V.A. Richards	b Griffiths	117
P.M. Roebuck	b Willey	14
I.T. Botham	b Lamb T.M.	27
V.J. Marks	b Griffiths	9
G.I. Burgess	c Sharp b Watts	1
D. Breakwell	b Lamb T.M.	5
J. Garner	not out	24
D.J.S. Taylor+	not out	1
K.F. Jennings		
Extras	(b 5,lb 3,nb 3)	11
TOTAL	(60 overs)(for 8 wkts)	269

NORTHAMPTONSHIRE

G. Cook	run out	44
W. Larkins	lbw b Garner	0
R.G. Williams	hit wicket b Garner	8
A.J. Lamb	st Taylor b Richards	78
P. Willey	c Taylor b Garner	5
T.J. Yardley	c Richards b Burgess	20
G. Sharp+	b Garner	22
Sarfraz Nawaz	not out	16
T.M. Lamb	b Garner	4
B.J. Griffiths	b Garner	0
P.J. Watts*	absent hurt	
Extras	(b 2,lb 9,nb 7)	18
TOTAL	(56.3 overs)	224

NORTHANTS	O	M	R	W	FALL OF WICKETS		
Sarfraz Nawaz	12	3	51	1		SOM	NOR
Griffiths	12	1	58	2	1st	34	3
Watts	12	2	34	2	2nd	95	13
Lamb T.M.	12	0	70	2	3rd	145	126
Willey	12	2	45	1	4th	186	138
					5th	213	170
SOMERSET	O	M	R	W	6th	214	186
Garner	10.3	3	29	6	7th	218	218
Botham	10	3	27	0	8th	268	224
Jennings	12	1	29	0	9th		224
Burgess	9	1	37	1	10th		
Marks	4	0	22	0			
Richards	9	0	44	1			
Breakwell	2	0	9	0			

had finally repaid them.

I felt so much a part of the area I could not imagine ever playing for any other county. Just think, it had taken the club over 100 years to achieve that success and we were the team to achieve it for them. We put Somerset on top of the world, we gave the county a place in cricket history. Whatever was to happen, nobody would ever be able to take that away from us and I think the people of Somerset – the people who really matter, the fans – will always respect us for that. Likewise, I will always respect them.

The guys at the top of the Somerset hierarchy became very big shots during our years of success. They changed completely from nice humble people, who would do anything to bring honours to the club, into arrogant types who thought they were special. I could see this happening but, as things continued to go so well for us for a number of years, nobody ever really saw the need to pass comment. After all, how can you knock success?

What they seemed to forget, however, was that we achieved that success for them. We spoilt those people – it is as simple as that. We spoilt them. The Somerset people know the truth. They know that it was the team which made the county great, not the committee.

I do not want to make too big an issue of the Somerset affair. I had great times there and I would rather remember the happy days than the disappointments which were to follow. But there are some things which still niggle, some things which I need to get off my chest.

One thing hurt me more than anything else. That was all the talk about Viv Richards not being a trier. That almost destroyed me at the time, much more than all the back-stabbing which went on behind the scenes .

Nobody could ever justify saying that Viv Richards is

not a trier. There are always times when you are going to have your indifferent days and, yes, I did suffer periods like that at Somerset. I do not deny that, in the later years, my concentration did suffer a bit. But certain people were openly accusing me of cricketing apathy and that was like a red rag to a bull to me. There were many awful and totally unjustifiable things said. I do still feel that the management of the club let us down badly. I believe that, throughout our years at Somerset, we had given sufficient service to the club to be treated with a bit of respect.

In the later years, I could feel a certain undercurrent of tension without fully understanding what it meant. Because I was a player, concentrating on my cricket, I never really saw some of the things that were going on – the scheming of the people who wanted Viv Richards out of the club.

There were hints. People would sneak bits of information out of committee meetings which seemed to signify that the end was in sight for me and Joel, but I did not take too much notice. There was a lot of talk about Viv Richards and Joel Garner being arrogant personalities and a disruptive influence on the team. Someone put the notion around that I was a bad influence on Ian Botham. How ridiculous. Ian, more than anyone else I have ever met, is his own man. If the truth be known there were other people who really *were* disruptive.

As far as I can understand it the club committee thought we were attracting the wrong sort of media coverage. Joel and I were seen as the big bad men. If I wore a Rastafarian wrist band it was assumed that I was subversive, some kind of radical. Some of the committee thought that by getting rid of me and Joel they would purify the club. Then there was a lot of talk about me being a 'money hawk', only concerned with money and not really interested in cricket or Somerset. That hurt.

Anyone who really knows me well will tell you that is simply not true. David Copp, who manages my commercial affairs, can tell you how many money-making opportunities I have turned down to concentrate on my cricket. I had been at my peak for Somerset for a number of years and we had enjoyed some success. We were pulling in new members and good crowds. Yet I never went to the manager's office to ask for more money. When I did finally talk to Colin Atkinson about a raise my request was for £12,500. Surely that was not an unreasonable request for an established Test player who had helped Somerset win honours and attract large crowds. Playing for Somerset meant more to me than money.

Then there was a repeated whisper that I was not trying. That was below the belt. I have tried hard never to just 'go through the motions' on the field. My passion for cricket makes me want to do well at all times. I am a competitor. Yes, it is true we did come into a very lean period at Somerset, but I'm telling you it was never through lack of trying. If my record is examined critically it will show that most of the time I did fairly well. My record for the county stands up along side other Test players' records for their counties. It seems to me that some of the less knowledgeable people expect you to be a run machine. You are not allowed to have off days, 'flu, family worries or simple bad luck. If you don't score you are accused of not trying.

Perhaps the real reason for much of this talk was Martin Crowe. Let's face it, I was getting on and there was a school of thought that said Martin Crowe would be a better investment for the club than me. Somerset had a reputation for selecting overseas players (Greg Chappell and Sunil Gavaskar had played for the county) and Martin

Crowe was certainly one of them. He had come to the county as second-choice overseas player. The idea was for me to stay first-choice and Martin to step in when the West Indies were touring England. However, Allan Border unwittingly upset the apple cart. He decided to cut short his two-year contract with Essex, and Essex asked Somerset's permission to approach Crowe. Somerset feared they might lose him.

I could understand that they wanted to keep Crowe but it was the duplicity, the way they went about getting rid of me which was so upsetting. Rumours were flying around about Crowe's position and a feeling of uneasiness built up over a number of weeks. During this time I was repeatedly assured that my situation at Somerset would not be in jeopardy. 'We want Martin for the future, Viv, but we will look after you.' But the rumours persisted and then the whispers that I was a 'money hawk' and that I was not really trying. Nobody likes that feeling of insecurity and it is true I exploded. I remember yelling, 'Don't speak to me about Crowe!' But I assure you it was more in frustration at all the uncertainty than jealousy, as some people suggested.

The sacking was sudden. It happened early one morning. We had been at a benefit function for Joel in Sherborne on the Friday night. The chairman, the secretary and the captain had all been expected but did not show up. It was a good party and there had been a limbo contest. We got home late. But early next morning we were called into Taunton and sacked. Bang! After eleven years' service I was told I was not wanted.

I don't think those guys really understood just how much playing for the County meant to me. Somerset for me was not just a cricket team but a second home. I had bought a house in Taunton and Miriam and I had settled happily there and built up a circle of friends. To be kicked out of Somerset in that way was deeply hurtful.

I am certain the whole business could have been handled better. If only the chairman or secretary had said, 'Look, Viv, we want Martin to stay at Somerset but we will honour our contract with you'. But all I got was lies and rumours. Maybe I would not have been happy playing second fiddle to Crowe. But surely after eleven years' service you deserve a little honesty. The lies and deceit were hurtful.

MR 'BOTH' AND ME

One good thing that came out of the whole affair was the support of Ian Botham. He rang me and said, 'Viv, I'm gonna resign'. I said, 'Look, don't get involved man; you just get on with your cricket'. But then he told me that his mind was made up and that a certain fixture would be his last game for Somerset. Tears came to my eyes. We had enjoyed a really special relationship both on and off the field. Until I die I will always harbour a ferocious respect for Ian Botham.

I consider myself really fortunate to have played alongside Ian for such a long time. He was not at all like other English cricketers. His whole attitude was different. He did not have that superior air about him. His approach to cricket seemed more West Indian than English. He was a marvellously destructive player, fuelled by pride and courage, the kind of player who would and could single-handedly take control of a game. No team could contain him when he was kickin'. That was part of his genius.

I responded to him because, as I say, he was like a West Indian in his attitude to the game. It was suggested that Ian and I were always competing with each other, that we were always trying to get one up on each other. We are similar players. We both have an explosive factor, it is true we both believe in our own ability, but we are both team players. Besides, in those days Ian's first love was bowling. My gentle off-spin did not compete with his speed and movement.

Off the field I have the greatest respect for the man because I know how humane he really is. Not many people know the real Ian Botham. They know the caricature that has been drawn, they know the image portrayed of the man. But they don't know the inner Ian Botham. He is a genuinely caring person, a real friend, and a truly great cricketer.

I think he has done a wonderful job for England. He has been a great ambassador for English cricket and indeed for England in the whole world of sport. From the first time we met, playing for the Somerset Under-25s in my own first season in England, we became instant friends, something just clicked. He has a special aura about him. I could feel the power of his warm, open personality. It contrasted strongly with some of the colder, more intense, cricketers I met at that time. I enjoy being in his company because he lifts you. I put it down to heart. Whatever peeople say about Ian Botham they will never destroy his heart. What he did for me that day I was sacked was to give me real support and courage on one of the blackest days of my life.

A CAPTAIN'S MANIFESTO

The Range Rover pulls to a slow halt, some way short of a crossroads in downtown St John's. It is a beautiful Antiguan night. The warmth, not at all oppressive, wraps itself around you like a comforting blanket.

The social atmosphere is no less enticing. People 'stroll' rather than briskly 'walk'. People smile and, as always, chat on street corners. Cars swish by on the uneven surfaces. Every isolated sound seems pronounced and totally separate from the omnipresent nightime squealing of the Caribbean crickets. It is the kind of night that seems to eclipse the power of money – when the size of your house, or car, seems irrelevant. Just to be there, on those streets, in that intoxicating air, seems enough.

Viv Richards has pulled to a halt outside the local basketball and netball courts. These courts are awash with furious sporting activity and are lined, like mini-versions of the aforementioned football match, with shouting, cheering spectators. Richards leaps across the street and joins this excitable maelstrom. Once again he sinks into a vast ocean of local sporting dialogue. Ten minutes later he re-emerges. 'Oh yes, ' he states enthusiastically, 'I want to talk about the man who has probably been the greatest single influence in my life. I want to talk about Clive Lloyd. I want to talk about captaincy.'

Captaincy, by its very nature, is the most difficult job in cricket. It is difficult, mainly, because the captain is dependent upon his particular team. There are times when a captain might make the right decision, but is let down by an unusually poor performance by one or more of his players.

When this happens, it seems as if he made the wrong decision. Somehow a captain is expected to be able to predict the future. He can set the best stage, make all the right moves in this strange chess match called cricket, but, ultimately, the team has to pull together as a cohesive unit.

I was very fortunate to learn my captaincy skills from two men I regard as just about the best around. Firstly, Brian Close at Somerset, who taught me so much about chanelling personal aggression in a professional way, and, of course, Clive Lloyd. Clive had a reputation for being a tactful captain rather than a hard man. But this was not always the case. He could be as tough as anyone. I have seen Clive hand out some real strong rollickings. He was not soft, quite the opposite.

THE GREAT MAN

Everybody had a go at Clive. They knocked him for many things – which he would always rise above – but mainly he was given stick for playing four fast bowlers. It was Clive's gift that he saw a particular trend in West Indies cricket. Nobody else spotted it. It took a great deal of cricket vision and you have to admire that. Where would we be without that vision?

Over the years the team has been able to pick from a variety of wonderful fast bowlers, but we always thought we should search for that particular balance where we would have two fast bowlers, a medium paced all-rounder and, maybe, a couple of spinners. Clive thought differently and I think people should give him credit, not blame, for spotting what would become the West Indies' true strength in international cricket.

It was one of my biggest privileges to be able to learn directly from Clive when he was captain. To see the way we were running, the way the team was moving. We had our bad times but, with Clive, I always thought that we were in a flow, that each match, even a bad one, was playing a part in the long-term plan. As far as I was concerned, things worked out very well and it was a perfect education for me to work with Clive as his vice-captain.

Without doubt, this experience was one of the highlights of my career. It moulded my perception of cricket, and provided me with the feel of captaincy. Clive was the first man who had the vision needed to create his team and the leadership to make it gel. And that was not all.

It was the beginning of a winning attitude in West Indies cricket. It was to become a winning habit. Although many people do not realise this, the backbone of that success came not from flashes of individual brilliance, but from sheer hard work.

Clive never wanted his team to go down in history as a brief explosion in international cricket, he wanted to form the basis of a team that would forever evolve – like Liverpool Football Club. Any young players coming into that team, or even those who got anywhere near the team, would find out in no uncertain terms that the route to success as a West Indian cricketer could only be achieved by falling in with our demanding code of discipline.

Today all the senior players – myself, Gordon Greenidge, Des Haynes, Malcolm Marshall – we all accept that it is our responsibility to instil this feeling into the newcomers. It is like handing down to them our pride. It feels good to have in the side that blend of experience and sheer raw pride. I look to my fellow Antiguan, Richie Richardson, who has come almost all the way down this path and may be the man to lead the West Indies into a new era. He fully understands the way of our professionalism. We want to make sure that it stays inbred. It is something we see solely as a love of the game. For us this is the only way. Even when we go through a bad patch – like at this particular moment, and when the whole cricketing world begins to cast doubts, this deep, deep love remains. I do not think any of the other cricketing nations can quite match us for this.

Certainly, we have helped all the other Test teams. I know that most of the players from the other nations have watched us very closely over the years. They have watched the way we train and our attitude towards fitness. They have watched our physio, Dennis Waight, and the things he puts us through. It is an extremely hard routine. He is a hard nut, he gets us into shape. The belief is that to play top-class cricket one has to attain a high degree of athleticism.

In the past, we have seen players from other teams look on in amazement at our workload. It is good to see it rubbing off on people like Graham Gooch who, in England, seems to be changing the image of the cricketer into that of a genuinely fit sportsman. I do not think that anyone can doubt that it has been largely the West Indies who have set this trend and, through it, have improved the overall standard.

I believed that at one time there was a conspiracy, of sorts, to prevent me from taking over the leadership of the squad. After we had lost the World Cup to India, Clive announced that he would be giving up the captaincy and that I would be his immediate successor. I had been his vice-captain for five years and I felt, at that particular time, that I had paid my dues. I had actually captained the West Indies, in Clive's absence, as far back as 1980 in England. Nobody knew the West Indies game more than me. I thought I had done my job as deputy very well throughout that period and, I am not trying to be big-headed, but the captaincy rightfully belonged to me.

Clive knew this, which is why he stated it, on a couple of occasions. But Clyde Walcott, the touring manager of the side, told Lloyd that he should not have made those statements, that the West Indies Cricket Board had not, at that point, decided that I was to be captain. They told Clive to think again, and carry on as captain. But I knew that was wrong. Clive had decided to quit and there was no way they should have persuaded him otherwise.

But they did and, although I know that Clive tried to ring me to tell me of his decision to carry on, he could not reach me. I heard the news on the radio when I was in Somerset. Of course, it was immensely frustrating for me, not because of Clive's decision to carry on, but because I knew why he had been persuaded to do so. I knew that there were people who did not want me to take over.

Everyone knew I was the obvious choice, but suddenly

ENGLAND vs. WEST INDIES (Fifth Test)
at Headingley on 7th, 8th, 9th, 11th, 12th August 1980
Toss: West Indies. Umpires: W.E. Alley and K.E. Palmer
Match drawn

ENGLAND

G.A. Gooch	c Marshall b Garner	14	lbw b Marshall	55
G. Boycott	c Kallicharran b Holding	4	c Kallicharran b Croft	47
B.C. Rose	b Croft	7	(5) not out	43
W. Larkins	c Kallicharran b Garner	9	(3) lbw b Marshall	30
M.W. Gatting	c Marshall b Croft	1	(4) lbw b Holding	1
I.T. Botham*	c Richards b Holding	37	lbw b Marshall	7
P. Willey	c Murray b Croft	1	c Murray b Holding	10
D.L. Bairstow+	lbw b Marshall	40	not out	9
J.E. Emburey	not out	13		
C.M. Old	c Garner b Marshall	6		
G.R. Dilley	b Garner	0		
Extras	(b 3,lb 3,w 1,nb 4)	11	(b 5,lb 11,w 2,nb 7)	25
TOTAL		143	(for 6 wkts dec)	227

WEST INDIES

C.G. Greenidge	lbw b Botham	34
D.L. Haynes	b Emburey	42
I.V.A. Richards*	b Old	31
S.F.A.F. Bacchus	c and b Dilley	11
A.I. Kallicharran	c Larkins b Dilley	37
C.L. King	c Bairstow b Gooch	12
D.L. Murray+	c Emburey b Dilley	14
M.D. Marshall	c Bairstow b Dilley	0
M.A. Holding	b Old	35
J. Garner	c Emburey b Gooch	0
C.E.H. Croft	not out	1
Extras	(b 2,lb 9,w 3,nb 14)	28
TOTAL		245

WEST INDIES	O	M	R	W	O	M	R	W
Holding	10	4	34	2	23	2	62	2
Croft	12	3	35	3	19	2	65	1
Garner	14	4	41	3	1	0	1	0
Marshall	11	3	22	2	19	5	42	3
King					12	3	32	0

ENGLAND	O	M	R	W	O	M	R	W
Dilley	23	6	79	4				
Old	28.5	9	64	2				
Botham	19	8	31	1				
Emburey	6	0	25	1				
Gooch	8	3	18	2				

FALL OF WICKETS

	ENG	WI	ENG	WI
1st	9	83	95	
2nd	27	105	126	
3rd	28	133	129	
4th	34	142	162	
5th	52	170	174	
6th	59	198	203	
7th	89	198		
8th	131	207		
9th	140	207		
10th	143	245		

a few stories started to fly around about possible alternatives. There were reports in the good old British press and suddenly there was speculation everywhere. It was hard for me because I had been psyched up, ready for the job and, all of a sudden, it seemed to be all out in the open again. I did my best just to carry on. I kept my head down, refused to comment and got on with the important job of playing my best cricket. But I cannot deny that it was unsettling.

I think, looking back, that the West Indies Board were probably nervous about my temperament. Clive always had the remarkable ability to suppress his true feelings. He had a temper but he would keep it hidden. I think they thought that I might be too volatile a character. But no two men are the same and there was no point in looking around for another Clive Lloyd. It would certainly have been very wrong of me to try to emulate his character.

They were, possibly, a little worried about my natural rebellious streak. True enough, my past had made me a little distrustful of authority, and quite rightly. I think they thought that I would not communicate with them in the proper professional manner. I knew, however, that I had matured enough to be able use my personality in a manner which suited a captain. I had an aggressive streak, true, but I would channel this in a positive way and try to help the players do likewise.

There was another reason for their reticence, and it is a subject, a very important subject which I will touch upon elsewhere. They knew that I had many Rastafarian friends. I had been told, on many occasions, that my career would not be helped by these links. As far as I was concerned, and I still feel exactly the same way, as long as my private life does not interfere with my cricket then it is no concern of anyone else.

I also think that I was seen as difficult because I came from Antigua, rather than one of the larger islands. There are political reasons for thinking this although, again, as far as I was concerned that too had little to do with what I could achieve on the cricket field. So, I had to wait, but I knew I would get the captaincy in the end.

It was always going to be hard to follow someone like Clive, I never had any illusions about that. There were many doubts cast as I took over and I cannot honestly say that I found it immediately to be an enjoyable experience. But I have always believed that you can never go into any job and expect to enjoy it from the first day.

If you are in charge you have to work hard in order to build respect. You can inherit a team, but you cannot inherit respect. In fact, following a figure as powerful as Clive made my task even more difficult.

In the first few months I made quite a few mistakes but with the help of a few of the senior players I managed to keep Clive's legacy rolling along. Nevertheless, I think I ruffled a few feathers because I was totally determined to do things my way.

I felt this was essential. Then, when criticised, I could at least defend myself with pride. It was a rocky sort of a period at first, but when we went down we had the kind of team who would really work to put things right. We had a positive attitude, no matter what had gone wrong.

TAKING HOLD OF THE REINS

There was no trouble within the ranks. Although it might have been expected, because we had not lost a Test match for some time when I took over and then we immediately fell into trouble. When this happens, everyone starts talking. But every team must go through those periods now and again. As for criticism, you will always get some

WEST INDIES vs. NEW ZEALAND (First Test)

at Port of Spain on 29th, 30th, 31st March, 2nd, 3rd April 1985
Toss : West Indies.   Umpires : C.E. Cumberbatch and D.M. Archer
Match drawn

WEST INDIES

Batsman	Dismissal	Score	2nd Innings	Score
C.G. Greenidge	b Boock	100		
D.L. Haynes	c Rutherford b Hadlee	0	c Crowe M.D. b Chatfield	78
H.A. Gomes	c Smith b Hadlee	0	c and b Chatfield	25
R.B. Richardson	c Hadlee b Coney	78	(2) c Smith b Chatfield	3
I.V.A. Richards*	b Hadlee	57	(4) b Cairns	78
A.L. Logie	b Chatfield	24	(5) b Cairns	42
P.J.L. Dujon+	b Chatfield	15	(6) b Chatfield	5
M.D. Marshall	c sub b Chatfield	0	(7) c Coney b Chatfield	1
R.A. Harper	c Howarth b Chatfield	0	(8) not out	11
M.A. Holding	lbw b Hadlee	12	(9) c Crowe J.J. b Chatfield	8
J. Garner	not out	0		
Extras	(b 1,lb 16,nb 4)	21	(lb 3,nb 7)	10
TOTAL		307	(for 8 wkts dec)	261

NEW ZEALAND

Batsman	Dismissal	Score	2nd Innings	Score
J.G. Wright	c Richardson b Harper	40	lbw b Holding	19
K.R. Rutherford	c Haynes b Marshall	0	run out	0
J.J. Crowe	c and b Harper	64	c Garner b Marshall	27
M.D. Crowe	lbw b Holding	3	c Haynes b Marshall	12
G.P. Howarth*	c sub b Holding	45	b Marshall	14
J.V. Coney	lbw b Marshall	25	c Dujon b Marshall	44
R.J. Hadlee	c Garner b Holding	18	not out	39
I.D.S. Smith+	c Logie b Holding	10	not out	11
B.L. Cairns	c Harper b Garner	8		
S.L. Boock	c sub b Garner	3		
E.J. Chatfield	not out	4		
Extras	(b 12,lb 11,nb 19)	42	(b 7,lb 6,nb 8)	21
TOTAL		262	(for 6 wkts)	187

NEW ZEALAND	O	M	R	W	O	M	R	W
Hadlee	24.3	6	82	4	17	2	58	0
Chatfield	28	11	51	4	22	4	73	6
Cairns	26	3	93	0	19	2	70	2
Boock	19	5	47	1	14	4	57	0
Coney	9	3	17	1				

WEST INDIES	O	M	R	W	O	M	R	W
Marshall	25	3	78	2	26	4	65	4
Garner	21.3	8	41	2	18	2	41	0
Holding	29	8	79	4	17	6	36	1
Harper	22	11	33	2	14	7	29	0
Richards	2	0	7	0	2	1	1	0
Gomes	1	0	1	0	2	1	2	0
Richardson					1	1	0	0
Logie					1	1	0	0

FALL OF WICKETS

	WI	NZ	WI	NZ
1st	5	1	10	0
2nd	9	110	58	40
3rd	194	113	172	59
4th	196	132	226	76
5th	236	182	239	83
6th	267	223	240	158
7th	267	225	241	
8th	269	248	261	
9th	302	250		
10th	307	262		

people who do not agree with your decisions. That is all part of the sport.

In our response we were professional. We stuck by our guns and when we went through that bad patch we did not panic. We slowly assessed the problems together – and brought more criticism on ourselves for doing so. To me it would be stupid for a captain never to listen to the views of individual players. But the fact that we held these discussions was widely interpreted the wrong way. Press people can twist a team discussion into something which looks like a mass falling-out. Maybe that is the job their editors give them but I do not see why we should start apologising for having team discussions. If the journalists then distort what happens, as they constantly do, then the public should be careful what they believe.

After I had followed Clive Lloyd, there were critics who wanted instantly to test my ability as a captain. Boy, did they leap onto my back. All of a sudden I found myself being measured against Clive, which was totally unfair. However, rising above such nonsense is part of the captain's job.

Then we started to win. Everything started to come together and we began working as a team. We were going well. During this period, maybe my batting declined a little bit. Suddenly the journalists leapt onto this. Really they had nothing to write about because our performances, in that initial series against New Zealand, began to improve. That had shaken them so they started in on my batting. The focus suddenly changed from the captaincy to my performance with the bat. Previously that had never been in question. It was all so stupid. When you take on such a formidable task as captaining a Test team, you are bound to get a few low scores. I expected it.

You cannot possibly take with you to the crease the

same degree of concentration as a captain. You suddenly have so many people to worry about, not just your own performance. I accepted that it was a part of the job. You have to bring some maturity to a job like that and partly it means you can no longer play in such a selfish manner. It would be a poor captain who still attempted to be so single-minded. I think I dealt with it in a reasonable way.

If the truth be told, I aged a lot, I actually became a far more mature player. I could still pick up the ball early, when batting, but I had to bat in a more responsible manner, no knocking about in the carefree manner of old.

Geoff Boycott said that Viv Richards's hard-hitting cricketing days were over. In a sense, although that hurt at the time, and it was meant to hurt, I now regard it as something of a compliment. I matured. It was as simple as that. As a team we just got on with our job.

The rocky times have helped us a great deal. We now make sure that no-one in the team feels left out. If younger players come into the team, and they are shy, we coax them into expressing themselves. When I started as captain, I encouraged open discussions in the dressing room. I wanted it to be like a debate and thought this would be a good thing for the general spirit of the team. I wanted each individual to make his point and be understood by the rest of the guys.

We always study the opposition together, in extreme detail. We examine the weak points and plan how to expose them. I want each person in my team to know exactly what his job is, exactly what is expected of him and how that job relates to the other players. Some teams insist on building some kind of atmosphere of intimidation, so that the newcomers have to fight to gain respect. We have never believed in that. We like to nurture young talent. We try to gain their trust. We involve them in crucial decisions, we make them feel important and they seem to return that with total commitment.

It is so satisfying to see their game begin to pick up, to see their confidence grow. Over the years, in various countries, I have seen so many promising cricketers fail, through shyness and lack of confidence. It is heartbreaking to see this happen and it does happen a lot, especially in English county cricket. Sometimes I can't help but wonder how many fabulous cricketing careers have been squandered because the people in charge were unable to break the ice.

All I can do is make sure that this does not happen in any of the teams that I am involved in. With the West Indies, any attention I have paid to young players is repaid in full when I lead the team onto the pitch. I have complete faith in every one of my players and they know this.

I am very close to my players, I have to be. There they are, fighting their guts out, diving here and there, giving one hundred per cent. A captain must stand fully behind them. There are times when you must draw the line, and there are certain things that you just cannot afford to get involved in, but in general it is the captain's duty to speak up on behalf of his team and he must never shirk from this even though there will be times when it gets him into trouble.

Sometimes you have to make a stand that will not exactly get you a good press. It can be about something that, to the casual observer, might not seem to be that important. The best example I can think of is what happened during the Test against England at St John's in 1986. I was heavily criticised for arguing with the umpires when they were looking at some replacement balls. It was said that I was trying to be the umpire myself, that I was taking the law into my own hands but this was not true.

We had started that series using Stuart Surridge balls and then, in the final Test, they wanted to use different ones. All I was doing was pointing out to the umpires the inconsistency of this. It was a simple point but I felt it was important for me to exercise my rights as a captain.

If I had not made that point then, in a small way, I would have neglected my duty. It was a mistake on the umpires' behalf and in the end they did use the Stuart Surridge balls.

When you are a captain you have to be extremely careful because practically everything you do is monitored by the press and, more often than not, is jumped upon and reported inaccurately. Again on that same tour I took a terrible bashing from the press after I had reportedly sulked and refused to entertain the media after we had lost a one-day game in which Graham Gooch hit a splendid century. As the captain I would have been more than willing to talk to the press had any one of them thought to ask me – none of them did. I would have been happy to give credit to Gooch for his match-winning innings.

It was another example of press stupidity. Why should I have wanted to sulk? We were one up in the Test series and had won the first one-day international. All was going pretty well, but I guess they saw it as one way to apply a bit more pressure to the captain.

Although I do have a reputation for being volatile I have matured constantly throughout my captaincy and I have always been prepared to take the flak whenever we performed badly. That is no problem, that is my job. But it has got to me sometimes when I have been unfairly attacked and I am always likely to fight back.

CHAMPIONS OF
THE WORLD

When I talk of the passion I have for the game, which I often do, I inevitably find myself thinking back to winning the Prudential World Cup, not once, but twice. The first time, in 1975, in England, proved to be a turning point in cricket history. It was the first real proof that the public actually wanted a more compact form of cricket – a game with a shorter time span and much faster action.

Until the first World Cup in England, few people really considered the one-day game to be such an important development, at least as far as international games were concerned. Before 1975, the one-day game had featured strongly in England but it was this particular competition that gave one-day international cricket a much-needed spur. When Packer came along, the trend towards the shorter, faster game was furthered considerably.

That first World Cup series was a delight to play in. Eight countries took part, West Indies, Australia, New Zealand, India, Sri Lanka, East Africa, Pakistan and England. It was quite confusing, at first, to be performing so fast, and against so many different teams in such a short period.

Cricketers in general are hardly geared for such competitions. Although I didn't have a particularly good series as an individual, it was a fabulous experience just to participate in it and I found myself developing a particular love for one-day cricket.

The final, against Australia, was dramatic enough for anyone. It was one of those games where Clive Lloyd really showed his class and took the game by the scruff of the neck. His 102 was one of the finest and most powerful centuries I have ever seen and, of course, it was produced despite the attentions of Lillee and Thomson who were both at their fearsome best. Although my batting may not have been up to scratch, I did field well, hitting the stumps on three occasions which was enough for me to feel rightly proud.

I still remember clearly the drama at the end of the game. Thomson and Lillee were batting very stubbornly at the tail of the Australians innings and were pushing their total steadily towards our innings of 291. It was strange because our section of the crowd, who had been prematurely jubilant, suddenly grew very silent as these two kept lashing out. Somehow, our total no longer seemed so big. The tension in the air was almost unbearable and, once again, I found myself thinking about the fans back home, their ears glued to their radios. Finally, I think it was Derryck Murray who hit the stumps after Thomson had attempted a run which was never on. Australia had made 274, just 17 short of us. Prince Philip presented the trophy and Clive, deservedly, was named Man of the Match. Although there were still some people who did not rate the one-day game, I felt more elated than ever before.

That, I felt, was the closest a cricketer could get to winning a gold medal at the Olympics. We had competed, successfully, against all the world's greatest players and to achieve that, to walk up and have the guy placing that medal in your hand, that just has to be the greatest feeling.

International cricket does seem, all too often, an

WEST INDIES vs. AUSTRALIA
at Lord's on 21st June 1975
Toss : Australia. Umpires : H.D. Bird and T.W. Spencer
West Indies won by 17 runs
Man of the Match: C.H. Lloyd

WEST INDIES

R.C. Fredericks	hit wicket b Lillee	7
C.G. Greenidge	c Marsh b Thomson	13
A.I. Kallicharran	c Marsh b Gilmour	12
R.B. Kanhai	b Gilmour	56
C.H. Lloyd*	c Marsh b Gilmour	102
I.V.A. Richards	b Gilmour	5
K.D. Boyce	c Chappell G.S. b Gilmour	34
B.D. Julien	not out	26
D.L. Murray+	c and b Gilmour	14
V.A. Holder	not out	6
A.M.E. Roberts		
Extras	(lb 6,nb 11)	17
TOTAL	(60 overs)(for 8 wkts)	291

AUSTRALIA

R.B. McCosker	c Kallicharran b Boyce	7
A. Turner	run out	40
I.M. Chappell*	run out	62
G.S. Chappell	run out	15
K.D. Walters	b Lloyd	35
R.W. Marsh+	b Boyce	11
R. Edwards	c Fredericks b Boyce	28
G.J. Gilmour	c Kanhai b Boyce	14
M.H.N. Walker	run out	7
J.R. Thomson	run out	21
D.K. Lillee	not out	16
Extras	(b 2,lb 9,nb 7)	18
TOTAL	(58.4 overs)	274

AUSTRALIA	O	M	R	W	FALL OF WICKETS		
Lillee	12	1	55	1		WI	AUS
Gilmour	12	2	48	5	1st	12	25
Thomson	12	1	44	2	2nd	27	81
Walker	12	1	71	0	3rd	50	115
Chappell G.S.	7	0	33	0	4th	199	162
Walters	5	0	23	0	5th	206	170
					6th	209	195
WEST INDIES	O	M	R	W	7th	261	221
Julien	12	0	58	0	8th	285	231
Roberts	11	1	45	0	9th		233
Boyce	12	0	50	4	10th		274
Holder	11.4	1	65	0			
Lloyd	12	1	38	1			

isolated kind of sport. There are long tours when you play
one team repeatedly. Sometimes there are years separating
a confrontation between the top two nations. The World
Cup seemed to be just the right antidote to that. It felt as
though all the players were in the right place at the right
time. How could anyone then say, 'Oh yes, they may have
beaten India but they wouldn't beat the present Australian
side', or whoever? This time it was all or nothing. The
winners proved their case and West Indies were champions
of the world.

Then, predictably, out came the doubters. Reporters
began saying that we had been lucky, that our success was
just a flash in the pan, that we would never win it again –
the usual old rubbish. Even in victory, we were made to
doubt ourselves. It was as though people did not want us
to enjoy the victory.

As it happened this prejudice served to work in our
favour. When the next World Cup came along, in 1979, it
was all the more important to us. Not only did we start as
defending world champions, but we were still fired by
those criticisms. I will never forget that feeling of euphoria
when we won it a second time. In the final against
England, I was playing just about at my best, scoring 138
not out and helping the West Indies to victory by 92 runs.
Now, I thought, there can be no argument about who are
the world champions.

This time we seemed to silence just about everybody
– at least, for a while. I knew that the knockers would
emerge from their hiding places eventually, but nobody
would be able to take it away from us. It was lovely to know
that we would be going down in the history books as
undisputed champions of the world. I think that really
was the turning point in West Indian cricket history. We
knew, deep down, that we could beat anybody and that we

WEST INDIES vs. ENGLAND
at Lord's on 23rd June 1979
Toss : England. Umpires : H.D. Bird and B.J. Meyer
West Indies won by 92 runs
Man of the Match: I.V.A. Richards

WEST INDIES
C.G. Greenidge	run out	9
D.L. Haynes	c Hendrick b Old	20
I.V.A. Richards	not out	138
A.I. Kallicharran	b Hendrick	4
C.H. Lloyd*	c and b Old	13
C.L. King	c Randall b Edmonds	86
D.L. Murray+	c Gower b Edmonds	5
A.M.E. Roberts	c Brearley b Hendrick	0
J. Garner	c Taylor b Botham	0
M.A. Holding	b Botham	0
C.E.H. Croft	not out	0
Extras	(b 1,lb 10)	12
TOTAL	(60 overs)(for 9 wkts)	286

ENGLAND
J.M. Brearley*	c King b Holding	64
G. Boycott	c Kallicharran b Holding	57
D.W. Randall	b Croft	15
G.A. Gooch	b Garner	32
D.I. Gower	b Garner	0
I.T. Botham	c Richards b Croft	4
W. Larkins	b Garner	0
P.H. Edmonds	not out	5
C.M. Old	b Garner	0
R.W. Taylor+	c Murray b Garner	0
M. Hendrick	b Croft	0
Extras	(lb 12,w 2,nb 3)	17
TOTAL	(51 overs)	194

ENGLAND	O	M	R	W	FALL OF WICKETS		
Botham	12	2	44	2		WI	ENG
Hendrick	12	2	50	2	1st	22	129
Old	12	0	55	2	2nd	36	135
Boycott	6	0	38	0	3rd	55	183
Edmonds	12	2	40	2	4th	99	183
Gooch	4	0	27	0	5th	238	186
Larkins	2	0	21	0	6th	252	186
					7th	258	188
WEST INDIES	O	M	R	W	8th	260	192
Roberts	9	2	33	0	9th	272	192
Holding	9	1	16	2	10th		194
Croft	10	1	42	3			
Garner	11	0	38	5			
Richards	10	0	35	0			
King	3	0	13	0			

had no reason at all to feel inferior. It was such a proud thing. Even if we were to stumble across bad times again, which would surely happen, we had proved what we could do – and we would do it again.

I must admit, and I make no apologies for this at all, I went a little bit wild. I was totally out of control. There were nights of celebrating, when I completely drowned myself in champagne. I would love to be able to relate to you now just what went on on those occasions, but I can't. To this day, I have no idea what really happened. Perhaps some reporter might like to tell me. I know it's not really acceptable to get into such a state, but in the Caribbean we believe in celebrating to the fullest...and I think the rest of the team did the same. I did not care about anything at all. I just promised myself that I would get into a hell of a state...and that is just what I did. It was glorious to be on top of the world and to know that we would be remembered for our achievement.

I may be wrong, but I sense that winning an ultimate contest like that is more important for a black person than anyone else. It feels like a vindication – the sense of pride attached to such wins is phenomenal. I do not know if the English or the Australians feel it in quite the same way; maybe they do.

Things had changed a bit by the time the third Prudential World Cup came around, in 1983, but we still approached the contest not just as champions but as champions who fully expected to retain our crown. We knew we were still the finest one-day team in the world and, perhaps more importantly, our supporters knew it as well. They were united in the belief that the World Cup was ours by right, and I think most of our team believed that.

Even after being beaten by India in the first match,

we still felt more than confident. That was a mere hiccup, or so we thought, and our confidence fully returned after we had beaten Australia and Pakistan and had to face that Indian team, once again, in the final. It was an extraordinary game. After India had been bowled out for 183 in 54.5 overs every Caribbean supporter had already begun to celebrate. The atmosphere at Lord's was fantastic. The drums were out and we could certainly sense that the same thing was happening back home.

Even when we began the innings badly – Haynes was out, I think, when we were on five – the atmosphere did not soften. I personally felt in good form, hitting three fours off Madan Lal in my first over. But when I was on 33, I fell to a magnificent catch by Kapil Dev and after that we collapsed for 140. I received a certain amount of criticism for the way I had played. Some people thought I was reckless but the truth was that I had been batting pretty well and Kapil Dev's catch really was something special.

It was a terrible day for us but the fact is that we had been winning for so long that our fans had come to expect West Indian victories every time. But life's not like that. Every team has its day, and its off day, and, although you can influence this by hard work, you are always going to suffer the odd bad result.

Some supporters were really upset, however, especially back in the Caribbean and starting saying that we had thrown the match. That really got to me. It reminded me of the old days, when I was banned in Antigua, the way people can be all for you one minute and then just turn against you. We did not throw the World Cup, it just was not our day. People seemed to expect absolute perfection at all times but no matter how hard you strive, you are never going to achieve that.

It was quite horrible in our hotel that night. Some

of our guys took it really badly, especially when the Indian drums began to pound.

That defeat also made us think a little. The Indian players were treated like gods in their own country after that final. For winning the World Cup, some of them were even given apartments. It all seemed a lot different to the way we had been treated. Some of our team became a little envious. It was part of our learning process. Suddenly, it became apparent that maybe something was amiss. We had achieved the peaks of professionalism and had put our little islands on the world's sporting map. Now, we thought, we too had a right to expect the proper rewards.

THE BEST OF
TIMES

Approach Antigua, for the first time, from the sea (if you are lucky enough) and you will be initially confronted by an island which looks deceptively uninteresting, especially when compared to the more mountainous and striking islands lying to the south.

This dullness vanishes, as the island draws nearer, for it soon becomes apparent that Antigua's coastline is a bewildering chain of secluded bays, empty tropical beaches, coves and inlets strung together to divide long stretches of dazzling white sand stretching from achingly beautiful turquoise waters. The guide books never tire of stating that Antigua boasts one beach for every day of the year, and although this might be stretching a point it is true that, even at the height of the tourist season, it is relatively easy to find a stretch of empty sand. Every Antiguan, when politely approached, seems only too happy to tell a stranger about their own favourite secluded beach. Every Antiguan, or so it seems, will take time off from the pressures of life, if only occasionally, to spend hours in such splendid isolation. Viv Richards is no different. He adores a contemplative stroll in such a place. It is as close as one can get to heaven and, what's more, it is free. Antiguans are eternally proud of their beaches – and eternally grateful. It is from such a place that Viv Richards chooses to talk about three significant West Indies victories.

There was one other factor about losing that third World Cup, and having to suffer humiliation in the face of the Indian supporters. We all knew that our next tour would be, ironically, to India. I think most of us would have preferred to go to Pakistan or Australia – *anywhere* other than India. Our confidence had been pretty unshakable up to then, so what could be a crueller, sterner test than to go straight to India. On the other hand it gave us a chance to avenge the defeat immediately. When the time came to set off for India the mood in our camp was pretty good, and remained that way, even when the subject of the World Cup kept cropping up to haunt us.

It must have been fantastic to have been an Indian, in India, at the time of the World Cup. Everywhere we went on that tour we found reminders of a mass national party. We saw banners that had been left over, and the victory was still celebrated on lots of local advertising hoardings. It was an odd experience for us because, as well as rubbing it in, it also seemed to signify the esteem in which the Indian team were held in their own country, not just by the people but by the authorities as well.

The rewards that the Indian players had received for their World Cup victory seemed enormous to us, way above what we would have received had we won. The thought was in the minds of most of the West Indies team, not from greed, but because it did not seem fair. There we were, still in many people's eyes the best team in the world, and yet we had never tasted the kind of rewards which the Indian team were enjoying.

That is the reason why this particular series was special. Like the Tony Greig 'grovel' incident, it was a situation which seemed to fire us up. Whenever we saw those advertisement hoardings, whenever we saw the Indian players enjoying so much attention, whenever we thought back to that night in the London hotel when we were surrounded by the noise of jubilant Indians, it served only to make us feel angry. Not at the Indian players personally, but at the situation. We were determined that we would to do well. We were going to avenge that defeat – and avenge it well.

The tour began with a series of one-day internationals, beginning at Srinagar. We won those fairly easily, and suddenly we had not only regained our confidence, but we were once again treated with respect by the Indian crowd. We knew we were the better of the two teams. It is always difficult to talk like that without sounding big-headed, and I am not saying that India did not deserve their victory in the World Cup. They did, but we all knew that it had been a very strange match.

In the first Test, in Kanpur, we began pretty badly. Desmond Haynes was caught for six and I too went quickly. Although I went out there in a very confident and aggressive mood and hit a couple of good drives off Kapil Dev, I was caught off an edge for 24. Thankfully, Gordon Greenidge powered his way to 194, which pulled us out of trouble but, if anything, the real honours belonged to Malcolm Marshall. He supported Greenidge and made a career-best of 92. He followed this with ferocious bowling, the best I have ever seen from him; his pace and accuracy were just mesmerising. It was particularly sweet because it had been Marshall who had been hit the hardest by the World Cup defeat and it was great to see him channelling his frustration in such a positive manner. Marshall and Holding were just too good, too fast. The Indians could not cope with them.

On a personal level, I was not at all happy with my form. I had been frustrated with the way I had got out in my first innings, especially as I had felt so confident. In the second Test things were made even worse. I was going really well and had got to 67 when the umpire gave me out after I was hit on the pads. It was a terrible decision. I was way down the wicket and there was no way the umpire could tell where the ball was going. I was annoyed, probably because I felt that I had not vindicated myself against the Indians. In the dressing room, I let my frustration show in no uncertain terms. I flung my bat about, which I should not have done. It was wrong of me but I just snapped. Yes, it was bad, but it was no big deal, really. I was not being 'anti-Indian' as was then reported. The Test ended in a draw and I was still left worrying about my 'lost touch'.

The third Test was even stranger. It was played at Ahmedabad and again my form deserted me. Although it was tempting, I could not really lay the blame on the peculiar wicket, which had been under-prepared, or the even more peculiar standard of umpiring, which caused Clive Lloyd to complain bitterly – and quite rightly. We had reached mid-tour and I felt that I should have been able to put a decent innings together.

What was interesting was that, despite the fact that the West Indies were winning, and that I was not playing particularly well, and despite the reports that I had been making anti-Indian remarks at that second Test, I received a lot of encouragement from many Indian supporters. It was quite moving. They really did wish me well, they really wanted me to make a century. It showed a tremendous spirit – the true spirit in which cricket should be played. I was quite touched.

The fourth Test began at Bombay and there was definitely something special about it. For a start, the Deputy Prime Minister of Antigua, Lester Bird, had arrived to watch the game. I think he had been at a conference in Delhi. It was a very good match, even if, in the end, it was drawn. For me it was a personal triumph. At last I broke through that mental barrier which had caused me to lose confidence. Mind you, it was a close thing. I had been playing well and, again, I was edging towards my half century. I hit a ball, from Shastri, I think, and Kapil Dev went to catch it. The next few moments were in slow motion. I thought to myself, 'No, not again, not another promising innings ruined just as it was getting under way'. But Dev just could not hold it. I was so relieved. That was the turning point. After that I knew I would reach a century. At the end of the day I was happily on 103 not out and, although Mr Bird had to leave before the end, he left me some money to buy the team a few drinks.

That night, we had a celebration. I received many calls of congratulation at the hotel. It had not been a particularly mighty innings, but it had been a significant one. I had broken through my bad form and I was delighted to discover that so many people were pleased. The next day, I added another 20 before finally falling to the spinners. If I have to be honest, I must admit that the entire innings was precarious and a number of times I thought I had blown it, but this time luck had been on my side.

In the next Test we managed to dismiss India for 90 in their second innings – their lowest-ever score against

INDIA vs. WEST INDIES (Fourth Test)
at Bombay on 24th, 26th, 27th, 28th, 29th November 1983
Toss : India.   Umpires : M.V. Gothaskar and Swaroop Kishen
Match drawn

INDIA

S.M. Gavaskar	lbw b Marshall	12	c Davis b Marshall	3
A.D. Gaekwad	b Holding	48	c Richards b Holding	3
D.B. Vengsarkar	c Richards b Davis	100		
A. Malhotra	c Dujon b Holding	32	(3) not out	72
R.J. Shastri	b Holding	77	(4) run out	38
R.M.H. Binny	lbw b Marshall	65	(5) lbw b Davis	18
Kapil Dev*	b Holding	8	(6) c Dujon b Daniel	1
Madan Lal	lbw b Marshall	0	(7) not out	26
S.M.H. Kirmani+	not out	43		
N.S. Yadav	b Daniel	12		
Maninder Singh	c Lloyd b Holding	9		
Extras	(b 16,lb 14,w 1,nb 26)	57	(b 1,lb 6,nb 5)	12
TOTAL		463	(for 5 wkts dec)	173

WEST INDIES

C.G. Greenidge	b Yadav	13	b Kapil Dev	4
D.L. Haynes	handled the ball	55	b Maninder Singh	24
R.B. Richardson	lbw b Yadav	0	b Shastri	26
I.V.A. Richards	st Kirmani b Shastri	120	c Kirmani b Shastri	4
H.A. Gomes	b Kapil Dev	26	not out	37
P.J.L. Dujon+	c Kirmani b Yadav	84		
C.H. Lloyd*	run out	67	(6) not out	9
M.D. Marshall	c Gavaskar b Yadav	4		
M.A. Holding	c and b Yadav	2		
W.W. Daniel	c Gavaskar b Shastri	0		
W.W. Davis	not out	4		
Extras	(b 4,lb 8,nb 6)	18		
TOTAL		393	(for 4 wkts)	104

WEST INDIES	O	M	R	W	O	M	R	W
Marshall	32	6	88	3	13	3	47	1
Holding	40.5	10	102	5	11	1	39	1
Davis	36	3	127	1	8	0	35	1
Daniel	30	3	113	1	14	3	45	1
Gomes	4	1	3	0				

INDIA	O	M	R	W	O	M	R	W
Kapil Dev	23	10	41	1	5	1	13	1
Shastri	35	8	98	2	13	4	32	2
Maninder Singh	27	7	71	0	15	7	25	1
Madan Lal	13	6	29	0	3	1	8	0
Binny	4	1	11	0				
Yadav	44.1	8	131	5	12	5	22	0
Gaekwad					1	0	4	0
Gavaskar					1	1	0	0
Malhotra					1	1	0	0

FALL OF WICKETS

	IND	WI	IND	WI
1st	12	47	4	4
2nd	145	47	6	40
3rd	190	128	91	48
4th	234	205	118	68
5th	361	238	121	
6th	372	357		
7th	373	377		
8th	385	383		
9th	433	384		
10th	463	393		

us. This clinched the series for us. It was very much Clive Lloyd's game. It was his last series in India and, although he had always performed well against spinners, I cannot remember him in a more ferocious mood. Really, to average around 90 over five Test matches against a team of such quality, against the world champions, was a magnificent acheivement. It was always a privilege to play alongside him but, on that tour, it felt even more special.

There was another Test series at around that time which showed Clive Lloyd's West Indian team at their very best and at their most powerful. I am talking about our tour of England in the summer of 1984.

We had just been victorious in Australia and arrived in England in a state of high confidence. We knew that we were a far better team, at that moment, than England. It was a well-rounded, fully professional unit, in which every player knew exactly what was expected of him. Of course, our true strength in the eyes of the world was our pace attack. But to draw too much attention to that particular aspect of our game, which was understandable because it was the pace bowlers who commanded the headlines, was wrong. We were also one of the most athletic fielding sides in the history of cricket.

That was no accident either. It was part of Clive's policy. It was part of the very nature of the team. We fielded in a state of exuberance. It takes great confidence to aspire to that. You have to be, at all times, very very sharp and, what's more, safe in the knowledge that those around you are equally highly tuned. It is an important point and I mention it here because I think we were probably at our very best during that tour. I hope I have managed to continue this state of mind during my own captaincy. Nobody can ever afford to suffer loss of concentration in a West Indian side or he will soon be out of it. Pride of performance is essential at all times.

If any side had an excuse to suffer a touch of complacency, then we did. As we arrived, there was already talk of a whitewash or, as they termed it at the time, 'blackwash'. This was silly talk. It had only been achieved four times in Test history, and only once by a West Indies team. (The West Indies, under Frank Worrell's guidance, had beaten India 5-0 in 1961-2 in the Caribbean.) I did not think about it at all. What was important was to win the series and this we knew we were capable of doing.

Our previous tour of England, although we had won one-nil, had been devastated by bad weather conditions. If the England team could not beat us in any of the Tests coming up, I was pretty sure that the English weather would. Much to our delight the weather of that summer proved to be warm and sunny. Things immediately seemed to be working in our favour. After a few good performances in the limited-overs games, including my own very enjoyable 189 not out at Old Trafford, we entered the first Test at Edgbaston in a perfect frame of mind.

Our first innings was remarkable. I think England had a taste of success when we stood at 35 for 2. However, the next wicket to be taken was mine (for 117) when we had reached 241. Larry Gomes took over from there, finally making 143 out of 606, one of our highest-ever totals. This gave us a lead of 415 and, with our pace bowlers in perfect form, it was way beyond the reach of any team.

In the second Test, England seemed a little more determined to do well and they began with 286 against our total of 245. In the second innings, Gower declared at 300 for 9 and the possibility of a West Indies blackwash did not

ENGLAND vs. WEST INDIES (Fifth Test)
at Kennington Oval on 9th, 10th, 11th, 13th, 14th August 1984
Toss : West Indies.   Umpires : D.J. Constant and B.J. Meyer
West Indies won by 172 runs

WEST INDIES

C.G. Greenidge	lbw b Botham	22	c Botham b Agnew	34
D.L. Haynes	b Allott	10	b Botham	125
H.A. Gomes	c Botham b Ellison	18	c Tavare b Ellison	1
I.V.A. Richards	c Allott b Botham	8	lbw b Agnew	15
P.J.L. Dujon+	c Tavare b Botham	3	(6) c Lamb b Ellison	49
C.H. Lloyd*	not out	60	(5) c Downton b Ellison	36
M.D. Marshall	c Gower b Ellison	0	(8) c Lamb b Botham	12
E.A.E. Baptiste	c Fowler b Allott	32	(7) c Downton b Allott	5
R.A. Harper	b Botham	18	c Downton b Allott	17
M.A. Holding	lbw b Botham	0	lbw b Botham	30
J. Garner	c Downton b Allott	6	not out	10
Extras	(b 1,lb 4,w 7,nb 1)	13	(lb 12)	12
TOTAL		190		346

ENGLAND

G. Fowler	c Richards b Baptiste	31	c Richards b Marshall	7
B.C. Broad	b Garner	4	c Greenidge b Holding	39
P.I. Pocock	c Greenidge b Marshall	0	(10) c and b Holding	0
C.J. Tavare	c Dujon b Holding	16	(3) c Richards b Garner	49
D.I. Gower*	c Dujon b Holding	12	(4) lbw b Holding	7
A.J. Lamb	lbw b Marshall	12	(5) c Haynes b Holding	1
I.T. Botham	c Dujon b Marshall	14	(6) c Marshall b Garner	54
P.R. Downton+	c Lloyd b Garner	16	(7) lbw b Garner	10
R.M. Ellison	not out	20	(8) c Holding b Garner	13
P.J.W. Allott	b Marshall	16	(9) c Lloyd b Holding	4
J.P. Agnew	b Marshall	5	not out	2
Extras	(b 2,lb 4,nb 10)	16	(lb 2,w 1,nb 13)	16
TOTAL		162		202

ENGLAND	O	M	R	W	O	M	R	W
Agnew	12	3	46	0	14	1	51	2
Allott	17	7	25	3	26	1	96	2
Botham	23	8	72	5	22.3	2	103	3
Ellison	18	3	34	2	26	7	60	3
Pocock					8	3	24	0

WEST INDIES	O	M	R	W	O	M	R	W
Garner	18	6	37	2	18.4	3	51	4
Marshall	17.5	5	35	5	22	5	71	1
Holding	13	2	55	2	13	2	43	5
Baptiste	12	4	19	1	8	3	11	0
Harper	1	1	0	0	8	5	10	0

FALL OF WICKETS

	WI	ENG	WI	ENG
1st	19	10	51	15
2nd	45	22	52	75
3rd	64	45	69	88
4th	64	64	132	90
5th	67	83	214	135
6th	70	84	237	181
7th	124	116	264	186
8th	154	133	293	200
9th	154	156	329	200
10th	190	162	346	202

seem on the cards at that point. I didn't even need to bat. Gordon Greenidge made 214 not out and we reached 334 for the loss of only Des Haynes, who was run out, to give us a nine-wicket victory.

This trend continued through the Manchester and Leeds Tests and, as we prepared for the final encounter, at The Oval, the tension ran high.

Actually, I felt really nervous as people kept talking of the blackwash, which was ridiculous. After all, we were four-nil up in a Test series away from home, and against England. What did we have to be nervous about? The English players, on the other hand, had plenty of things to ponder. However, things were not all on our side. Had we been 3-1 up, then the series would have been all but over. But at 4-0, there was still a lot to play for and England, surely, would fight like tigers to avoid the ultimate humiliation. Needless to say, the atmosphere at The Oval was fairly wild. We began very badly. We collapsed to 70 for 6 and although we eventually reached 190 I could see our chances slipping away. Thankfully, our pace attack came to the rescue, practically destroying England for 162. Eventually we won the game by 172 runs. It was the moment when Clive Lloyd's West Indies team felt truly dominant. The World Cup defeat was (almost) just a dim memory – we were definitely the best team in the world.

There is one other Test series which remains of particular importance to me. The two I have already mentioned stand as a tribute to Clive Lloyd's West Indies team while this third series is a more personal thing for me because it represents my successful continuation of the Clive Lloyd legacy. It was the series when I felt that, as captain, I had finally stamped my own mark on the team. It was when I began to feel secure and happy with my own authority. I am talking about the visit to the Caribbean by England in 1986. (The later, more explosive tour of 1990 I will talk about in a forthcoming chapter).

We had more or less dominated world cricket for a number of years and I do not think that anybody even entertained the possibility that we might lose the series. Confidence among both the West Indies team and the supporters was running so high that there was very little tension in the air as the series approached. Normally, on such occasions, I tend to get a bit jittery, as if terrified of complacency. I should have felt this before that opening game at Sabina Park Oval, in Kingston, Jamaica – but, strangely, I did not. It had been an awful long time since we had lost a Test series and we were going to win. The only question was, could we possibly repeat the blackwash?

Actually, that's not strictly true. There was a little more at stake, at least there was for me. This was only my second Test series as captain. Against New Zealand we had managed to win the series but, along the way, I had picked up a lot of unfair criticism on my captaincy. It *had* been unfair, too. When a captain as mighty as Clive Lloyd steps down he leaves behind him a huge gulf. I have mentioned my frustration about this criticism elsewhere, but it was this particular series against England that really gave me a chance to make those stupid critics eat their words.

In a sense, I could not personally win against New Zealand. If we lost it would have been total disaster, if we won then people would say that New Zealand were not a stern enough test for my captaincy. It was frustrating and it is a peculiarly West Indian trait that, no matter how good things look, a portion of the people will always look for defeat, for weakness. It comes from our insecurity, I think.

But I was hungry, I was confident and relished the prospect of attacking England. In the first Test, at Sabina Park, we coasted to a ten-wicket victory, which was expected and, of course, meant that we had won a record six Tests in a row against England. We had won that Test in three days and we soon went on to coast through the next three Tests with varying degrees of ease.

There was a terrific difference between the two teams – not in terms of skill because England had some of the finest players in the world in that team. They had Gooch, Lamb, Gower, Smith, Botham – hardly no-hopers. However, in terms of attitude, we had the upper hand. We could enjoy the continuation of what I have already spoken about – our athleticism, taking the game of cricket very seriously indeed and preparing for each Test in a thoroughly professional manner. This professionalism is the main reason behind our years of dominance.

Take our fast bowlers, much maligned as they may be, but they have climbed to their position because of simple hard graft. A West Indies bowler, for instance, will always be on a strict diet. He will know all about maintaining the balance betwen proteins and carbohydrates – he will be very sophisticated in this sense. Our physio will put him through just the correct amount of weight-training. In short, he will be a complete athlete, performing to the peak of his power.

The difference between the West Indian players and the English was particularly significant during this series. I had carried on Lloyd's belief in a tough disciplinarian regime. The English players, I have to say, just did not aspire to the same level of athleticism. The big match, as far as I was concerned, was the last one. Needless to say, it took place at the Recreation Ground in St John's. It was massively important to me.

Five years earlier, I had played here against England and this had also been a very important occasion for me. Not only was it in front of my home crowd but I had just got married and I wanted everything to be perfect. I did score a hundred but, in truth, it had been a pretty edgy innings. I allowed the occasion to get to me.

In 1986 I had the bit between my teeth. It was the final match and we were on the verge of achieving the second blackwash. What could be more perfect than to achieve this in front of all my family and friends? Also, my father had just suffered a mild stroke. That was the main reason for my determination. I was going to play well for my father – as simple as that. But when we batted my first innings proved to be a terrible disappointment (caught Gooch bowled Botham 26).

I felt a little different in the second innings. As I strode to the wicket, the crowd gave me a truly thunderous ovation. It was true that my batting performances of the previous year had not been my best, and there had been talk that 'Richards is no longer hungry'. But this crowd seemed to cast all that talk to the wind.

I went to the wicket with about half an hour to go to tea, and when we went into the break I had got to 28. I felt particularly good. I remember hitting a couple of sixes, off Ellison and Emburey, which seemed to set the ground alight. I was happy because my form was with me on my home ground. But I was not thinking about setting records, or anything like that. I had no selfish strategy, I just wanted to play well. After the break, it just flowed. I started hitting fours and sixes and with every strike the crowd's noise seemed to intensify. When I made 100 off 56 balls, I began to realise what it must be like to score for Liverpool at Anfield. It was a world record but I didn't know it at the time. In fact, I never gave it a thought until

WEST INDIES vs. ENGLAND (Fifth Test)

at St John's, Antigua on 11th, 12th, 13th, 15th, 16th April 1986
Toss : England.   Umpires : L.H. Barker and C.E. Cumberbatch
West Indies won by 240 runs

WEST INDIES

C.G. Greenidge	b Botham	14			
D.L. Haynes	c Gatting b Ellison	131	(1) run out		70
R.B. Richardson	b Emburey	24	(2) c Robinson b Emburey		31
H.A. Gomes	b Emburey	24			
I.V.A. Richards*	c Gooch b Botham	26	(3) not out		110
P.J.L. Dujon+	b Foster	21			
M.D. Marshall	c Gatting b Gooch	76			
R.A. Harper	c Lamb b Foster	60	(4) not out		19
M.A. Holding	c Gower b Ellison	73			
J. Garner	run out	11			
B.P. Patterson	not out	0			
Extras	(b 2,lb 11,w 1)	14	(b 4,lb 9,w 1,nb 2)		16
TOTAL		474			246

ENGLAND

G.A. Gooch	lbw b Holding	51	lbw b Holding		51
W.N. Slack	c Greenidge b Patterson	52	b Garner		8
R.T. Robinson	b Marshall	12	run out		3
D.I. Gower*	c Dujon b Marshall	90	(5) c Dujon b Harper		21
A.J. Lamb	c and b Harper	1	(6) b Marshall		1
M.W. Gatting	c Dujon b Garner	15	(7) b Holding		1
I.T. Botham	c Harper b Garner	10	(8) b Harper		13
P.R. Downton+	c Holding b Garner	5	(9) lbw b Marshall		13
R.M. Ellison	c Dujon b Marshall	6	(4) lbw b Garner		16
J.E. Emburey	not out	7	c Richardson b Harper		0
N.A. Foster	c Holding b Garner	10	not out		0
Extras	(b 5,lb 6,nb 40)	51	(b 10,lb 10,w 2,nb 21)		43
TOTAL		310			170

ENGLAND	O	M	R	W	O	M	R	W
Botham	40	6	147	2	15	0	78	0
Foster	28	5	86	2	10	0	40	0
Ellison	24	3	114	2	4	0	32	0
Emburey	37	11	93	2	14	0	83	1
Gooch	5	2	21	1				

WEST INDIES	O	M	R	W	O	M	R	W
Marshall	24	5	64	3	16.1	6	25	2
Garner	21.4	2	67	4	17	5	38	2
Patterson	14	2	49	1	15	3	29	0
Holding	20	3	71	1	16	3	45	2
Harper	26	7	45	1	12	8	10	3
Richards	2	0	3	0	3	1	3	0

FALL OF WICKETS

	WI	ENG	WI	ENG
1st	23	127	100	14
2nd	63	132	161	29
3rd	137	157		84
4th	178	159		101
5th	232	205		112
6th	281	213		124
7th	351	237		147
8th	401	289		164
9th	450	290		168
10th	474	310		170

I was told about it in the dressing room.

Apparently, the whole of the Caribbean had come to a standstill in celebration. I was so happy that it had happened at the Recreation Ground. I knew then that, as long as I lived in St John's, I would always remember that day. More importantly, a lot of other people would remember it too. We had beaten the English 5-0, home and away. What more could a cricketer aspire to?

PRIDE AND PREJUDICE

In the centre of St John's sits the old court house which contains the Antigua Historical Museum. A handsome building, it is described by the guide books as 'a good example of West Indian Georgian style'. It has a military feel to it, made all the more impressive by the distinct lack of uniformity in the buildings which surround it. A solid, officious fence guards its perimeter. Once past the fence, and through the archways, the visitor finds a museum of a rather dusty, basic nature.

The island's remarkable naval history – including many shipwrecks with the places of rest immaculately charted – is mixed with many Amerindian artifacts found on the island. Antiguans do seem to enjoy the museum and it is, of course, important to the schoolchildren of the island. There is, perhaps, nowhere else on the island where those who wish to lose themselves in Antiguan lore can do so and, along the way, learn a great deal. Antigua's history is tumultuous and fascinating and this museum is cherished by the locals.

Initially, the casual observer or tourist may feel that the museum hardly typifies the mood of the island. This is a misconception which is rectified as the visitor, having circled the building, finally comes face to face with the museum's, and the island's, proudest artifact: a cricket bat which had once been held firmly in the hands of Vivian Richards.

I have always felt that, when you come from one of the smaller Caribbean islands, it is that much harder to climb the sporting ladder that eventually leads to playing for the West Indies cricket team.

There are so many hurdles. To begin with, you have to overcome that feeling of smallness or irrelevance that you suffer when you grow up in a place which is often ignored in favour of the larger islands. It makes it that much harder to break through at representative level. On the other hand there can be advantages. When you come from a small country you are filled with a natural feeling of comradeship and pride. It seems to make you all the more determined to make your mark in the world, and when you do your country is more likely to rally behind you. In return you have to take on the responsibility of acting for the whole island.

Another good thing is that you are never allowed to get too above yourself on an island like Antigua. There is no point in becoming aloof or precious – it just does not work.

As I said, there are many hurdles to cross. For a cricketer the first task is to represent your island. Believe me, that alone is quite an achievement. Small as islands such as Antigua and St Kitts may be, competition is ferocious and the standard is always high.

Once established at this level, you find yourself

playing in one of the local tournaments – say between Antigua, St Kitts and Montserrat. After that, if you perform well enough and happen to be the kind of cricketer that the selectors are searching for, you may get to play for the Leeward Islands team. Luck does play an important role. If there are established players in that team whose game is similar to your own, then it is all the more difficult for a newcomer to break through. Remember also that, even at the Leeward Islands stage you are still far from being a professional sportsman, even though you are expected to perform at the highest level. At this point you are effectively in the same category as Barbados, Trinidad and Jamaica. You will get to play in the Red Stripe Cup, which used to be the Shell Shield. From this base, you stand a chance of being selected for the West Indies.

To some extent I have simplified the ladder here. In reality it is a long, difficult climb and one that, statistically speaking, gives the young player little chance of making it all the way.

I have seen so many local players with real class and fine technique who failed to climb that ladder. I have seen some really talented cricketers play in the Shell Shield tournament. They were full of promise and yet, for some reason way beyond their control, they never proceeded further than that.

As I personally progressed, I gradually became aware that something was seriously wrong. Some players, especially from the smaller islands, were failing to progress in a way that paid tribute to their potential. We Antiguans have always felt strangely handicapped in that way. I am not saying that there has been a conspiracy to keep down players from the smaller islands. It is just that the system has never favoured the smaller-island players. When we do achieve victory in the Red Stripe, as we did in 1990, our islands went totally potty. They exploded in a way that even certain legendary West Indies victories could not match.

There is no competition in the world that is more fiercely fought than the Red Stripe. And yet people still attack us for using aggressive pace bowling in international matches. 'How would you like to face your own?' they say. What a stupid question. We face our own all the time. In the Red Stripe, that bowling is every bit as fierce as in any Test match and each team has a battery of fast bowlers all with their eyes on a Test place.

In the Leewards we have had many potentially great players such as Derek Michael and Sydney Wallis whose talent was never allowed to mature fully. The West Indies Cricket Board, at least in those days, never had any particular programme nor, so it seemed, any desire to encourage talent from the smaller islands. That was one of the biggest let-downs. That is why in the small islands we were so late in getting our due representation in the West Indies team. Things have improved a little, but not enough.

We lived with this injustice for many years and it created something of a pressure-cooker effect in the small islands. The talent was in evidence but then it would boil away, unnurtured, which was a great tragedy. This historical neglect could still have a serious fall-out. Frank Worrell foresaw this when he once noted that if the West Indies were to survive, they would have to start looking towards the smaller islands in the future.

We have come a long way since then, but there is still a lot of political wrangling. The old discontent has created a separatist movement in the smaller islands. This works at regional and international level. People want each island to go it alone and not merge into a Leeward Islands team. They also want more power and recognition at top level for representatives from the smaller islands.

   There are good grounds for these demands. For instance, we put up Andy Roberts to be a West Indies selector and, for some reason, the Leeward Islands Cricket Association turned him down. It made us suspicious that people at the top do not want a Leeward Islander. Similarly, we in Antigua feel that we do not get a fair deal in the Leeward Islands set-up. Although we supply the nucleus of the players, Antiguan cricket delegates find it difficult to have their say.

   Antigua needs to be fully represented at Leeward Islands level. I would even support a move for Antigua to go it alone and enter the Red Stripe tournament as Antigua & Barbuda – not because I want separation, but simply to state a point. I am tired of all that wrangling. We should have, we must have, more say in Leeward Islands cricket. If the power struggles do not end shortly I am going to pledge my support for the Antigua Cricket Association to go it alone in the Red Stripe Cup. I would put all my support and energy behind that venture.

I have always stated that I am, first and foremost, a sportsman and I have never expressed any real desire to get involved with politics. As far as party politics are concerned, I tend to shy away from them. I prefer to speak through my cricket and this is one of the key factors which makes cricket so special in the West Indies. It is a way of expressing ourselves, and doing so in a way that is totally pure.

   Of course, you cannot evade the point that playing cricket is in itself a political action. You cannot get away from that. During my career the question of South Africa has, sadly, occurred many times. It has been widely reported that I have received all kinds of offers to play in South Africa and these reports have been true.

Once I was offered one million Eastern Caribbean dollars, and there have been all kinds of similar proposals. They all carried a political burden and in each case it was a very simple decision for me. I just could not go.

As long as the black majority in South Africa remains suppressed by the *apartheid* system, I could never come to terms with playing cricket there. I would be letting down my own people back in Antigua and it would destroy my self-esteem.

What would happen when I was over there? Would I be treated like a lord on the cricket pitch and yet still be denied access to places when I was away from that spotlight? How could I live with myself knowing that I was only being treated well because of my cricket? How could I accept special treatment? No, I could not, it would be impossible. Try to imagine how I would justify this to the people back home.

I could go on for pages about this but there is little point. I do, however, have one further thing to say. I have always believed that in this game of cricket, which is not as yet a particularly high-paid sport for most people, every player has a right to exploit his talent to the full. I really do believe that. I myself could not play in South Africa because of the way I personally feel, and everyone has to look upon it in a similar way.

With this in mind, I would never hold a grudge against the players who have gone out there. They have had to justify it to themselves and if they can do that, then fine. I do not think that playing in South Africa automatically makes someone a racist, although many people do take that view.

It is a different situation for the white players and I

respect their right to come to terms with it in their own way. Bearing a grudge will not help the situation. Nevertheless, from my own viewpoint I think they are wrong to go. I was therefore very moved when Ian Botham refused to go by stating that if he went he could never look Viv Richards in the face again.

The whole issue is quite central for me, coming as I do from the West Indies at the very end of colonialism. I believe very strongly in the black man asserting himself in this world and over the years I have leaned towards many movements that follow this basic cause. It was perfectly natural for me to identify, for example, with the Black Power movement in America and, to a certain extent, with the Rastafarians.

I cannot say that I have ever reconciled myself totally to Rastafarianism. However I have many Rastafarian friends and I have always despised the way they have been discriminated against. Even in Antigua I have been put down in the past for simply having Rastafarian friends. It was hinted once that my career might not progress as far as it might simply because I was friendly with Rastafarians. Now that is certainly a case of prejudice and it goes back a long way in the Caribbean, back to when the Rastaman was initially regarded as nothing more than a subversive influence. Many people in the Caribbean have treated them in a bad way.

Rastafarians have always been put down in West Indian cricketing circles. Why else do you think that there has not been a Rastafarian influence in the West Indies national team? There have certainly been one or two players around but it was always seen as a great pity that they would not cut their hair and generally toe the orthodox line. Surely everyone has a basic right to be what they want to be, on a cricket field or anywhere else.

UP NORTH

After leaving Somerset I felt embittered. Above all else, I wanted to have the chance to prove to people that, whatever anyone may have said about me, I really did love my cricket.

I did not want to be instantly involved with another county. I needed something else, something pure. I was not interested in boardroom politics and I certainly was not interested in business.

When the opportunity came along to play for Rishton CC in the Lancashire League, I jumped at the chance.

It was a man from Rishton called Wilf Woodhouse who initially instigated this move. In the Lancashire League, all the clubs are allowed one professional and, sensing that I might be available and interested, Wilf was on the phone almost every night to my manager, David Copp. He even called me, at one point, in Australia. This man was so insistent that, eventually, David went up to look at the place. They treated him like royalty. David realised that I would be very happy in such a community and told me so.

I saw it as an opportunity to salvage my pride. I was not bothered about going for big money deals and I wanted to show people that cricket is what makes Viv Richards tick. The more I thought about it, the more the idea of spending time with a little club like Rishton began to appeal to me. It would be uncomplicated. It might also be fun, and that was something that had been lacking in the last days at Somerset.

When I arrived in Rishton, I was instantly stunned. The first time I ever saw the place was when we landed on the outfield in a helicopter. It was a beautiful little ground and I found myself immediately swamped by Lancastrian hospitality. It was a real royal welcome and I quickly found myself feeling at home in the company of the local lads. Something seemed to click straight away. That first night, all the lads in the team wanted me to meet their wives and generally show me around, make me feel comfortable.

At first, I stayed in a lovely hotel on the edge of the village. It was nice accommodation but, to be honest, I felt a little lonely there so I used to hop in my car – supplied by Rishton – and drive round to the club. In a place like Rishton, the club is the very centre of the community, so it was the perfect place to get to know everyone.

I think that, after a while, the novelty of having me there began to wear off, in a nice way, and I felt as if I had been truly accepted. I had the odd drink and game of snooker and, generally, just chatted about cricket and sport. It was a lovely situation and one which reminded me strongly of the bars back home in Antigua. I was happy again. All I had to do was concentrate on cricket. My duties at Rishton were fairly simple. I had to play for the club each Saturday. I was expected to bowl a number of overs each match and also, of course, to perform well with the bat.

Some people can be forgiven for thinking that this would be easy for me, but the standard of cricket up there was very high indeed. They are experienced players in the League and some of the captains could be very crafty. They knew exactly where to put their fielders on those grounds

Above Another big hit off Ian Botham in my 56-ball century against England at St John's in 1986.
Right Once again it was nice to play a memorable innings in front of an Antiguan crowd.

Lighter moments from the 1986 season.
Above At Bournemouth for Somerset's match against Hampshire.
Below A drink in the Taunton dressing room to celebrate Ian Botham's recall to the Test side.

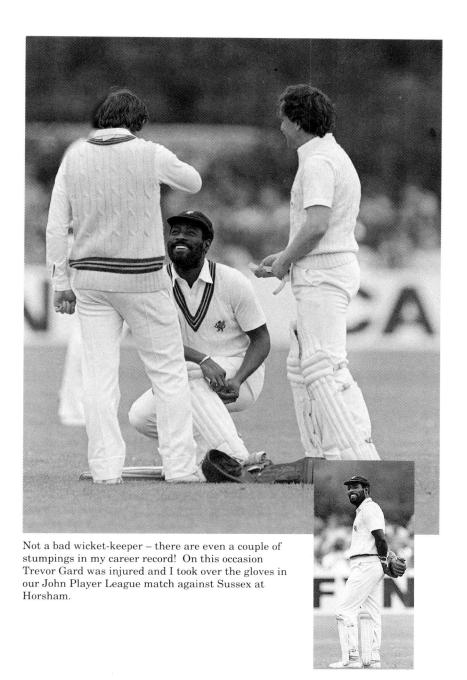

Not a bad wicket-keeper – there are even a couple of
stumpings in my career record! On this occasion
Trevor Gard was injured and I took over the gloves in
our John Player League match against Sussex at
Horsham.

Left A pause during my 48-ball century against Glamorgan at Taunton in May 1986. **Below** With Ian Botham at a 25th Anniversary party for Amnesty International hosted by Richard Branson.

The University of Exeter generously conferred on me an honorary doctorate. I was proud to attend a Congregation of the University in July 1986 to receive the degree of Doctor of Letters *honoris causa*.

A sad end to many happy years with Somerset.
Above left Tony Brown, club Secretary in 1986.
Above right Roy Kerslake, who had been chairman for some of the club's most successful years.
Right Peter Roebuck talks to Mrs Bridget Langdon who organised a petition to try to reverse the committee's decision.
Below A wreath left at the County Ground.

Above left and right It was good to have so many people who wanted us to stay.
Left Our last appearance for Somerset in a Championship match at Taunton.

Above left The next generation – a left-handed Mali Richards.
Above right A rare chance to relax on the beach between cricket commitments.
Below A recent family group.

Pain and joy – training and
celebration West Indian style.
Left Recovering from a spinal
fracture at Lord's in 1980.
Below World Cup warm-up in
India, 1987
Below left Success for the West
Indies in the Nehru Cup series,
1989
Bottom Jubilation in the Lord's
Test of 1980.

Left Arriving by helicopter on the Rishton ground in May 1987.
Below It was good to be made to feel so welcome.

Right It actually
snowed during my
first game at
Rishton!
Below left With
rugby internationals
Steve Smith (right)
and Fran Cotton at
a leisurewear launch
in 1987.
Below right I very
much enjoyed the
social side during
my season at
Rishton.

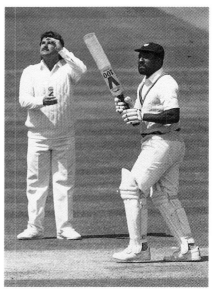

The 1988 Test series in England.
Above left With friends Tim and Maxi Hudson before the Lord's Test.
Above right Allan Lamb tries to follow the flight towards the Tavern stand.
Below left A word of warning to a member of the Headingley crowd.
Below right The anguish of being bowled by David Capel for 47 at Old Trafford.

Above My 100th first-class 100 at the Sydney Cricket Ground in 1988. Greg Dyer, the New South Wales wicket-keeper offers his congratulations. **Left** Not as rare as many people would believe – the Viv Richards forward defensive stroke. On this occasion it was at Adelaide during the fifth Test against Australia in February 1989

West Indies vs England 1990.
Above Allan Lamb is a good friend... even if we may have differing views out in the middle.
Right A lot of unnecessary heat. Christopher Martin-Jenkins and myself are interviewed during the Barbados Test.
Below A more relaxed chat with Tony Greig after we had won the series in Antigua

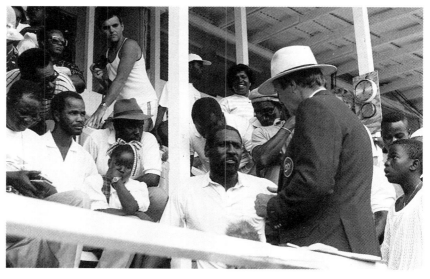

Back to county cricket in 1990 and happy to be
playing for Glamorgan, even if my return to
England after the Test series in the West Indies
was felt to require a police escort at Heathrow.

A handshake from Allan Border after I had passed Gary Sobers's record – for the most runs by a West Indian in Test cricket – during the first Test against Australia at Sabina Park, Jamaica in March 1991.

which were inclined to be damp on top. Quite often I would unleash what I thought to be a scorching drive, only to see it slowing rapidly and heading straight for a perfectly-positioned fielder. I adopted the attitude that, if I could not go for a clear six, I would settle for a single.

It took a good deal of concentration to play in that league, and I loved every minute of it. Other than just playing, I was expected to turn up at the practice sessions and take an interest in the promising youngsters of the area. Although this was a pleasure, I never have liked to tell others how to play. When you are a professional cricketer, people often think that you are able to coach and guide the game of every young hopeful. But that is against my principles. I would offer encouragement, of course, but I prefer to see youngsters developing their own game. I like to see them discovering their strengths and weaknesses in a perfectly natural way. I am reluctant to start telling a youngster, for instance, to get bat and pad together. That is against the very idea of 'hitting across the line'. On the other hand, I would be happy to try and get the youngster to feel comfortable and relaxed. Not technical stuff, but just common sense.

As the season progressed, I hope I became a worthwhile investment for Rishton. They had a good season, and the idea of a cricket club being an important part of village life seemed to be accepted by almost everyone. I cannot recall one unhappy incident. Friends of mine travelled from all over England, even from overseas, to spend time with me in this community. It was a time which also helped me to get back to basics. To rediscover what was truly important to me.

I remember one day in particular, when I was due to play in a match up at Jesmond. This was part of an annual Festival organised by Callers-Pegasus, a Newcastle-based company. They would attract players from across the world to play in the two-day event. It was great fun because it gave you a chance to play alongside the likes of Chappell and Pollock and you were also very well looked after. But Rishton had got involved in the semi-final of the Lancashire League Knockout Cup. This match had been rained off on several previous occasions and had ended up becoming one of the longest-running matches in Lancashire cricket.

I had batted and bowled some of my overs but had not made a very good job of either. It looked as if we were going to lose when the rain came down again. I had to phone the Pegasus people to say that I could not make the game at Jesmond.

People could not understand why I turned down the opportunity to earn some extra money and stayed with Rishton, whose cause in this particular match seemed to have been already lost. I felt that to leave would have been to let down the club and my friends. I wanted to share this match with them, however it went.

THE CASE FOR CHANGE

Monday 6th August 1990.

Head held aloft, shoulders back, purposeful stride. Vivian Richards, gracefully steering himself around endless magnetic greetings, strolls around the Lord's periphery before climbing to a relatively obscure area at the rear of the Warner stand and settling into conversation about his forthcoming book. His eyes continually dart down to the field where Mike Gatting's euphoric Middlesex – already anticipating the silverware to come – are entertaining an awkwardly spirited and much improved Glamorgan.

As Richards finally relaxes, and just as he is in full flow, he is approached by an awestruck if tentative fan, no doubt seeking an autograph and a few precious moments of attention. Richards, in refusing to allow his concentration to be broken, politely and expertly halts the fan's approach and sends him shuffling, sans autograph, back down to his seat at the front of the stand.

Thirty minutes later after Richards's meeting is over and as his tiny entourage stands to leave, he makes a point of wading downwards through the awkwardly ranged mass of spectators to find the aforementioned fan. He has a friendly word and signs his autograph.

Viv Richards had earlier been talking about many things. His flow of thought, not surprisingly, is initially inspired by the evocative nature of his surroundings.

I love this place. I have always dreamed about it from my boyhood days in Antigua, my ear glued to the transistor. After tasting its special magic there is nowhere else to go after Lord's. This is the ultimate, the Mecca. And you can feel it here, at all times. That history, that legacy. How can anyone fail to feel respect for that? It's like playing in a cathedral, there is something so grand, so permanent, so stately.

However, when I play here I always feel a slight pang of guilt. Even though I respect the place and love its magic, I find myself often looking towards the Long Room and I know that, even in this day and age, in these supposedly liberated times, women are not allowed to enter in there on a normal, everyday basis. Although I gather that women are now allowed in on official tours and that the MCC is considering a proposal to admit lady members.

Women have played a very important role in cricket, and for a long time, and deserve better rights of access to this place which is the very heart of cricket. It is a beautiful room and when you walk in there you are swamped with cricket history. We should not deny this pleasure to women along with the pleasure they would derive from being full members of the MCC. I am glad to see, by the way, that Lancashire County Cricket Club have finally come to their senses on this issue. I think it is important, and today should be seen as a matter of principle. It is I believe a thorn in the side of cricket. We must not have any discrimination against women in cricket

I have seen quite a lot of women's cricket both in England and the West Indies. There are some very good cricketers. I have certainly been entertained, on many occasions, by their skill and their talent has often surprised me.

Admittedly, they don't really get mixed up with the same degree of rough stuff as the men, but they are still fine athletes. I love to see them play. I would love to see more importance placed on their brand of cricket too because, like tennis, their game may not be as furious as the men's, but it can be just as exciting. It can also be far more elegant and stylish and, in that sense, maybe they could steal a little of our limelight in the same way that the ladies do on the tennis circuit.

Cricket is a stylish sport, perhaps the most stylish sport and, with that thought in mind, women's cricket could well be something quite exquisite. I suppose it is a different sport, in a sense, but just as valid as the men's game. I hope it is allowed to expand.

Talking about women's cricket may seem, to some people, an anarchic thing to do in a book like this, but I see it as one more purely natural extension of our game. It is another way in which we can encourage the entertainment factor. While I am pushing this theme I want to talk a little more about other innovative, and, as far as I am concerned, very entertaining strands of cricket and how they are treated by the purists.

INDOOR CRICKET

I have played some indoor cricket, mostly in exhibitions many of which were in Australia. It is a particularly important development for the working man who wants to indulge in a little light sport in the evening.

In no way do I see this as an intrusion into the traditional game. It is an exciting and entertaining variation. When professional cricketers try it they tend to find it a little strange. The basic speed of the game is something of a mind-blower. But I think it must be regarded as a good thing, especially if it keeps the game of cricket pumping.

One of the eternal problems of cricket, especially in England, is the fact that it is so much a summer sport. So if, in the winter, indoor cricket keeps the feel for the game alive, then this can only be a good thing. That is not meant to sound patronising to the serious indoor cricketer. It is now remarkably well-organised both in England and Australia. There are regular leagues and the game has also become a popular inter-company activity.

When I first went over to England that cold November twenty years ago, I would have loved the odd game of indoor cricket. And, speaking as someone whose basic sporting philosophy is one of fitness and sporting involvement for a whole community, the more indoor cricket there is, the better. It is lively, healthy and a terrific introduction to the sport.

Five-day cricket will, however, always be the ultimate challenge. I have to make this point clear. This is what cricket is really about. This is where all the subtleties come into play and, it goes without saying, that is where my heart lies. But I don't see indoor cricket, or one-day cricket, or women's cricket as being any kind of threat to that.

This is where we see the paranoia within the game. The purists are wrong. The game they love, the five-day game, will always be there but the other strands of cricket act, not in opposition to it, but as a necessary promotion of it. This is the only attitude we can take if we are truly to survive as a major sport. Let us welcome these innovative strands, not despise them.

Indoor cricket is a fine spectator sport and it must be treated seriously. There is no point in pretending otherwise, and in any case it is never going to go away. The same can be said of one-day cricket which, of course, is extremely well-established. It may not be as sophisticated as the five-day game, and it will never replace it, but it is something that is very much in demand from the spectators.

Day-night cricket is another fascinating development and one of the most exciting things I have ever taken part in. It's extremely intoxicating. It attracts a large number of people who, generally, would not call themselves cricket lovers.

The establishment have got to come to terms with all this. We are fighting for survival here. Let's go for it. Let's change cricket. I don't want to be involved in a nostalgia sport. I want to be involved in a sport that is very much a part of the times. If it's handled properly, then the Test match cricketer will stay firmly at the top of the tree which is how it should be. However if you alienate these new ideas, then sooner or later they will set up in direct opposition with no regard for the five-day game. The Test match cricketer could become largely obsolete. Now that really would be a disaster and, ironically, I believe it is the people who wish to safeguard it, and are most paranoid about it, who are most likely to instigate its demise.

Personally I would find life intolerable without Test matches. But the very nature of them hardly makes them the most commercially perfect events and, of course, we now rely on the one-day games to subsidise a Test series. This is a complex issue and I fully sympathise with people who stress that the one-day matches are killing Test cricket. I would agree that in some cases the limited-overs game has caused good Test players to fall into bad habits and has perhaps prevented a few top-class cricketers from achieving greatness. I accept that. But one-day cricket is still a highly skilled game, especially the way it has been played over the past few years. Even though it has still got many problems one-day cricket must be encouraged. Without it I believe that cricket as a whole would be in much worse shape.

For the professional cricketer it will always be very hard to adjust from playing five-day cricket to the one-day game. But I do believe they are compatible and, if there is a fault, then it lies not with the one-day game itself but with the extensive playing schedules that top-class cricketers are expected to fulfil. Cricket is a mental process. It is an extremely stressful sport and to be constantly changing from the deep concentration needed over five days to the quick-fire business of the one-day game puts the cricketer under horrendous pressure.

The pressure is not visible, and that I think is part of the problem. The game looks easy to people who do not understand just what is involved. However disciplined you are, there are times when a heavy itinerary can throw you into confusion. It is especially bad on Test match tours. If, for instance, you are pitched into a Test match after playing a couple of one-day games in quick succession, then you are not really being allowed to get yourself mentally prepared for the big game.

Under sound imaginative management there is room for all kinds of cricket. All can feed off each other and benefit each other. It is a wonderful game in all its various shapes. But the five-day Test match must never lose its position as the ultimate showcase.

ENTERTAINING
MR LAWTON

September 1990.
With U2's 'The Joshua Tree' pumping
mercilessly from the in-car stereo, the Vauxhall
attracts more than the odd passing glance as it
sweeps past Cardiff Castle and over the bridge
spanning the calm waters of the River Taff.
Turning right, the car eases through the
parklands and past the frontage of the National
Centre for Sports before swinging to a halt in the
comparatively modest forecourt belonging to
Glamorgan County Cricket Club.

Viv Richards, resplendent in Tim Hudson
tracksuit and, as ever, Nike trainers, leaps
energetically from the vehicle and strides through
the reception area and into an office where, head
down, Glamorgan captain Hugh Morris is
scribbling autographs on a weighty stack of
replies to fan letters.

After collecting his post, and enjoying five
minutes of rampant camaraderie, Richards
strides across the ghostly ground before choosing
a suitable seat in the low-lying Glamorgan
stands. As he talks, and as the cold autumn
wind rips through the aforementioned tracksuit,
his Glamorgan teammates slowly gather around
the nets. It is to be the last practice of the season.
It is, he admits, difficult to imagine that a full
cricket season, and one packed with incident,
has passed since that explosive 1990 Test series
against England in the West Indies. Intriguingly,
Richards recalls with good humour the events of
that now legendary encounter, only occasionally
allowing his damaged pride to surface.

I thought that the series against England in the West Indies was generally played in a very light-hearted manner. I cannot recall any serious tensions between the players at all. Most of them knew each other very well and, while that does not always mean that things will run smoothly, I think most of my players would agree that the series went very well. In fact I cannot think of a better example of two teams, although highly competitive on the field, enjoying such mutual friendship off it. One example I can think of was a party held at the St James's Club in Antigua, when both teams mixed freely, chatting, laughing, listening to the music and generally having a good time. That was the true mood of the tour.

But that was not the way it was reflected in some of the English papers. Sometimes I look up at the press box and despair. England played superbly in Jamaica and thoroughly deserved their win. We had to face up to defeat, learn from it and go down to Guyana determined to do better. Guyana was washed out and in Trinidad we were lucky not to go two down. Again, England played well and I have to admit we were probably saved by the rain. I had sympathy with England because they got into a position to win the game and the rain ruined it for them. I know how it feels to be 'done' by the rain, but that is part of cricket's unpredictability. Desmond Haynes took a lot of stick for his captaincy, but he had no choice but to limit

WEST INDIES vs. ENGLAND (First Test)

at Sabina Park, Kingston on 24th, 25th, 26th, 28th February, 1st March 1990
Toss : West Indies.   Umpires : L.H. Barker and S. Bucknor
England won by 9 wickets

WEST INDIES

C. G. Greenidge	run out	32	c Hussain b Malcolm	36
D.L. Haynes	c and b Small	36	b Malcolm	14
R.B. Richardson	c Small b Capel	10	lbw b Fraser	25
C.A. Best	c Russell b Capel	4	c Gooch b Small	64
C.L. Hooper	c Capel b Fraser	20	c Larkins b Small	8
I.V.A. Richards*	lbw b Malcolm	21	b Malcolm	37
P.J.L. Dujon+	not out	19	b Malcolm	15
M.D. Marshall	b Fraser	0	not out	8
I.R. Bishop	c Larkins b Fraser	0	c Larkins b Small	3
C.A. Walsh	b Fraser	6	b Small	2
B.P. Patterson	b Fraser	0	run out	2
Extras	(b 9,lb 3,nb 4)	16	(b 14,lb 10,w 1,nb 1)	26
TOTAL		164		240

ENGLAND

G.A. Gooch*	c Dujon b Patterson	18	c Greenidge b Bishop	8
W. Larkins	lbw b Walsh	46	not out	29
A.J. Stewart	c Best b Bishop	13	not out	0
A.J. Lamb	c Hooper b Walsh	132		
R.A. Smith	c Best b Bishop	57		
N. Hussain	c Dujon b Bishop	13		
D.J. Capel	c Richardson b Walsh	25		
R.C. Russell+	c Patterson b Walsh	26		
G.C. Small	lbw b Marshall	4		
A.R.C. Fraser	not out	2		
D.E. Malcolm	lbw b Walsh	0		
Extras	(b 23,lb 12,w 1,nb 12)	48	(lb 1,nb 3)	4
TOTAL		364	(for 1 wkt)	41

ENGLAND	O	M	R	W	O	M	R	W
Small	15	6	44	1	22	6	58	4
Malcolm	16	4	49	1	21.3	2	77	4
Fraser	20	8	28	5	14	5	31	1
Capel	13	4	31	2	15	1	50	0

WEST INDIES	O	M	R	W	O	M	R	W
Patterson	18	2	74	1	3	1	11	0
Bishop	27	5	72	3	7.3	0	17	1
Marshall	18	3	46	1				
Walsh	27.2	4	68	5	6	0	12	0
Hooper	6	0	28	0				
Richards	9	1	22	0				
Best	4	0	19	0				

FALL OF WICKETS

	WI	ENG	WI	ENG
1st	62	40	26	35
2nd	81	60	69	
3rd	92	116	87	
4th	92	288	112	
5th	124	315	192	
6th	144	315	222	
7th	144	325	222	
8th	150	339	227	
9th	164	364	237	
10th	164	364	240	

WEST INDIES vs. ENGLAND (Third Test)

at Port of Spain on 23rd, 24th, 25th, 27th, 28th March 1990
Toss : England.   Umpires : C.E. Cumberbatch and L.H. Barker
Match drawn

WEST INDIES

Batsman	First Innings		Second Innings	
C.G. Greenidge	c Stewart b Malcolm	5	lbw b Fraser	42
D.L. Haynes*	c Lamb b Small	0	c Lamb b Malcolm	45
R.B. Richardson	c Russell b Fraser	8	c Gooch bSmall	34
C.A. Best	c Lamb b Fraser	10	lbw b Malcolm	0
P.J.L. Dujon+	lbw b Small	4	b Malcolm	0
A.L. Logie	c Lamb b Fraser	98	c Larkins b Malcolm	20
C.L. Hooper	c Russell b Capel	32	run out	10
E.A. Moseley	c Russell b Malcolm	0	c Lamb b Malcolm	26
C.E.L. Ambrose	c Russell b Malcolm	7	c Russell b Fraser	18
I.R. Bishop	b Malcolm	16	not out	15
C.A. Walsh	not out	8	lbw b Malcolm	1
Extras	(lb 4,nb 7)	11	(b 2,lb 13,w 1,nb 12)	28
TOTAL		199		239

ENGLAND

Batsman	First Innings		Second Innings	
G.A. Gooch*	c Dujon b Bishop	84	retired hurt	18
W. Larkins	c Dujon b Ambrose	54	c Dujon b Moseley	7
A.J. Stewart	c Dujon b Ambrose	9	c Bishop b Walsh	31
A.J. Lamb	b Bishop	32	lbw b Bishop	35
R.A. Smith	c Dujon b Moseley	5	lbw b Walsh	2
R.J. Bailey	c Logie b Moseley	0	b Walsh	0
D.J. Capel	c Moseley b Ambrose	40	not out	17
R.C. Russell+	c Best b Walsh	15	not out	5
G.C. Small	lbw b Bishop	0		
A.R.C. Fraser	c Hooper b Ambrose	11		
D.E. Malcolm	not out	0		
Extras	(b 10,lb 9,w 3,nb 16)	38	(b 2,lb 7,nb 6)	15
TOTAL		288	(for 5 wkts)	120

ENGLAND	O	M	R	W	O	M	R	W
Small	17	4	41	2	21	8	56	1
Malcolm	20	2	60	4	26.2	4	77	6
Fraser	13.1	2	41	3	24	4	61	2
Capel	15	2	53	1	13	3	30	0

WEST INDIES	O	M	R	W	O	M	R	W
Ambrose	36.2	8	59	4	6	0	20	0
Bishop	31	6	69	3	10	1	31	1
Walsh	22	5	45	1	7	0	27	3
Hooper	18	5	26	0				
Moseley	30	5	70	2	10	2	33	1

FALL OF WICKETS

	WI	ENG	WI	ENG
1st	5	112	96	27
2nd	5	125	100	74
3rd	22	195	100	79
4th	27	214	100	85
5th	29	214	142	106
6th	92	214	157	
7th	93	243	200	
8th	103	244	200	
9th	177	284	234	
10th	199	288	239	

England's batting time. If I had been playing I would have done the same. What's more, I think England would have employed the same tactics if the positions had been reversed. Desmond did a marvellous job in holding the side together and I was proud of him. But the press labelled us a bunch of villains; we had unfairly deprived their boys of victory. Such talk is pathetic and unmanly.

Desmond took a lot of criticism in Trinidad and then it was my turn in Barbados. I took a catch behind the wicket and did a ceremonial jig, advancing towards the umpire, which I admit was something I do not normally do. The umpire thought for a while and finally gave the player out. In the commentary box Christopher Martin-Jenkins passed a remark about cheating. He stated that he thought both teams had been guilty of cheating and adopting a win-at-all-costs attitude. It is true that both teams were fired up, and rightly so. It was highly competitive Test cricket – the best of all cricket. But I am not a cheat and my dance was not intended to induce a bad decision. It was a genuine appeal – maybe a bit dramatic – but not an unusual feature of Test match cricket.

Much of the press coverage of this incident was critical but fair. But a lot of it was very personal and abusive. During the whole tour the pressure for new stories was intense. There were 70 or 80 journalists following the tour – more in Barbados and Antigua where the series would be decided. Some papers sent two or three reporters; not all of them were cricket correspondents. These 'extra' journalists were all vying for exclusive stories or 'different angles'. But there weren't any – we were too busy playing Test cricket – so they had to fabricate some.

On the rest day of the Antigua Test, James Lawton of the *Daily Express* came up to me and asked why I had made a V sign at Allan Lamb on the previous day. The

WEST INDIES vs. ENGLAND (Fourth Test)
at Bridgetown on 5th, 6th, 7th, 8th, 10th April 1990
Toss : England.   Umpires : D.M. Archer and L.H. Barker
West Indies won by 164 runs

WEST INDIES

C. G. Greenidge	c Russell b DeFreitas	21	lbw b Small	3
D.L. Haynes	c Stewart b Small	0	c Malcolm b Small	109
R.B. Richardson	c Russell b Small	45	lbw b DeFreitas	39
C.A. Best	c Russell b Small	164		
I.V.A. Richards*	c Russell b Capel	70	(4) c Small b Capel	12
A.L. Logie	c Russell b Capel	31	(5) lbw b DeFreitas	48
P.J.L. Dujon+	b Capel	31	(8) not out	15
M.D. Marshall	c Lamb b Small	4	(7) c Smith b Small	7
C.E.L. Ambrose	not out	20	c Capel b DeFreitas	1
I.R. Bishop	run out	10	not out	11
E.A. Moseley	b DeFreitas	4	(6) b Small	5
Extras	(lb 8,nb 18)	26	(lb 12,w 1,nb 4)	17
TOTAL		446	(for 8 wkts dec)	267

ENGLAND

A.J. Stewart	c Richards b Moseley	45	c Richards b Ambrose	37
W. Larkins	c Richardson b Bishop	0	c Dujon b Bishop	0
R.J. Bailey	b Bishop	17	c Dujon b Ambrose	6
A.J. Lamb*	lbw b Ambrose	119	(6) c Dujon b Moseley	10
R.A. Smith	b Moseley	62	(7) not out	40
N. Hussain	lbw b Marshall	18	(8) lbw b Ambrose	0
D.J. Capel	c Greenidge b Marshall	2	(9) lbw b Ambrose	6
R.C. Russell+	lbw b Bishop	7	(5) b Ambrose	55
P.A.J. DeFreitas	c and b Ambrose	24	(10) lbw b Ambrose	0
G.C. Small	not out	1	(4) lbw b Ambrose	0
D.E. Malcolm	b Bishop	12	lbw b Ambrose	4
Extras	(b 14,lb 9,w 3,nb 25)	51	(b 8,lb 9,w 1,nb 15)	33
TOTAL		358		191

ENGLAND	O	M	R	W	O	M	R	W
Malcolm	33	6	142	0	10	0	46	0
Small	35	5	109	4	20	1	74	4
DeFreitas	29.5	6	99	2	22	2	69	3
Capel	24	5	88	3	16	1	66	1

WEST INDIES	O	M	R	W	O	M	R	W
Bishop	24.3	9	70	4	20	8	40	1
Ambrose	25	3	82	2	22.4	10	45	8
Moseley	28	3	118	2	19	4	44	1
Marshall	23	6	55	2	18	8	31	0
Richards	9	4	14	0	10	5	11	0
Richardson					2	1	3	0

FALL OF WICKETS

	WI	ENG	WI	ENG
1st	6	1	13	1
2nd	67	46	80	10
3rd	108	75	109	10
4th	227	268	223	71
5th	291	297	228	97
6th	395	301	238	166
7th	406	308	238	173
8th	411	340	239	181
9th	431	340		181
10th	446	358		191

question annoyed me, firstly because real cricket correspondents don't approach cricketers on a rest day with such trivial questions. Secondly, Lawton had got his facts wrong: what he had seen was me making a gesture to some Antiguan supporters in the crowd. It was absolutely nothing to do with Allan Lamb or any other England player. Thirdly, anyone who really follows cricket would know that Allan Lamb and I are very good friends. We have played against each other for years and get on well both on and off the field. Allan is usually the first of the English players to come across to our dressing room and have a beer and a chat at the end of a day's play.

But Lawton persisted with his stupid questions; it seemed to me as if he was deliberately trying to provoke me. He succeeded. I answered him threateningly. He replied that he would headline my remarks. I told him that if he did I would come looking for him in the press box.

The next morning before play started I heard that the *Daily Express* had indeed run Lawton's story on the front page. I was really angry and went in search of Lawton to tell him my opinion of him in no uncertain terms.

As a result of this altercation I was late on to the field of play and had to apologise to the West Indies Board of Control and my team-mates. But I really felt that the limits of good reporting had been pushed too far, and I wanted to make a stand against such journalism.

What happened next was even more upsetting. A journalist wrote a piece saying that I should be banned from playing in England and that Glamorgan should terminate my contract. That created a hostile atmosphere and when I returned to England I received a lot of offensive, openly racist letters. I thank God for my thick skin. Writing letters like that is so cowardly.

Bad reporting can have this sort of consequence. I

know that I have enemies because of the colour of my skin; I can't help that. But I do resent reporters who incite their readers to write the sort of offensive letters that I received. I repeat that I am not afraid of fair criticism of my performance on the field. As I have said, I have had many happy associations with the press. What I appeal against is the trivial reporting that led to the run-in with James Lawton and irresponsible reporting which can lead to increased racial tension. I have to ask why it is that we have all these problems with the English press? In the Caribbean cricket is reported accurately. All right, a little bias for local players in some islands, but the reports concentrate on the action on the field. In Australia reporters also seem much more professional. They want to understand what has really happened on the field, they ask fair questions and they are helpful. They don't go sneaking around looking for some dirt to dredge up.

Sometimes off the field we do have a bit of fun, but I forget how many times I have seen reporters going out on the town and making fools of themselves. Nobody monitors their activities. Nobody tries to work up hatred against them. Nevertheless, they feel they can pass judgement on others. They are forever hiding behind the excuse that what they do is 'just part of journalism'. What hypocrites! I hope they get their comeuppance.

As you will gather I am very critical of a section of the press. Thank heavens it is the minority. But they do a lot of harm to the reputation of real cricket correspondents. It would be really great if we could get back to the days of mutual trust and confidence when cricket journalists were professional commentators off the field and cricketers were professional on it.

Perhaps cricket journalists need to look at better ways of reporting the game, analysing batting and bowling performances in greater depth, going beyond the instant coverage of radio and television. Maybe, too, the British tabloid press needs to review much of its approach to cricket and cricketers – the game and journalism would be the better for that!

REFLECTIONS
FROM THE PATIO

The Volvo – as opposed to the Range Rover which is being used by Miriam – makes a confident right turn and rises through one of Antigua's softer regions. To the left squats the house belonging to Viv Richards. To be honest, casual passers-by do not much notice Viv's house, for it lacks the expected ostentation of a superstar's abode. It is a handsome house which, far from being a manifestation of arrogant wealth, sits unpretentious and unthreatening.

Viv Richards strides from the Volvo, opens the gate and states, 'This is it...this is where I live' and, just in case one is fazed by the prevailing normality, a portrait of Richards in majestic pose, stares down from above the patio doorway.

Sitting on the patio, Red Stripe in hand, Richards begins to talk. As always, his flow suffers from constant interruptions. Every passer-by – and there are many – on noticing the reclining cricketer, halts and begins yet another jovial, apparently in-depth debate. Richards accepts the interruptions in good humour and seems to be at his most relaxed. In half an hour he will take the Range Rover, guide it to some of the more remote areas of St John's, picking up along the way a variety of small boys who will make up the football team he helps to run.

It is not difficult to imagine Richards, in just a small handful of years, settling back into this scenario. He admits this as he begins to reflect, initially on his plans for life after cricket and then, intermittently, through a web of loose ends. 'Oh yes, the loose ends,' he laughs. 'We must tie up the loose ends.'

Sportsmen are used to life being something of a gamble. It is a gamble from day one. I suppose that, statistically, it is a crazy career to go into and the chances of success are minute. But there is something inside you which urges you onward and, God willing, you will be able to take whatever talent you have and nurture it and edge your way up the ladder.

It is a gamble all along the way. Nobody really knows how far your talent will stretch, least of all yourself. I have seen supremely talented youngsters fail for many reasons. Not just because of problems they might have on a personal level with people in power. I have seen people who seem to be in a perfect state of mind, have just the right attitude, just the right skill and are in just the right teams at the right time – and still they fail. Nobody really knows why. It is a gamble and the line between success and failure is terrifyingly small. I could have failed so easily. My life could have been so different but somehow I managed to get through.

Even when you are on top of the world and everything seems to be going superbly, the risk is still there. At the back of every successful sportsman's mind is that big question mark. What will I do when this is all over? And, of course, it is such a short life. It is over in a flash. You are so busy throughout your sporting life, then suddenly you see the end hurtling towards you. Many people panic and we all know stories of top sportsmen who have come unstuck and slipped into bad times. I think the general situation has improved, partly because sportsmen are far better advised these days and they do, generally, make more money – even cricketers.

I chose an adviser with commercial experience of sport but with an understanding of cricket and the demands on the first-class player. I told him that my cricket commitments came first. I don't want to get involved with personality appearances and commercial activities while I am trying to concentrate on a match. I try hard for my sponsors but the best return I can give Slazenger is a good performance on the field.

Lots of people approach me with ideas about how to invest my money. Some of them are very speculative. It is tempting to speculate because you have such a short time at the top and you want to secure the future for your family. But I am not a gambler, nor a speculator on the Stock Exchange. I have heard stories about the piles of money that can be made. But that is not for me; it is out of my league. I have a natural suspicion of get-rich-quick ideas. I don't dream of wealth but I do want to be comfortable. I have seen too much poverty. In India I have seen people who have nothing. It makes me realise how fortunate I am, so the investments I make are generally sound. I like to get involved in local projects that I know something about or in which I am interested. I have an interest in a small clothing factory in Antigua, which makes beautiful hand-painted and printed T-shirts as well as a range of Viv Richards Activewear. We make for the domestic market but would like to export more. I also have an interest in the Spinnakers Club in St Johns where we have created what we hope is a special atmosphere. Recently I have taken a share in a fishing trawler. Miriam has a small shop of her own and we have some property. I am ploughing my money back into Antigua because that is what I really want. My roots are there and that is where I want to be rather than in New York or London. The Antiguan government is trying to encourage small business and I am keen to play some small part in helping my fellow Antiguans to succeed in doing their own thing. I am not cut out to be a big-time entrepreneur.

The things that are important to me are firmly planted in Antiguan life. In a sense I am laying down more and more roots, because that is what I want. I have no great desire to carry on travelling around the world once my playing days are over. That type of lifestyle holds no attraction for me.

I am very enthusiastic about Antiguan cricket. Even now this little island boasts seven players of Test standard and, believe me, there are many more on the way. That is something that I am very proud of.

However, although I dream of a united Caribbean, I am sometimes upset by the insularity which still persists and is even growing in the region.

Cricket is a great leveller and one thing which does not change from island to island is the amount of enthusiasm and genuine expertise you can find in the crowd. Of course, across the world, you will find self-appointed experts in any crowd, but in the West Indies these experts are, more often than not, spot on. They know and understand every aspect of the game. They often know just as much as the professionals and I am not joking.

One story, to illustrate this fact, concerns an old guy who was watching Malcolm Marshall bowling in his early days. In those days, Malcolm was bowling medium-pace. This old guy, after studying him for some time, went up to him and said, 'Y'know, with your bowling action you could bowl real quick. You have an arm action which would be perfectly suited to a fast bowler.' And so, Malcolm did indeed begin to bowl quick.

This little story says a great deal about the West Indian attitude towards cricket. It was remarkable that that old boy managed to see the potential in Malcolm. It is remarkable, also, that Malcolm actually listened to him and acted upon the unsolicited advice. Can you imagine that happening in England?

Over in the West Indies, the crowds are very much a part of the game. There is none of this cold aloofness, none of this superstar stuff. The game involves everyone.

I am not saying that there is not stardom in the West Indies, of course there is, but it is a different kind of stardom. It draws you closer to the people, rather than making you isolated. Even so, I have not always been able to cope with it.

In Antigua, I have never really come to terms with all the red-carpet treatment. It is not as bad now as it used to be. There was a time, for me and Andy Roberts, when the entire country would seem to be going out of its way to entertain us, to embrace and cherish us. It was terrifying. I was just a humble little island lad and I did not like this feeling, which might sound a bit ungrateful, but there you have it.

The first few years were the worst. The heads of Andy Roberts and myself were printed on postage stamps.

For us everything in the island was free. By nature I am far more suited to anonymity. I am not like 'Both', I can't always cope and I prefer to go off on my own. Sometimes I upset a few people because I don't always respond by returning, or receiving calls. There are times when I demand privacy. I will always find time to talk to people, but I do not always want to talk cricket. I find it necessary just to relax, and find myself.

Fame is a peculiar thing, it screws up so many people. I have seen many charming people become totally ruined by it. Some people can handle it perfectly, they relish it, which is fine. But not me. It makes me uncomfortable and I know that many people, who perhaps are working in some job that they hate, will think me appallingly arrogant for saying such a thing. After all, am I not fantastically lucky to be making a good living playing cricket? Not only that, I have people praising me for it, even idolising me.

Of course I am lucky. I do appreciate that, but it does not mean that I am happy or receptive all of the time. It does not mean that I have to enjoy being pursued by people when I am trying to concentrate, or am going through some kind of crisis. I think that is the part that people cannot quite understand. They expect you to be in a certain all-welcoming mood all the time and be forever friendly. But who, if they are totally honest about it, is really like that one hundred per cent of the time? Nobody. Being in a privileged position, as I am, does not change that. It does not stop me from being human – feeling miserable from time to time.

On the whole, I am an easy-going guy, but I do find it hard sometimes to mask how I am really feeling. Perhaps that is a weakness. One thing I do know: I am never false. That is not in my nature.

I suppose I must say a little about girls. Yes, there have been many stories in the media, most of them false – some of them true.

I do not have an untarnished reputation. I admit this although, needless to say, the press have exaggerated some stories to an outrageous degree. However, as I have said before, I have not been an angel. There have been times, at nightclubs or wherever, when I have thrown caution to the wind, and have had a great time.

I think it is fair to say that Antiguan men do have a very macho attitude towards sex. Some people would certainly call it sexist, but that is a very simple view and, to be honest, a view that does not really understand West Indian society. However, I don't really want to get into that, other than to say that in the West Indies a man's virility is considered extremely important. It is a measure of his status. That may sound appalling to some people, but that is how it is.

I have always had a lot of female friends, especially in England. But they were always friends, and just friends. I was an active young man, alone in England, and surrounded by people in the same situation. Of course we got up to things. Again, it may seem arrogant, but I always saw it as harmless. I am neither proud nor ashamed of that part of my life. That is just how it was. As for my relationship with Miriam, that was always a far deeper thing, and always will be.

Miriam and I got married in 1981. It was an emotional occasion, not just for us but, at least so it seemed, the whole of Antigua. It was a joyful occasion with almost a carnival atmosphere and we were literally swamped with greetings. It was a big wedding in a tiny place and I like to think that the entire island shared our joy.

Ian Botham was present, as was Clive Lloyd, Joel Garner, Michael Holding, Andy Roberts, Gordon Greenidge, my friend Pete McCoombe and the Prime Minister. I was exhilarated and terrified, so much so that I decided not to make a speech. We were so happy, our lives flashed before us. We saw smiling faces everywhere to remind us of our humbler days. It is all a lovely, hazy memory.

When you are a sportsman, or perhaps in any kind of occupation which keeps you away from home for so long, you need to find an extra special kind of person who will keep the family together. That person has to be utterly selfless and immensely strong. I have seen too many sportsmen meet girlfriends along the line. Quite often they have got married but when that glamorous veneer begins to fade, as it always does, those marriages usually become very shaky.

Ours is not a glamorous life, it is not an easy life either. It is especially difficult for the wives. At the start of this book, I mentioned my fantastic luck in finding someone like Miriam, and so early in my life. Even though she knew all about the pressures of professional sport, she has still been a quite remarkable wife. We have had two children, a son, Mali, and a daughter, Matara.

Miriam's role, more often that not, has been one of both ma and pa combined because I have been missing on so many occasions. Nevertheless, she has handled things superbly. She has seen our kids through some very difficult times when I was away. Her role in this whole story is a vital one. She has been totally magnificent and I am very grateful to her.

ON HEALTH AND EXERCISE

Throughout my career, but especially in the latter years,

there has always been a certain amount of speculation about my health. My problem with haemorrhoids is not something that I have enjoyed being repeatedly referred to in the press and I certainly do not wish to spend much time talking about it here. But it is important for me to clear up one or two points.

In winter 1988-89 I signed a two-year contract with Glamorgan. At that time I was in Australia and David Copp negotiated the agreement on my behalf. I told David that although I had an operation (during the Oval Test in 1988) in an attempt to clear everything up, I was still not feeling very well. The contract had to include a clause 'subject to fitness'. David openly discussed this matter with Glamorgan and they accepted that I should only come if I was fully fit.

When I got back home from Australia I was feeling worse than ever. My own consultant strongly recommended changing my diet, lots of rest and no stress. I felt awful about letting Glamorgan down so I came over to Wales to explain my situation to Tony Lewis and to reassure the Glamorgan members that I would honour my contract next season and try to make up for my absence in 1989.

The problem with me is that I have always been healthy. Just look through my career and you will see that I have missed very few matches through illness. I have always been a very fit person and it is that feeling – the feeling of being on top of the world – that has provided the base for my cricket. If I do not have that feeling then I cannot give my best to my team. As a batsman I rely on timing and anything which might impair that timing is a cause for great concern.

I do admit that I was a little caught out by the haemorrhoid problem. It is something that can be caused by stress and maybe it was a sign that I was beginning to feel my age. Des Haynes came up with the most acceptable solution. He said that I was not drinking enough Guinness.

There were also a number of cancer scare stories around at the time. This stemmed from the same problem. I was told that after having two or three operations there is a very slight risk of developing cancer of the bowel. Obviously this played on my mind, but thankfully those fears were without substance. I came to the Barbados Test in 1990 fully fit and raring to go.

BATS AND PADS AND GLOVES

As I have matured, I have grown to appreciate more and more the value of good cricketing equipment. When I was young, I was not too bothered about it. I had this macho idea that I could play with anything and still whack the ball out of the ground. Looking back, I have been a little too casual at times.

During my first season at Somerset I did not even wear a box until about midsummer. I can't remember what it was that persuaded me to change my mind, but I am sure it was painful. This was partly my naivety. Boxes were practically unheard of at the level I was playing in Antigua. Also, I think I had a macho idea that I would not be seriously hurt. That attitude fades in time. In recent years I have begun to want, and need, the confidence which good equipment instils in you. Playing in a Test match, the last thing you want to worry about is having your finger caught up in a faulty glove. It is just common sense really, but a player should always want to feel comfortable. The very best equipment allows you to concentrate one hundred per cent on your game, that is why I contracted to use Slazenger bats, pads and gloves.

Leg-guards have changed enormously over the years. You used to get little flimsy ones which could leave you at the mercy of the cleverer fast bowlers. Pads or not, you really knew it if you got hit.

After that, the trend was towards really heavy pads. I can remember some which weighed down on the top of my foot, which was the last thing I needed when I was looking to get a few quick singles.

Things have changed an awful lot since those days. The Slazenger pads I now use have got double protection, really strong padding inside, good side wings, and impact-absorbing foam to protect the shins. I like extra padding around the knee and a good fastening which makes them more comfortable to wear. These pads are so light that, like the gloves, you can forget that you are wearing them at all.

I have a very good relationship with Slazenger. I talk to them and they understand my individual needs. Contrary to popular belief, cricket equipment for the professional cricketer is a very complex issue and new and better products are being tried out all the time, be it a synthetic glove material, which is both flexible and very strong, or whatever. I like to know that I am dealing with professionals. Yes, at times it seems an awful long way from beach cricket in Antigua.

For me, of course, the most important piece of equipment is the bat. I, like most professional cricketers, go up to the factory about once a year to talk, at great length, to the bat-maker. I tell him about my different needs, about what kind of wickets I expect to be playing on during the coming season. To put it simply, on faster wickets one would want a lighter bat whereas on heavy English wickets I would prefer a bit more weight for that extra bit of power. These days, I stand a little bit straighter at the crease. I do not crouch like I used to and my bats are about an inch longer than in the old days. I usually have about three bats with me and, from these, I will usually have one firm favourite. This is the bat which feels just right. It is partly a matter of balance and craftsmanship, but however perfectly they are made some bats do not have the right feel. This may be a mental thing, I do not know, but if I have what I believe to be a really good piece of wood, it can last me throughout a season.

Although I am very fussy, if I break my favourite bat I will not allow it to play on my mind. Good equipment is there to help you, but you should never become too dependent on it. That is very dangerous. I have seen players become far too superstitious about all kinds of favourite equipment. When you reach that point it just adds to the pressure, rather than easing it.

I use Slazenger bats, specially made from hand-selected close-grain willow. They certainly helped me to win the National Power Six-Hit Award in 1990, which I will talk about shortly. They are classically shaped with superb balance and pick-up. The sweet spot is easy to find.

Gloves are one of the most important pieces of equipment in any cricketer's bag. Look at the number of top-class players who have spent a month or more out of the game because of finger injuries. English readers, in particular, will understand this point. The gloves I use at the moment are perfect for me. They are the V5 Test from Slazenger. They are light and comfortable to wear, which is essential for me, and, although they have lots of padding, I cannot feel any of it. These gloves are specifically designed to reduce the chance of broken fingers. They have side bars, double layers of padding inside to spread any shock if you do get hit, and a shaped cup to protect the thumb. Basically, I need gloves that give me good contact with the bat and do not restrict the movement of my fingers.

If I have only come to terms in later years with the full importance of equipment, the opposite can be said of my attitude towards preparation. This is something that I have never underestimated.

I am a pretty good sleeper and, before an innings, I often get in a snooze at the back of the dressing room. Once again, this is something that the textbooks would hardly recommend. They would tell you to sit outside, watching the game and getting used to the light. For some people that may be the right thing to do but I do not like to watch too much when I am batting. (Unless I am acting as captain, of course, where it is my duty to watch everything.) I feel I must be careful because, if I am watching a cricket match unfold, I get too involved in it. If I am waiting to bat, and I watch too much, I make up my mind just what I am going to do. I will begin to over-analyse everything and this will affect my performance. I prefer to watch a little bit and then go and have a sleep.

It is my way of relaxing, of feeling refreshed when I walk on. And, of course, that's another problem with me – the slow walk-ons which have become something of a trademark. I know that many people regard this as just my arrogance, or even a touch of gamesmanship, but that is not what it's about at all. It is my way of preparing myself. It is my way of getting into a very determined mood, of getting ready for the immense degree of concentration which is needed. If that makes me look arrogant, then that is just too bad.

A LITTLE REST AND RELAXATION

I spend hours listening to music, it is my favourite form of relaxation. I have always been pretty wide open when it comes to choice. I have never restricted myself to any one kind of music, which is fairly typical of someone who is from a small part of the world like the West Indies. We ourselves have a fine musical tradition and, while being very proud of that, I also like to enjoy other kinds of good music.

I grew up with calypso and that must be regarded as my basic music. Calypso, and reggae of course, are the rhythms of the Caribbean. Those forms of music will always play a big part in my life but I don't restrict myself to them. Although I am a music fanatic, I am no expert.

I do not ever think of any kind of division in music. I do not really like it when people refer to something as 'black music'. I never look at music like that. It is just music to me and, although it may not be particularly hip to like some of the stuff I do like, that never bothers me. I got into listening to U2 for instance, quite late on. In fact 'The Joshua Tree' was the first thing I heard of theirs. When I first listened to it, it meant very little to me. But then I found it to be very thoughtful music. There is a serious message in there. It transcends colour or culture and means as much to me as it does to somebody in Dublin. That is the measure of good music, the fact that it can cross such boundaries. U2 do manage to achieve that.

I pick up on all kinds of things that put me in certain moods. I might listen to Michael Bolton or Chris De Burgh, but I have never really been into heavy stuff. I just like to listen and relax to music. I simply adjust the music to suit my moods.

For sporting relaxation I play a lot of tennis. I am not really a guy who likes to go running. I find that really boring. But tennis is my main form of non-cricketing exercise. It loosens up the muscles. In cricket you can find yourself spending long, inactive periods. I love playing tennis because it is an antidote to the inactivity. It helps me to flow, makes me feel good. And so does squash, although I have to be careful not to injure myself. It is so easy to pull a muscle, and it would be stupid to do this when only playing for relaxation. Injury is always at the back of your mind.

If you are a professional sportsman, then that professionalism stays with you twenty-four hours a day. Sometimes it is difficult to relax. I feel at my most content when I am simply sitting at home, maybe drinking a little Red Stripe beer, not too much, and watching Liverpool winning a League game on television.

BEST MEMORIES
My time with Somerset remains with me and always will. It gives me a warm glow to think back to the time in 1979 when we won a trophy for the first time in 100 years. Those were wonderful days.

Other highlights are when the combined Leeward and Windward Islands team won the Shell Shield tournament for the first time in 1981. And then as the Leeward Islands we won it again in 1990. I was also thrilled when West Indies won the first World Cup final. My greatest memories are definitely the team victories. The camaraderie derived from a really good team performance always beats the satisfaction of an individual achievement.

It is a bit empty to look back on your own personal greatest innings. Cricket is a team game. I like to place everything within the context of teams. I regard it as a pleasure and a privilege to have played alongside, and against, so many great players. If I must talk about individual achievements, I think my proudest memory is of the day I completed 100 Test catches in my 100th Test match, against Australia at Brisbane in 1988. It was also a great feeling to become the first West Indian to score one

AUSTRALIA vs. WEST INDIES (First Test)
at Brisbane on 18th, 19th, 20th, 21st November 1988
Toss : Australia.   Umpires : P.J. McConnell and A.R. Crafter
West Indies won by 9 wickets

AUSTRALIA

G.R. Marsh	c Logie b Ambrose	27	(2) lbw b Ambrose	2
D.C. Boon	lbw b Marshall	10	(1) c Dujon b Marshall	12
M.R.J. Veletta	b Hooper	37	c Hooper b Walsh	10
G.M. Wood	c Greenidge b Ambrose	6	(5) lbw b Walsh	0
A.R. Border*	c Dujon b Ambrose	4	(6) c Haynes b Ambrose	41
S.R. Waugh	lbw b Marshall	4	(4) c Haynes b Marshall	90
I.A. Healy+	c Logie b Walsh	27	c Ambrose b Marshall	28
C.J. McDermott	c Logie b Walsh	2	(9) not out	32
A.I.C. Dodemaide	c Richards b Walsh	22	(8) c Richards b Marshall	7
C.D. Matthews	c Dujon b Walsh	1	c sub b Walsh	32
T.B.A. May	not out	4	c Hooper b Ambrose	5
Extras	(b 1,lb 5,w 1,nb 16)	23	(b 4,lb 5,nb 21)	30
TOTAL		167		289

WEST INDIES

C.G. Greenidge	b May	80	c Healy b Dodemaide	16
D.L. Haynes	c Healy b Waugh	40	not out	30
R.B. Richardson	lbw b Dodemaide	81	not out	7
C.L. Hooper	c Border b Waugh	1		
I.V.A. Richards*	c McDermott b May	68		
A.L. Logie	c Border b May	19		
P.J.L. Dujon+	c May b McDermott	27		
M.D. Marshall	c Border b McDermott	11		
C.E.L. Ambrose	not out	19		
C.A. Walsh	lbw b McDermott	0		
B.P. Patterson	lbw b Dodemaide	0		
Extras	(b 5,lb 9,w 6,nb 28)	48	(b 4,w 3,nb 3)	10
TOTAL		394	(for 1 wkt)	63

WEST INDIES	O	M	R	W	O	M	R	W
Marshall	18	3	39	2	26	2	92	4
Patterson	3.1	1	5	0				
Ambrose	16.5	5	30	3	26.1	5	78	3
Walsh	18.3	3	62	4	19	3	61	3
Hooper	12	2	24	1	4	0	23	0
Richards	1	0	1	0	11	4	26	0

AUSTRALIA	O	M	R	W	O	M	R	W
McDermott	28	3	99	3	4	0	12	0
Matthews	21	3	62	0	3.5	0	18	0
Dodemaide	16.4	2	60	2	5.2	1	15	1
May	18	6	90	3	6	0	14	0
Waugh	18	2	61	2				
Border	1	0	8	0				

FALL OF WICKETS

	A	WI	A	WI
1st	19	135	14	43
2nd	52	156	16	
3rd	64	162	65	
4th	76	270	65	
5th	86	307	157	
6th	126	359	199	
7th	138	361	212	
8th	140	389	212	
9th	150	393	270	
10th	167	394	289	

hundred centuries. And to score a century in the first-ever Test match in Antigua, against England in 1981. Then to do so again in Antigua in the next series, breaking the world record for the fastest Test hundred in terms of number of balls received. That took place in front of our Prime Minister and my family, friends and supporters. That, I suppose, must be the greatest highlight.

GOING TO GLAMORGAN

There were many people, towards the end of the Eighties, who said I was finished as a player, that I was just a shadow of my former self, so I went to Glamorgan to prove them all wrong. I still feel that I have much to offer in first-class cricket. My Test career is not, I hope, at an end yet, and although I may not be the batsman of yesteryear, I would like to think that I am still up there amongst the best. I still have much to give and this is not just blind pride. When it is time for me to step down, I will know it.

I have just signed a three-year contract with Glamorgan although much of 1991 is likely to be taken up with West Indian commitments. The club means an awful lot to me. When I first went there, I instantly knew it would be a happy move. The sheer warmth of the Welsh people got to me. It rubbed off. I could tell, immediately, that I was going to enjoy myself in Cardiff.

When I started playing I determined to give these warm-hearted people my all. I wanted to give them something special for being so patient and so welcoming. I wanted to thank them for their hospitality by playing as often as possible at my very best. I could have decided to take things easy, not play in every match. But I did not want my career to end on a note of apathy. That would be for me a terrible way to go. For these people my heart governed my actions. I felt a new excitement for the game and was confident that together we could achieve something. The talent was there already. The passion and the commitment were there. The team gave *me* inspiration. From the first one-day match at Edgbaston we began to win, or at least to account well for ourselves. You could feel the confidence beginning to ooze.

Membership and support at away matches were building up. There was an optimism just like in the early days at Somerset. Alan Butcher and Hugh Morris were in tremendous form but everyone chipped in. I said that I treasure team performances above individual performances. There was one that was doubly pleasing. Against Hampshire at Southampton we were chasing 363 to win. At 139-5 we were struggling but Cowley and Metson stayed with me and we whittled down the difference so that we needed twelve from the last over. Malcolm Marshall bowled it and I managed to drive two fours and hook a six to take us home. Malcolm said it was the biggest-ever six off his bowling, but I think he just wanted a beer off me.

There was one other notable episode to recall. The Warwickshire off-spinner, Adrian Pierson, made some critical comment about one of my shots when I was struggling on a misleading wicket. You do not say things like that to Viv Richards. I hit the next ball over the pavilion.

At the end of the season I was proud to receive the National Power Six-Hit Award. I think it is a very good award because it encourages exciting cricket. It was a shame that I got 'flu at the end of the season and missed the last three matches. Ten more sixes (I had hit 40) and I would have won the £10,000 jackpot and Glamorgan would have received an identical amount. Certainly the last few matches of the season were not that important and I would have had every incentive to hit out. But there you are, that's the way it goes.

The 1990 season proved to be one of the most enjoyable of my career. The glare of the spotlight was a little less harsh and I welcomed this.

I have always felt an affinity with the Welsh. They play their rugby with the same sort of passion as the Antiguans play cricket. And they are always having to stand up for themselves against larger countries and higher authorities. I was really pleased to have helped to win a few matches. Losing regularly eats away at the very heart of a club. The future looks good, although we are 'bat heavy'; we need bowlers like Steve Watkins, Steve Bastien, Mark Frost and Robert Croft to live up to their true potential .

We have got back the winning habit and we play as a team under Alan Butcher. To win something with Glamorgan would give me as big a thrill as any victory in the past.

Let's hope the buzz in the city continues, let's hope the crowd feeds off the team and, in return, the team feeds off the crowd... an upward spiral. Whatever happens, I feel sure Glamorgan will not fail through want of trying and that is what truly matters.

Viv's concentration snaps – his eyes soften, if only for a few seconds, and his hands are held open in a friendly gesture of apology.
'Look, I'm going to have to go. In ten minutes I'm supposed to be picking up some of the boys for the football team...'
And off he goes, relieved, I sense, to have finished talking. The Range Rover (having been returned by Miriam) spins around in a crackle

of dust, and is gone. Soon it will be filled with precocious young footballers, an explosive mass of young sporting chatter and rant. And Viv, happy to be amongst them. Not to coach, but to share their genuine love of sport, their burgeoning athleticism and, maybe, to guide them a little.

Later, no doubt inspired by an afternoon spent within the camaraderie of this little team, a buoyant Viv Richards will offer one final outburst. Succinct and optimistic, it sums up the man himself.

I don't want hero worship from these youngsters. I hope they can glean more from me than that. I hope I can give them some kind of inspiration which extends beyond all that. Some of them, perhaps, might grasp the true meaning of this phrase 'hitting across the line' which is not merely a cricketing term or even a concept for this book. It is about self-belief, about finding that inner strength, that sense of determination to develop your talents naturally, in the face of all manner of adversity and negative influence. That's what I mean by 'hitting across the line'. It's the only way I know.

CAREER RECORD

TEST MATCHES

MATCH BY MATCH

1974-75 - in India

Opposition	Venue	Date	Batting		Bowling		Ct
India	Bangalore	22 Nov	4	3			2
India	Delhi	11 Dec	192*				1
India	Calcutta	27 Dec	15	47			
India	Madras	11 Jan	50	2			
India	Bombay	23 Jan	1	39*	0-10		2

1974-75 - in Pakistan

Opposition	Venue	Date	Batting		Bowling		Ct
Pakistan	Lahore	15 Feb	7	0			1
Pakistan	Karachi	1 March	10			1-17	2

1975-76 - in Australia

Opposition	Venue	Date	Batting		Bowling		Ct
Australia	Brisbane	28 Nov	0	12			
Australia	Perth	12 Dec	12				1
Australia	Melbourne	26 Dec	31	36	0-2		1
Australia	Sydney	3 Jan	44	2		0-4	1
Australia	Adelaide	23 Jan	30	101			3
Australia	Melbourne	31 Jan	50	98		0-38	

1975-76 - in West Indies

Opposition	Venue	Date	Batting		Bowling		Ct
India	Bridgetown	10 March	142				2
India	Port of Spain	24 March	130	20	0-17		
India	Port of Spain	7 April	177	23			1
India	Kingston	21 April	64				

1976 - in England

Opposition	Venue	Date	Batting		Bowling		Ct
England	Trent Bridge	3 June	232	63	0-8	0-7	1
England	Old Trafford	8 July	4	135			
England	Headingley	22 July	66	38			1
England	The Oval	12 Aug	291		0-30	1-11	

1976-77 - in West Indies

Opposition	Venue	Date	Batting		Bowling		Ct
Pakistan	Bridgetown	18 Feb	32	92	0-3	0-16	
Pakistan	Port of Spain	4 March	4	30		0-27	1
Pakistan	Georgetown	18 March	50			0-11	
Pakistan	Port of Spain	1 April	4	33	2-34		1
Pakistan	Kingston	15 April	5	7			2

1977-78 - in West Indies

Opposition	Venue	Date	Batting	Bowling	Ct
Australia	Port of Spain	3 March	39		1
Australia	Bridgetown	17 March	23		2

1979-80 - in Australia

Opposition	Venue	Date	Batting		Bowling	Ct
Australia	Brisbane	1 Dec	140			1
Australia	Melbourne	29 Dec	96			1
Australia	Adelaide	26 Jan	76	74	0-7	1

1980 - in England

Opposition	Venue	Date	Batting		Bowling		Ct
England	Trent Bridge	5 June	64	48	0-9		4
England	Lord's	19 June	145		0-24	0-1	
England	Old Trafford	10 July	65			0-31	1
England	The Oval	24 July	26		0-5	0-15	
England	Headingley	7 Aug	31	*		0-0	1

1980-81 - in Pakistan

Opposition	Venue	Date	Batting		Bowling		Ct
Pakistan	Lahore	24 Nov	75		1-31	2-20	2
Pakistan	Faisalabad	8 Dec	72	67	1-0		4
Pakistan	Karachi	22 Dec	18			0-10	1
Pakistan	Multan	30 Dec	120*	12			2

1980-81 - in West Indies

Opposition	Venue	Date	Batting		Bowling		Ct
England	Port of Spain	13 Feb	29		0-16	1-9	1
England	Bridgetown	13 March	0	182*		2-24	1
England	St John's	27 March	114		0-26	1-54	1
England	Kingston	10 April	15		0-29	1-48	

1981-82 - in Australia

Opposition	Venue	Date	Batting		Bowling	Ct
Australia	Melbourne	26 Dec	2	0	0-17	1

Australia	Sydney	2 Jan	44	22	0-21	0-33	
Australia	Adelaide	30 Jan	42	50		0-38	

1982-83 - in West Indies

Opposition	Venue	Date	Batting		Bowling		Ct
India	Kingston	23 Feb	29	61	0-0		1
India	Port of Spain	11 March	1			1-14	2
India	Georgetown	31 March	109		0-24		2
India	Bridgetown	15 April	80				2
India	St John's	28 April	2		0-13	0-36	1

1983-84 - in India

Opposition	Venue	Date	Batting		Bowling	Ct
India	Kanpur	21 Oct	24			3
India	Delhi	29 Oct	67	22	0-8	2
India	Ahmedabad	12 Nov	8	20		
India	Bombay	24 Nov	120	4		2
India	Calcutta	10 Dec	9			
India	Madras	24 Dec	32			1

1983-84 - in West Indies

Opposition	Venue	Date	Batting		Bowling		Ct
Australia	Georgetown	2 March	8		0-3	0-8	1
Australia	Port of Spain	16 March	76		1-15	2-65	1
Australia	Bridgetown	30 March	6				
Australia	St John's	7 April	178		0-7		1
Australia	Kingston	28 April	2			0-13	

1984 - in England

Opposition	Venue	Date	Batting		Bowling	Ct
England	Edgbaston	14 June	117			1
England	Lord's	28 June	72			1
England	Headingley	12 July	15	22*		
England	Old Trafford	26 July	1		0-2	
England	The Oval	9 Aug	8	15		3

1984-85 - in Australia

Opposition	Venue	Date	Batting		Bowling		Ct
Australia	Perth	9 Nov	10			0-4	
Australia	Brisbane	23 Nov	6	3*		0-1	1
Australia	Adelaide	7 Dec	0	42			1
Australia	Melbourne	22 Dec	208	0	0-9	1-7	
Australia	Sydney	30 Dec	15	58	0-11		1

1984-85 - in West Indies

Opposition	Venue	Date	Batting		Bowling		Ct
New Zealand	Port of Spain	29 March	57	78	0-7	0-1	
New Zealand	Georgetown	6 April	40	7 *	0-22		1
New Zealand	Bridgetown	26 April	105			0-25	1
New Zealand	Kingston	4 May	23			1-34	

1985-86 - in West Indies

Opposition	Venue	Date	Batting		Bowling		Ct
England	Kingston	21 Feb	23		0-0		
England	Port of Spain	7 March	34			0-7	
England	Bridgetown	21 March	51		0-9	0-7	
England	Port of Spain	3 April	87				2
England	St John's	11 April	26	110 *	0-3	0-3	

1986-87 - in Pakistan

Opposition	Venue	Date	Batting		Bowling		Ct
Pakistan	Faisalabad	24 Oct	33	0			
Pakistan	Lahore	7 Nov	44			1-9	
Pakistan	Karachi	20 Nov	70	28			1

1986-87 - in New Zealand

Opposition	Venue	Date	Batting		Bowling		Ct
New Zealand	Wellington	20 Feb	24		1-32	1-86	1
New Zealand	Auckland	27 Feb	14				1
New Zealand	Christchurch	12 March	1	38	0-29		3

1987-88 - in India

Opposition	Venue	Date	Batting		Bowling		Ct
India	Delhi	25 Nov	9	109 *			
India	Bombay	11 Dec	37				4
India	Calcutta	26 Dec	68		1-39		
India	Madras	11 Jan	68	4	1-36	1-28	1

1987-88 - in West Indies

Opposition	Venue	Date	Batting		Bowling		Ct
Pakistan	Port of Spain	14 April	49	123		2-17	4
Pakistan	Bridgetown	22 April	67	39	0-19	1-8	2

1988 - in England

Opposition	Venue	Date	Batting		Bowling		Ct
England	Trent Bridge	2 June	80		0-2	0-26	
England	Lord's	16 June	6	72			2
England	Old Trafford	30 June	47				1

England	Headingley	21 July	18				
England	The Oval	4 Aug	0				

1988-89 - in Australia

Opposition	Venue	Date	Batting		Bowling		Ct
Australia	Brisbane	18 Nov	68		0-1	2-26	2
Australia	Perth	2 Dec	146	5	0-43		1
Australia	Melbourne	24 Dec	12	63		0-12	
Australia	Sydney	26 Jan	11	4	1-68	1-12	
Australia	Adelaide	3 Feb	69	68*	0-73	1-64	

1988-89 - in West Indies

Opposition	Venue	Date	Batting		Bowling		Ct
India	Georgetown	25 March	5		0-17		1
India	Bridgetown	7 April	1		0-18	0-16	2
India	Port of Spain	15 April	19	0	1-28	0-13	2
India	Kingston	28 April	110		0-36		5

1989-90 - in West Indies

Opposition	Venue	Date	Batting		Bowling		Ct
England	Kingston	24 Feb	21	37	0-22		
England	Bridgetown	5 April	70	12	0-14	0-11	2
England	St John's	12 April	1				2

1990-91 - in West Indies

Opposition	Venue	Date	Batting		Bowling	Ct
Australia	Kingston	1 March	11	52*		

TEST AVERAGES

SERIES BY SERIES

Batting and Fielding

Year	Opposition	Mtchs	Inns	NO	Runs	HS	Avge	100	50	Ct
1974-75	India	5	9	2	353	192*	50.43	1	1	5
1974-75	Pakistan	2	3	0	17	10	5.66	-	-	3
1975-76	Australia	6	11	0	426	101	38.72	1	2	6
1975-76	India	4	6	0	556	177	92.66	3	1	3
1976	England	4	7	0	829	291	118.43	3	2	2
1976-77	Pakistan	5	9	0	257	92	28.55	-	2	4
1977-78	Australia	2	2	0	62	39	31.00	-	-	3
1979-80	Australia	3	4	0	386	140	96.50	1	3	3
1980	England	5	6	0	379	145	63.16	1	2	6
1980-81	Pakistan	4	6	1	364	120*	72.80	1	3	9
1980-81	England	4	5	1	340	182*	85.00	2	-	3
1981-82	Australia	3	6	0	160	50	26.66	-	1	1
1982-83	India	5	6	0	282	109	47.00	1	2	8
1983-84	India	6	9	0	306	120	34.00	1	1	8
1983-84	Australia	5	5	0	270	178	54.00	1	1	3
1984	England	5	7	1	250	117	41.66	1	1	5
1984-85	Australia	5	9	1	342	208	42.75	1	1	3
1984-85	New Zealand	4	6	1	310	105	62.00	1	2	2
1985-86	England	5	6	1	331	110*	66.20	1	2	2
1986-87	Pakistan	3	5	0	175	70	35.00	-	1	1
1986-87	New Zealand	3	4	0	77	38	19.25	-	-	5
1987-88	India	4	6	1	295	109*	59.00	1	2	5
1987-88	Paksitan	2	4	0	278	123	69.50	1	1	6
1988	England	5	6	0	223	80	37.16	-	2	3
1988-89	Australia	5	9	1	446	146	55.75	1	4	3
1988-89	India	4	5	0	135	110	27.00	1	-	10
1989-90	England	3	5	0	141	70	28.20	-	1	4

Bowling

Year	Opposition	Overs	Mdns	Runs	Wkts	Avge	Best	5wI	10wM
1974-75	India	7	2	10	0	-	-	-	-
1974-75	Pakistan	9	2	17	1	17.00	1-17	-	-
1975-76	Australia	8.1	0	44	0	-	-	-	-
1975-76	India	6	0	17	0	-	-	-	-
1976	England	31	12	56	1	56.00	1-11	-	-
1976-77	Pakistan	40.3	11	91	2	45.50	2-34	-	-
1977-78	Australia	-	-	-	-	-	-	-	-
1979-80	Australia	2	0	7	0	-	-	-	-
1980	England	36	12	85	0	-	-	-	-
1980-81	Pakistan	26.2	6	61	4	15.25	2-20	-	-
1980-81	England	100	35	206	5	41.20	2-24	-	-
1981-82	Australia	49	13	109	0	-	-	-	-

Year	Opposition	Overs	Mdns	Runs	Wkts	Avge	Best	5wI	10wM
1982-83	India	36	9	87	1	87.00	1-14	-	-
1983-84	India	3	1	8	0			-	-
1983-84	Australia	53	13	102	3	34.00	2-65	-	-
1984	England	1	0	2	0			-	-
1984-85	Australia	16	4	32	1	32.00	1-7	-	-
1984-85	New Zealand	39	7	89	1	89.00	1-34	-	-
1985-86	England	20	7	29	0			-	-
1986-87	Pakistan	5	2	9	1	9.00	1-9	-	-
1986-87	New Zealand	67	19	147	2	73.50	1-32	-	-
1987-88	India	50	11	103	3	34.33	1-28	-	-
1987-88	Pakistan	17	6	44	3	14.66	2-17	-	-
1988	England	10	1	28	0			-	-
1988-89	Australia	117	12	299	3	99.66	1-12	-	-
1988-89	India	51	8	128	1	128.00	1-28	-	-
1989-90	England	28	10	47	0			-	-

AGAINST EACH OPPOSITION

Batting and Fielding

Opposition	Mtchs	Inns	NO	Runs	HS	Avge	100	50	Ct
England	32	42	3	2493	291	63.92	8	9	25
Australia*	30	48	3	2155	208	47.88	5	13	22
New Zealand	7	10	1	387	105	43.00	1	2	7
India	28	41	3	1927	192*	50.71	8	7	39
Pakistan	16	27	1	1091	123	41.96	2	7	23
Total	112	168	11	8053	291	51.29	24	39	116

Bowling

Opposition	Overs	Mdns	Runs	Wkts	Avge	Best	5wI	10wM
England	226	77	453	6	75.50	2-24	-	-
Australia	247.5	42	593	7	84.71	2-65	-	-
New Zealand	106	26	236	3	78.66	1-32	-	-
India	153	31	353	5	70.60	1-14	-	-
Pakistan	267.3	25	232	11	21.09	2-17	-	-
Total	833.4	201	1857	32	58.03	2-17	-	-

* as at 6.3.91 including West Indies v Australia (First Test) 1991

ALL FIRST-CLASS

MATCH BY MATCH

1971-72 - in West Indies (for Leeward Islands & Combined Islands)

Opposition	Venue	Date	Batting		Bowling		Ct
(for Leeward Islands)							
Windward Islands	Roseau	15 Jan	20	26	0-9		
(for Combined Islands)							
Jamaica	Kingston	21 Jan	15	32			
Trinidad & Tobago	Basseterre	27 Jan	55	16			
Barbados	Roseau	3 Feb	5	13			
(for Leeward Islands)							
New Zealanders	St John's	25 Feb	82	0			
(for Combined Islands)							
Guyana	Berbice	3 March	23	58			

1972-73 - in West Indies (for Leeward Islands, Combined Islands & President's XI)

Opposition	Venue	Date	Batting		Bowling		Ct
(for Leeward Islands)							
Windward Islands	St John's	19 Sept	28			0-2	3
Windward Islands	St John's	23 Sept	55		0-28	2-38	1
(for Combined Islands)							
Barbados	Bridgetown	6 Jan	11	52	1-62		
Guyana	St John's	20 Jan	1	15	0-12	1-1	1
Trinidad & Tobago	Port of Spain	2 Feb	5	0	3-49	0-14	1
(for President's XI)							
Australians	Montego Bay	9 Feb	18	5		0-30	
(for Leeward Islands)							
Australians	St John's	24 Feb	5		1-31	2-54	1
(for Combined Islands)							
Jamaica	Kingstown	1 March	14	4	1-11	0-11	

1973-74 - in West Indies (for Leeward Islands & Combined Islands)

Opposition	Venue	Date	Batting		Bowling		Ct
(for Combined Islands)							
Barbados	Basseterre	5 Jan	11	21	1-0	0-23	
Jamaica	Kingston	11 Jan	40	7	0-57		
Trinidad & Tobago	Castries	9 Feb	64	45*	0-3		
(for Leeward Islands)							
MCC	St John's	23 Feb	42	52*	0-15	1-25	
(for Combined Islands)							
Guyana	Berbice	28 Feb	4	78		0-2	1

1974 - in England (for Somerset)

Opposition	Venue	Date	Batting		Bowling		Ct
Indians	Taunton	1 May	7				1
Lancashire	Taunton	8 May	36	7 *			1
Oxford University	The Parks	11 May		5		1-5	
Sussex	Hove	22 May	74			2-53	1
Gloucestershire	Bristol	25 May	102	20	1-13	2-53	
Northamptonshire	Taunton	5 June	1	62			3
Kent	Taunton	8 June	85	6		0-41	
Yorkshire	Bath	15 June	107	19	0-11		
Glamorgan	Bath	19 June	73				
Pakistanis	Bath	22 June	14	43	0-51	0-27	
Northamptonshire	Northampton	29 June	4				
Essex	Taunton	6 July	0	36			1
Middlesex	Taunton	13 July	39	27			1
Essex	Westcliff	17 July	4	13			
Glamorgan	Swansea	27 July	7			0-10	2
Surrey	The Oval	3 Aug	32	50			1
Nottinghamshire	Trent Bridge	7 Aug	10	31			
Worcestershire	Worcester	10 Aug	31				1
Leicestershire	Weston-s-Mare	17 Aug	2	41			
Warwickshire	Weston-s-Mare	21 Aug	41	22			2
Gloucestershire	Weston-s-Mare	24 Aug	67	18			2
Hampshire	Bournemouth	28 Aug	45	4			
Derbyshire	Derby		38			0-9	2

1974-75 - in India, Sri Lanka & Pakistan (for West Indies)

Opposition	Venue	Date	Batting		Bowling		Ct
West Zone	Pune	7 Nov	102 *	3	0-5		1
Indian Universities	Indore	11 Nov	34 *			2-25	
India	Bangalore	22 Nov	4	3			2
President's XI	Jaipur	30 Nov	16	9	0-0	1-8	
North Zone	Jullundur	6 Dec	103 *	53 *	0-6		
India	Delhi	11 Dec	192 *				1
Central Zone	Nagpur	20 Dec	45				1
India	Calcutta	27 Dec	15	47			
East Zone	Cuttack	4 Jan	77				1
India	Madras	11 Jan	50	2			
Karnataka	Ahmedabad	18 Jan	75 *	27		0-44	2
India	Bombay	23 Jan	1	39 *	0-10		2
Sri Lanka	Colombo	3 Feb	151				1
Sri Lanka	Colombo	7 Feb	3	77			
Pakistan	Lahore	15 Feb	7	0			1
Patron's XI	Rawalpini	22 Feb	79	43			1
Pakistan	Karachi	1 March	10			1-17	2

1974-75 - in West Indies (for Combined Islands)

Opposition	Venue	Date	Batting		Bowling		Ct
Guyana	St George's	14 March	112	59		0-31	2
Barbados	Bridgetown	29 March	13	54		1-14	2
Jamaica	St John's	4 April	101		0-34	0-17	
Trinidad & Tobago	Port of Spain	11 April	14	10	0-6		1

1975 - in England (for Somerset & International XI)

Opposition	Venue	Date	Batting		Bowling		Ct
Sussex	Taunton	30 April	20				
Northamptonshire	Northampton	7 May	0	0			1
Middlesex	Lord's	14 May	1				1
Gloucestershire	Bristol	24 May	33				3
Oxford University	The Parks	28 May	38	5			
Yorkshire	Harrogate	28 June	217*	1	0-25	0-11	3
Lancashire	Old Trafford	5 July	15	0	0-23		2
Northamptonshire	Taunton	12 July	6	0	0-22		1
Worcestershire	Weston-s-Mare	23 July	32	49	1-15		4
Hampshire	Weston-s-Mare	26 July	79	0	2-38	0-14	2
Australians	Taunton	6 Aug	0	12	1-26		
Essex	Leyton	9 Aug	7	25	0-5	0-8	2
Gloucestershire	Taunton	16 Aug	128		2-10		2
Nottinghamshire	Taunton	23 Aug	77	23	0-23		1
Kent	Folkestone	27 Aug	122	23	0-21	1-28	1
Glamorgan	Cardiff	30 Aug	24	35	0-24	2-38	
Essex (for International XI)	Taunton	3 Sept	44	39	0-14	0-1	4
Yorkshire (for Somerset)	Scarborough	10 Sept	3	20		1-6	2
Glamorgan	Taunton	13 Sept	45	51	1-12		

1975-76 - in Australia (for West Indies)

Opposition	Venue	Date	Batting		Bowling		Ct
Victoria	Melbourne	7 Nov	2		0-9	0-47	2
New South Wales	Sydney	14 Nov	26	43			
Queensland	Brisbane	21 Nov	61				
Australia	Brisbane	28 Nov	0	12			
Western Australia	Perth	6 Dec	175	40		2-42	
Australia	Perth	12 Dec	12				1
South Australia	Adelaide	21 Dec	8	59*			
Australia	Melbourne	26 Dec	41	36	0-2		1
Australia	Sydney	3 Jan	44	2		0-4	1
Tasmania	Hobart	16 Jan	160	107*		0-1	2
Australia	Adelaide	23 Jan	30	101			3
Australia	Melbourne	31 Jan	50	98		0-38	

1975-76 - in West Indies (for Leeward Islands & West Indies)

Opposition	Venue	Date	Batting		Bowling		Ct
(for Leeward Islands)							
Indians	Montserrat	1 March	27*		0-10		2
(for West Indies)							
India	Bridgetown	10 March	142				2
India	Port of Spain	24 March	130	20			
India	Port of Spain	7 April	177	23			1
India	Kingston	21 April	64				

1976 - in England (for West Indies)

Opposition	Venue	Date	Batting		Bowling		Ct
Surrey	The Oval	12 May	46	13			
Hampshire	Southampton	15 May	176				3
MCC	Lord's	22 May	5	113			1
Somerset	Taunton	26 May	51				1
England	Trent Bridge	3 June	232	63	0-8	0-7	1
Lancashire	Old Trafford	12 June	37				
Derbyshire	Chesterfield	3 July	0	16*			3
England	Old Trafford	8 July	4	135			
Warwickshire	Edgbaston	17 July	71				
England	Headingley	22 July	68	38			1
Middlesex	Lord's	31 July	4	53			3
Minor Counties	Torquay	4 Aug	98	15			2
Glamorgan	Swansea	7 Aug	121				1
England	The Oval	12 Aug	291		0-30	1-11	
Worcestershire	Worcester	18 Aug	57				1
T.N.Pierce's XI	Scarborough	4 Sept	4	15			1 St

1976-77 - in Australia (for Queensland)

Opposition	Venue	Date	Batting		Bowling		Ct
Victoria	Brisbane	29 Oct	12				2
Western Australia	Brisbane	5 Nov	62	2			
South Australia	Brisbane	12 Nov	17				
New South Wales	Brisbane	26 Nov	73	15			
Pakistanis	Brisbane	9 Jan	143	25	0-34	0-6	2

1976-77 - in West Indies (for Leeward Islands, Combined Islands & West Indies)

Opposition	Venue	Date	Batting		Bowling		Ct
(for Leeward Islands)							
Pakistanis	St John's	2 Feb	60	34	1-42	1-20	
(for West Indies)							
Pakistan	Bridgetown	18 Feb	32	92	0-3	0-16	
Pakistan	Port of Spain	4 March	4	30		0-27	1

Pakistan	Georgetown	18 March	50				0-11	
Pakistan	Port of Spain	1 April	4	33	2-34			
(for Combined Islands)								
Barbados	Bridgetown	9 April	124	45	0-31			
(for West Indies)								
Pakistan	Kingston	15 April	5	7				2

1977 - in England (for Somerset)

Opposition	Venue	Date	Batting		Bowling		Ct
Glamorgan	Taunton	4 May	70				
Nottinghamshire	Bath	14 May	15	28	0-23	1-5	1
Australians	Bath	18 May	18	53			1
Hampshire	Southampton	28 May	76	41	1-7		
Warwickshire	Taunton	1 June	65	118	1-38		1
Gloucestershire	Bristol	4 June	5	241*	0-63		1
Glamorgan	Cardiff	15 June	6				1
Yorkshire	Harrogate	18 June	96	0	0-9		1
Leicestershire	Leicester	25 June	104	25*	0-7		
Sussex	Hove	29 June	204				3
Hampshire	Taunton	2 July	60	73			
Sussex	Taunton	6 July	38	89	0-8	0-16	1
Warwickshire	Edgbaston	9 July	101	0	0-7		
Worcestershire	Taunton	23 July	13	27	0-9	0-5	
Lancashire	Southport	30 July	189	19			1
Northamptonshire	Weston-s-Mare	6 Aug	32	8		0-14	2
Surrey	Weston-s-Mare	10 Aug	204	48		3-15	1
Essex	Taunton	13 Aug	22	0	0-12		
Kent	Canterbury	20 Aug					1
Gloucestershire	Taunton	27 Aug	70	3		1-10	

1977-78 - in West Indies (for Combined Islands and West Indies)

Opposition	Venue	Date	Batting		Bowling		Ct
(for West Indies)							
Australia	Port of Spain	3 March	39				1
(for Combined Islands)							
Trinidad & Tobago	St John's	11 March	51	0	2-29	0-31	4
(for West Indies)							
Australia	Bridgetown	17 March	23				2

1978 - in England (for Somerset)

Opposition	Venue	Date	Batting		Bowling		Ct
Derbyshire	Burton	3 May	8				1
Glamorgan	Taunton	10 May	7	41*			
Kent	Taunton	24 May	60	0	0-4	1-31	1
Gloucestershire	Taunton	27 May	67				1

Surrey	The Oval	31 May	8	34	0-18	1-23	
Sussex	Hove	3 June	118	82			2
Lancashire	Bath	10 June	26	71		0-0	2
Sussex	Bath	14 June	36			2-11	
Nottinghamshire	Trent Bridge	17 June	35	5	0-39		
Yorkshire	Taunton	24 June	61	41			
Warwickshire	Nuneaton	28 June	87	55		1-31	
Glamorgan	Cardiff	8 July	47				1
Essex	Colchester	12 July	14	33			1
Leicestershire	Taunton	15 July	99	110			
Worcestershire	Taunton	26 July	80	18			
Hampshire	Bournemouth	29 July	8	39*	0-0	1-10	1
Warwickshire	Weston-s-Mare	5 Aug	6	24*		1-10	4
Hampshire	Weston-s-Mare	9 Aug	49	21		0-2	3
Northamptonshire	Wellingborough	12 Aug	35	50*	1-25		
Middlesex	Taunton	19 Aug	4	39	0-18		3
Gloucestershire	Bristol	26 Aug	12	28	0-39		2

1979 - in England (for Somerset)

Opposition	Venue	Date	Batting		Bowling		Ct
Surrey	Taunton	16 May	26				
Warwickshire	Edgbaston	30 May	33				
Hampshire	Taunton	2 June	18	41			
Worcestershire	Taunton	27 June	31	48	0-21		2
Yorkshire	Harrogate	30 June	41	116	0-9	0-2	2
Glamorgan	Swansea	7 July	14		0-0	0-8	2
Warwickshire	Taunton	10 July	60		0-8		
Leicestershire	Leicester	14 July	106	26	0-5	2-47	2
Indians	Taunton	28 July	39	8	2-62		1
Hampshire	Southampton	1 Aug	51		0-5		
Lancashire	Old Trafford	4 Aug	36		0-1	0-6	2
Sussex	Weston-s-Mare	11 Aug	65	1	0-1		
Nottinghamshire	Weston-s-Mare	15 Aug	10				
Middlesex	Lord's	18 Aug	156	0	0-28	0-4	
Gloucestershire	Taunton	25 Aug	0	10			
Derbyshire	Taunton	1 Sept	8	89		1-63	2

1979-80 - in Australia (for West Indies)

Opposition	Venue	Date	Batting		Bowling		Ct
South Australia	Adelaide	16 Nov	79				3
Tasmania Invitation XI	Devonport	23 Nov	127		0-1	0-1	1
Australia	Brisbane	1 Dec	140				1
Australia	Melbourne	29 Dec	96				1
Australia	Adelaide	26 Jan	76	74	0-7		1

1979-80 - in West Indies (for Combined Islands)

Opposition	Venue	Date	Batting		Bowling		Ct
Jamaica	Kingston	21 March	1	0	1-17	1-35	1
Guyana	Charlestown	5 April	78	47		3-30	1
Trinidad & Tobago	Kingstown	11 April	36		1-35	0-22	
Barbados	Bridgetown	25 April	0	3	2-71		1

1980 - in England (for Somerset & West Indies)

Opposition (for West Indies)	Venue	Date	Batting		Bowling		Ct
Worcestershire	Worcester	10 May	5	0			3
Leicestershire	Leicster	14 May	4				
Northamptonshire	Milton Keynes	17 May	131	27 *	0-17		1
Derbyshire	Chesterfield	24 May	4				
England	Trent Bridge	5 June	64	48	0-9		4
Sussex	Hove	14 June	55		0-10	0-17	2
England	Lord's	19 June	145		0-24	0-1	
Glamorgan	Swansea	28 June	100				1
Somerset	Taunton	5 July	103				
England	Old Trafford	10 July	65			0-31	1
England	The Oval	24 July	26		0-5	0-15	
Warwickshire	Edgbaston	2 Aug	62	41	0-11	1-37	
England	Headingley	7 Aug	31			0-0	1
(for Somerset)							
Leicestershire	Taunton	16 Aug	75	25	0-28		4
Hampshire	Bournemouth	20 Aug	22	0		3-12	
Gloucestershire	Bristol	23 Aug	170	0	0-24		1
Warwickshire	Taunton	3 Sept	14	0	0-25	0-21	1

1980-81 - in Pakistan (for West Indies)

Opposition	Venue	Date	Batting		Bowling		Ct
Board President's XI	Rawalpindi	5 Nov	18				2
NWFP Governor's XI	Peshawar	9 Nov	8				1
Sind Governor's XI	Sukhur	14 Nov	21	32			
Pakistan	Lahore	24 Nov	75		1-31	2-20	2
Pakistan	Faisalabad	8 Dec	72	67	1-0		4
Pakistan Combined XI	Bahawalpur	15 Dec		0			
Pakistan	Karachi	22 Dec	18			0-10	1
Pakistan	Multan	30 Dec	120 *	12			2

1980-81 - in West Indies (for Combined Islands & West Indies)

Opposition (for Combined Islands)	Venue	Date	Batting		Bowling		Ct
Trinidad & Tobago	Port of Spain	17 Jan	168 *	1	0-0	0-26	

Jamaica	Basseterre	23 Jan	106			0-20	1
Guyana	St George's	7 Feb	14	17	2-4	0-28	1
(for West Indies)							
England	Port of Spain	13 Feb	29			0-16	1-9	1
(for Combined Islands)							
Barbados	Bridgetown	21 Feb	4	13	0-38		
(for West Indies)							
England	Bridgetown	13 March	0	182*		2-24	1
England	St John's	27 March	114			0-26	1-54	1
England	Kingston	10 April	15			0-29	1-48	

1981 - in England (for Somerset)

Opposition	Venue	Date	Batting		Bowling		Ct
Lancashire	Old Trafford	13 May	82	12			1
Australians	Taunton	23 May			0-17		1
Sussex	Hove	3 June	13	22	0-10		1
Middlesex	Lord's	6 June	92	3			
Gloucestershire	Bath	13 June	2	37	0-26	0-53	
Nottinghamshire	Bath	17 June	106		2-31		1
Worcestershire	Worcester	20 June	63	118		1-61	
Glamorgan	Swansea	27 June	2	15*		1-18	
Surrey	Taunton	1 July	4	68			2
Leicestershire	Leicester	4 July	196			0-44	
Sussex	Taunton	11 July	8	26	0-15	0-50	1
Derbyshire	Taunton	18 July	16	130	0-66		1
Glamorgan	Taunton	29 July	17	47*	4-55	2-15	
Yorkshire	Sheffield	1 Aug	8	153			2
Northamptonshire	Weston-s-Mare	8 Aug	1	23		0-23	2
Worcestershire	Weston-s-Mare	12 Aug	150	41			1
Hampshire	Taunton	22 Aug	30	9*	3-21	0-12	
Kent	Folkestone	26 Aug	37		0-7	0-1	1
Essex	Taunton	9 Sept	128			0-16	3
Warwickshire	Taunton	12 Sept		59	0-54		1

1981-82 - in Australia (for West Indies)

Opposition	Venue	Date	Batting		Bowling		Ct
South Australia	Adelaide	13 Nov	1				2
New South Wales	Sydney	27 Nov	44	53*	0-4	1-71	1
Tasmania	Hobart	7 Dec	57				
Queensland	Brisbane	11 Dec	121		0-32	5-88	
Australia	Melbourne	26 Dec	2	0		0-17	1
Australia	Sydney	2 Jan	44	22	0-21	0-33	
Australia	Adelaide	30 Jan	42	50		0-38	

1981-82 - in West Indies (for Leeward Islands)

Opposition	Venue	Date	Batting		Bowling		Ct
Windward Islands	Roseau	4 March	92	1	0-15	1-11	2
Jamaica	Kingston	12 March	73	50	0-29	0-9	4
Barbados	Basseterre	20 March	4	46	0-12	0-2	5
Trinidad & Tobago	St John's	2 April	167		0-19	0-6	1

1982 - in England (for Somerset)

Opposition	Venue	Date	Batting		Bowling		Ct
Worcetsershire	Worcester	19 May	5	1	0-16	3-34	
Kent	Taunton	29 May	146				
Glamorgan	Swansea	2 June	11	9	0-14	3-6	
Essex	Chelmsford	5 June	3	0	0-9		1
Northamptonshire	Northampton	12 June	6*		0-10	0-57	2
Hampshire	Bath	19 June	25		1-28	0-2	
Gloucestershire	Bath	23 June	12		3-26		
Warwickshire	Edgbaston	26 June	135		0-42		2
Pakistanis	Taunton	7 July	181*		0-36	0-12	
Sussex	Hove	10 July	33	69		1-27	
Glamorgan	Taunton	17 July	11	36	1-35		1
Surrey	The Oval	21 July	64	9	0-4		1
Middlesex	Weston-s-Mare	7 Aug	35	0	0-4		
Yorkshire	Weston-s-Mare	11 Aug	36		0-52		
Nottinghamshire	Trent Bridge	14 Aug	29	3	1-25	1-4	
Leicestershire	Taunton	21 Aug	36	0	0-16	0-61	
Gloucestershire	Bristol	28 Aug	58		0-13	2-79	1
Warwickshire	Taunton	1 Sept	26	85	0-41	0-18	
Worcestershire	Taunton	8 Sept	77				1
Lancashire	Taunton	11 Sept	178	5			2

1982-83 - in West Indies (for Leeward Islands & West Indies)

Opposition	Venue	Date	Batting		Bowling		Ct
(for Leeward Islands)							
Barbados	Bridgetown	21 Jan	0	45			2
(for West Indies)							
India	Kingston	23 Feb	29	61	0-0		1
India	Port of Spain	11 March	1			1-16	1
India	Georgetown	31 March	109		0-24		2
India	Bridgetown	15 April	80				2
India	St John's	28 April	2		0-13	0-36	1

1983 - in England (for Somerset)

Opposition	Venue	Date	Batting	Bowling	Ct
Worcestershire	Worcester	11 May	20		

Sussex	Taunton	25 May	2	30	0-32			
Leicestershire	Leicester	9 July	216			2-75	1	
Kent	Maidstone	13 July	32	82	2-28	0-42	2	
Surrey	Taunton	16 July	142 *	76	2-29	3-56	2	
Northamptonshire	Northampton	27 July	117 *		0-23	1-56		
Lancashire	Old Trafford	30 July	37	0	1-41		1	
Northamptonshire	Weston-s-Mare	6 Aug	61	128 *	0-27			
Yorkshire	Weston-s-Mare	10 Aug	25	27 *	0-12	0-4		
Middlesex	Lord's	20 Aug	35	20				
Hampshire	Bournemouth	24 Aug	7	44	1-32	0-5		
Kent	Taunton	7 Sept	103					

1983-84 - in India (for West Indies)

Opposition	Venue	Date	Batting		Bowling		Ct
Central Zone	Jaipur	4 Oct	16				
South Zone	Hyderabad	8 Oct	109		2-25		
North Zone	Amritsar	15 Oct	24	61	0-13	1-37	1
India	Kanpur	21 Oct	24				3
India	Delhi	29 Oct	67	22	0-8		2
India	Ahmedabad	12 Nov	8	20			
West Zone	Kalhapur	19 Nov	11		0-5		1
India	Bombay	24 Nov	120	4			1
India	Calcutta	10 Dec	9				
India	Madras	24 Dec	32				1

1983-84 - in West Indies (for Leeward Islands & West Indies)

Opposition	Venue	Date	Batting		Bowling		Ct
(for Leeward Islands)							
Trinidad & Tobago	St John's	23 Feb	37		1-31	0-27	2
(for West Indies)							
Australia	Georgetown	2 March	8		0-3	0-8	1
Australia	Port of Spain	16 March	76		1-15	2-65	
Australia	Bridgetown	30 March	6				
Australia	St John's	7 April	178		0-7		1
Australia	Kingston	28 April	2			0-4	

1984 - in England (for West Indies)

Opposition	Venue	Date	Batting		Bowling		Ct
Worcestershire	Worcester	19 May	12		0-10		
Glamorgan	Swansea	26 May	170				1
Northamptonshire	Milton Keynes	9 June	41		0-10	0-17	
England	Edgbaston	14 June	117				1
Essex	Chelmsford	23 June	9	60	0-27	0-22	2
England	Lord's	28 June	72				1
Leicestershire	Leicester	7 July	2		2-60	1-27	3

Opposition	Venue	Date	Batting		Bowling		Ct
England	Headingley	12 July	15	22*			
Derbyshire	Derby	21 July	0		0-10		1
England	Old Trafford	26 July	1		0-2		
Nottinghamshire	Trent Bridge	1 Aug	81				
England	The Oval	9 Aug	8	15			3

1984-85 - in Australia (for West Indies)

Opposition	Venue	Date	Batting		Bowling		Ct
Queensland	Brisbane	19 Oct	23		0-3		3
South Australia	Adelaide	26 Oct	80	102	0-23	1-20	
Western Australia	Perth	2 Nov	1		0-26		
Australia	Perth	9 Nov	10			0-4	
New South Wales	Sydney	16 Nov	27	4	0-20	4-18	1
Australia	Brisbane	23 Nov	6	3*		0-1	1
Australia	Adelaide	7 Dec	0	42			1
Tasmania	Devonport	14 Dec	16	11	1-33		1
Australia	Melbourne	22 Dec	208	0	0-9	1-7	1
Australia	Sydney	30 Dec	15	58	0-11		

1984-85 - in West Indies (for West Indies)

Opposition	Venue	Date	Batting		Bowling		Ct
New Zealand	Port of Spain	29 March	57	78	0-7	0-1	
New Zealand	Georgetown	6 April	40	7*	0-22		1
New Zealand	Bridgetown	26 April	105			0-25	1
New Zealand	Kingston	4 March	23			1-34	

1985 - in England (for Somerset)

Opposition	Venue	Date	Batting		Bowling		Ct
Hampshire	Taunton	22 May	0	186	2-55	0-34	
Gloucestershire	Bristol	25 May	26				
Yorkshire	Headingley	29 May	105	53	0-21	0-14	1
Warwickshire	Taunton	1 June	322		1-31		
Gloucestershire	Bath	8 June	27		0-62		
Lancashire	Bath	12 June	65		1-14		
Surrey	The Oval	22 June	5				1
Glamorgan	Cardiff	26 June	100		1-40		
Leicestershire	Taunton	6 July	47		0-17		1
Middlesex	Lord's	13 July	135		1-32	1-34	2
Warwickshire	Edgbaston	24 July	65	53	0-26		1
Essex	Taunton	27 July	5				
Northamptonshire	Weston-s-Mare	10 Aug	58		0-8		
Middlesex	Weston-s-Mare	14 Aug	8				
Lancashire	Old Trafford	24 Aug	120			0-30	
Derbyshire	Derby	28 Aug	123		0-20		
Sussex	Taunton	31 Aug	112				

Worcestershire	Worcester	4 Sept	44	0				2
Worcestershire	Taunton	11 Sept	52	125	0-56			1

1985-86 - in West Indies (for Leeward Islands & West Indies)

Opposition	Venue	Date	Batting		Bowling		Ct
(for Leeward Islands)							
Jamaica	Kingston	16 Jan	2	5	0-24		1
Barbados	Charlestown	24 Jan	16		0-24	0-60	
Trinidad & Tobago	Basseterre	31 Jan	132		3-40	4-80	2
Guyana	Georgetown	12 Feb	32		0-1	0-7	1
(for West Indies)							
England	Kingston	21 Feb	23		0-0		
England	Port of Spain	7 March	34			0-7	
England	Bridgetown	21 March	51		0-9	0-7	
England	Port of Spain	3 April	87				2
England	St John's	11 April	26	110*	0-3	0-3	

1986 - in England (for Somerset)

Opposition	Venue	Date	Batting		Bowling		Ct
Yorkshire	Taunton	26 April	25		0-11		
Derbyshire	Chesterfield	30 April	22		4-36	1-56	1
Glamorgan	Taunton	7 May	102			1-25	4
Gloucestershire	Taunton	21 May	4			0-7	3
Glamorgan	Cardiff	24 May	136	15	0-31	0-23	
Nottinghamshire	Trent Bridge	4 June	6	65	0-40	0-3	
Hampshire	Bournemouth	7 June	9	29	0-25		1
Kent	Bath	14 June	128				
Northamptonshire	Bath	18 June	59	0	2-55		
Kent	Maidstone	2 July	29	31	0-7	0-7	3
Hampshire	Taunton	5 July	12		1-30		
Gloucestershire	Bristol	19 July	35	0	0-17		2
Worcestershire	Weston-s-Mare	2 Aug	36	4	0-41	0-40	1
Warwickshire	Weston-s-Mare	6 Aug	74*	115	0-10	0-6	1
Northamptonshire	Wellingborough	9 Aug	0	43			1
Surrey	Taunton	16 Aug		7	0-30		
Sussex	Tuanton	20 Aug	41				
Essex	Taunton	27 Aug	53	94			2

1986-87 - in Pakistan (for West Indies)

Opposition	Venue	Date	Batting		Bowling		Ct
Balu'stan Governor's XI	Quetta	12 Oct	47				2
President's XI	Rawalpindi	19 Oct	54				
Pakistan	Faisalabad	24 Oct	33	0			
Punjab Governor's XI	Sahiwal	3 Nov	0		0-26		1
Pakistan	Lahore	7 Nov	44			1-9	

Pakistan	Karachi	20 Nov	70	28			1

1986-87 - in New Zealand (for West Indies)

Opposition	Venue	Date	Batting		Bowling		Ct
New Zealand	Wellington	20 Feb	24		1-32	1-86	1
New Zealand	Auckland	27 Feb	14				1
Shell XI	Napier	6 March	117*				
New Zealand	Christchurch	12 March	1	38	0-29		3

1986-87 - in West Indies (for Leeward Islands)

Opposition	Venue	Date	Batting		Bowling	Ct
Jamaica	St John's	18 April	42	16	1-35	

1987-88 - in India (for West Indies)

Opposition	Venue	Date	Batting		Bowling		Ct
Under 25 XI	Chandigarh	20 Nov	138*		1-20		
India	Delhi	25 Nov	9	109*			
India	Bombay	11 Dec	37				3
BCCI President's XI	Visakhatnam	18 Dec	6			1-8	
India	Calcutta	26 Dec	68		1-39		
India	Madras	11 Jan	68	4	1-36	1-28	1

1987-88 - in West Indies (for Leeward Islands & West Indies)

Opposition	Venue	Date	Batting		Bowling		Ct
(for Leeward Islands)							
Guyana	St John's	19 Feb	119			0-2	
Barbados	Bridgetown	26 Feb	70		1-18		2
(for West Indies)							
Pakistan	Port of Spain	14 April	49	123		2-17	4
Pakistan	Bridgetown	22 April	67	39	0-19	1-8	1

1988 - in England (for West Indies)

Opposition	Venue	Date	Batting		Bowling		Ct
Sussex	Hove	7 May	128		0-22		1
Gloucestershire	Bristol	25 May	10	63	0-24	0-7	1
Worcestershire	Worcester	28 May	50		0-33		
England	Trent Bridge	2 June	80		0-2	0-26	
Northamptonshire	Northampton	11 June	39	6			1
England	Lord's	16 June	6	72			2
Kent	Canterbury	25 June	7				
England	Old Trafford	30 June	47				1

Glamorgan	Swansea	13 July	23 *			
Leicestershire	Leicester	16 July	0		1-7	3
England	Headingley	21 July	18			
Nottinghamshire	Trent Bridge	27 July	75	2-1		
England	The Oval	4 Aug	0			

1988-89 - in Australia (for West Indies)

Opposition	Venue	Date	Batting		Bowling		Ct
South Australia	Adelaide	4 Nov	136		0-4	3-78	2
New South Wales	Sydney	11 Nov	101		2-46	0-13	
Australia	Brisbane	18 Nov	68		0-1	0-26	2
Australia	Perth	2 Dec	146	5	0-43		1
Australia	Melbourne	24 Dec	12	63		0-12	
Australia	Sydney	26 Jan	11	4	1-68	1-12	
Australia	Adelaide	3 Feb	69	68 *	0-73	1-64	

1988-89 - in West Indies (for West Indies)

Opposition	Venue	Date	Batting		Bowling		Ct
India	Georgetown	25 March	5		0-17		1
India	Bridgetown	7 April	1				2
India	Port of Spain	15 April	19	0	1-28	0-13	2
India	Kingston	28 April	110		0-36		5

1989-90 - in West Indies (for Leeward Islands & West Indies)

Opposition	Venue	Date	Batting		Bowling		Ct
(for Leeward Islands)							
Barbados	Bridgetown	3 Jan	25 *				
Jamaica	Kingston	9 Feb	16	17	2-74	0-5	1
(for West Indies)							
England	Kingston	24 Feb	21	27	0-22		
England	Bridgetown	5 April	70	12	0-14	0-11	2
England	St John's	12 April	1				2

1990 - in England (for Glamorgan)

Opposition	Venue	Date	Batting		Bowling		Ct
Leicestershire	Cardiff	26 April	3	119		0-9	
Somerset	Cardiff	3 May	16	16	0-22	0-68	1
Gloucestershire	Bristol	15 May	32	1			2
Sussex	Hove	19 May	118 *		2-27	0-14	2
Kent	Swansea	23 May		21	0-34		
Northamptonshire	Northampton	9 June	25	109	0-30		1
Hampshire	Southampton	16 June		164 *	1-32		
Somerset	Bath	20 June		21			

Yorkshire	Cardiff	23 June	38			0-19	
Surrey	Cardiff	30 June	0	14		0-10	
Gloucestershire	Swansea	4 July	41				
Leicestershire	Hinckley	7 July	14	68 *	0-13		1
Worcestershire	Abergavenny	21 July	41	43	0-31		
Warwickshire	Swansea	25 July	11	65 *			
Middlesex	Lord's	4 Aug	80	9	0-22		
Essex	Southend	8 Aug	111	118 *	0-32	2-63	1
Nottinghamshire	Worksop	11 Aug	127				
Derbyshire	Cardiff	29 Aug	0				

1990-91 - in West Indies (for Leeward Islands & West Indies)

Opposition	Venue	Date	Batting		Bowling		Ct
(for Leeward Islands)							
Trinidad & Tobago	Port of Spain	4 Jan	12		0-19	0-13	1
Windward Islands	St George's	11 Jan	73				1
Barbados	St John's	18 Jan	19	7	1-28	1-24	3
Guyana	Georgetown	26 Jan	0		4-55	0-21	1
Jamaica	Bassterre	1 Feb	112	8*	1-24	0-5	
(for West Indies)							
Australia	Kingston	1 March	11	52*			

FIRST-CLASS AVERAGES

SEASON BY SEASON

Batting and Fielding

Year	Country	Mtchs	Inns	NO	Runs	HS	Avge	100	50	Ct
1971-72	West Indies	6	12	0	345	82	28.75	-	3	-
1972-73	West Indies	8	13	0	213	55	16.38	-	2	7
1973-74	West Indies	5	10	1	362	78	40.22	-	3	1
1974	England	23	38	1	1223	107	33.05	2	6	18
1974-75	Ind, SL, Pak & WI	21	35	7	1630	192*	58.21	6	8	21
1975	England	19	34	1	1174	217*	35.57	3	3	29
1975-76	Australia & WI	17	28	3	1690	177	67.60	7	5	16
1976	England	16	25	1	1724	291	71.83	6	7	17 (& 1St)
1976-77	Australia & WI	12	21	0	869	143	41.38	2	5	7
1977	England	20	35	2	2161	241*	65.48	7	9	15
1977-78	West Indies	3	4	0	113	51	28.25	-	1	7
1978	England	21	38	4	1558	118	45.82	2	10	22
1979	England	16	26	0	1043	156	40.11	3	4	14
1979-80	Australia & WI	9	13	0	757	140	58.23	2	5	9
1980	England	17	25	1	1217	170	50.70	5	5	19
1980-81	Pakistan & WI	16	23	3	1106	182*	55.30	5	3	18
1981	England	20	33	3	1718	196	57.26	7	5	17
1981-82	Australia & WI	11	18	1	869	167	51.11	2	6	16
1982	England	20	31	2	1324	181*	45.65	4	5	11
1982-83	West Indies	6	8	0	327	109	40.87	1	2	9
1983	England	12	20	4	1204	216	75.25	4	3	6
1983-84	India & WI	16	20	0	834	178	41.70	3	3	14
1984	England	12	15	1	625	170	44.64	2	3	12
1984-85	Australia & WI	14	23	2	916	208	43.61	3	4	11
1985	England	19	24	0	1836	322	76.50	9	6	9
1985-86	West Indies	9	11	1	518	132	51.80	2	2	6
1986	England	18	28	1	1174	136	43.48	4	5	19
1986-87	Pak, NZ & WI	11	15	1	518	132	51.80	2	2	6
1987-88	India & WI	10	14	2	906	138*	75.50	4	4	12
1988	England	13	16	1	624	128	41.60	1	5	9
1988-89	Australia & WI	11	16	1	818	146	54.53	4	4	15
1989-90	West Indies	5	8	1	199	70	28.42	-	1	5
1990	England	18	28	5	1425	164*	61.95	7	3	8

Bowling

Year	Country	Overs	Mdns	Runs	Wkts	Avge	Best	5wI	10wM
1971-72	West Indies	1	0	9	0	-	-	-	-
1972-73	West Indies	141	23	268	11	24.36	3-49	-	-
1973-74	West Indies	54	10	125	2	62.50	1-0	-	-
1974	England	95	33	273	8	34.12	2-53	-	-
1974-75	Ind, SL, Pak & WI	59	32	217	5	43.40	2-25	-	-

1975	England	132	34	364	11	33.09	2-10	-	-
1975-76	Australia & WI	41.4	7	153	2	76.50	2-42	-	-
1976	England	31	12	56	1	56.00	1-11	-	-
1976-77	Australia & WI	82.3	18	224	4	56.00	2-34	-	-
1977	England	89.5	24	248	7	35.42	3-15	-	-
1977-78	West Indies	27	11	60	2	30.00	2-29	-	-
1978	England	89.5	16	268	8	33.50	2-11	-	-
1979	England	77.3	11	270	5	54.00	2-47	-	-
1979-80	Australia & WI	89	24	219	8	27.37	3-30	-	-
1980	England	98	23	287	4	71.75	3-12	-	-
1980-81	Pakistan & WI	176.3	56	383	11	34.81	2-4	-	-
1981	England	185.5	38	595	13	45.76	4-55	-	-
1981-82	Australia & WI	162.5	36	407	7	58.14	5-88	1	-
1982	England	265.3	75	671	16	41.93	3-6	-	-
1982-83	West Indies	36	9	89	1	89.00	1-16	-	-
1983	England	188	61	462	12	38.50	3-56	-	-
1983-84	India & WI	98.3	25	248	7	35.42	2-25	-	-
1984	England	74	20	185	3	61.66	2-60	-	-
1984-85	Australia & WI	133	33	264	8	33.00	4-18	-	-
1985	England	183	48	494	7	70.57	2-55	-	-
1985-86	West Indies	141	34	265	7	37.85	4-80	-	-
1986	England	161	32	500	9	55.55	4-36	-	-
1986-87	Pak, NZ & WI	90	22	217	4	54.25	1-9	-	-
1987-88	India & WI	91	24	195	9	21.66	2-17	-	-
1988	England	45.4	10	122	3	40.66	2-1	-	-
1988-89	Australia & WI	204.1	25	534	9	59.33	3-78	-	-
1989-90	West Indies	62	18	126	2	63.00	2-74	-	-
1990	England	137	26	426	5	85.20	2-27	-	-

ON TOUR WITH WEST INDIES

Batting and Fielding

Year	Country	Mtchs	Inns	NO	Runs	HS	Avge	100	50	Ct
1974-75	Ind, SL & Pak	17	28	7	1267	192*	60.33	4	6	16
1975-76	Australia	12	21	2	1107	175	58.26	4	4	11
1976	England	16	25	1	1724	291	71.83	6	7	17
										(& 1St)
1979-80	Australia	5	6	0	592	140	98.66	2	4	6
1980	England	13	17	1	911	145	56.93	4	4	13
1980-81	Pakistan	8	11	1	443	120*	44.30	1	3	13
1981-82	Australia	7	11	1	436	121	43.60	1	3	4
1983-84	India	10	14	0	527	120	37.64	2	2	10
1984	England	12	15	1	625	170	44.64	2	3	12
1984-85	Australia	10	17	1	606	208	37.87	2	2	9
1986-87	Pakistan	6	8	0	276	70	34.50	-	2	4
1986-87	New Zealand	4	5	1	194	117*	48.50	1	-	5
1987-88	India	6	8	2	439	138*	73.16	2	2	5
1988	England	13	16	1	624	128	41.60	1	5	9
1988-89	Australia	7	11	1	683	146	68.30	3	4	5

Bowling

Year	Country	Overs	Mdns	Runs	Wkts	Avge	Best	5wI	10wM
1974-75	India, SL & Pak	43	12	115	4	28.75	2-25	-	-
1975-76	Australia	30.4	2	143	2	71.50	2-42	-	-
1976	England	31	12	56	1	56.00	1-11	-	-
1979-80	Australia	5	1	9	0	-	-	-	-
1980	England	68	21	177	1	177.00	1-37	-	-
1980-81	Pakistan	26.2	5	61	4	15.25	2-20	-	-
1981-82	Australia	120.5	28	304	6	50.66	5-88	1	-
1983-84	India	21.3	5	88	3	29.33	2-25	-	-
1984	England	74	20	185	3	61.66	2-60	-	-
1984-85	Australia	94	26	175	7	25.00	4-18	-	-
1986-87	Pakistan	14	3	35	1	35.00	1-9	-	-
1986-87	New Zealand	67	19	147	2	73.50	1-32	-	-
1987-88	India	59	16	131	5	26.20	1-8	-	-
1988	England	45.4	10	122	3	40.66	2-1	-	-
1988-89	Australia	168.1	20	440	8	55.00	3-78	-	-

COUNTRY BY COUNTRY

In West Indies

Batting and Fielding

Year	Team	Mtchs	Inns	NO	Runs	HS	Avge	100	50	Ct
1971-72	Lee / Comb Is	6	12	0	345	82	28.75	-	3	-
1972-73	Lee / Comb Is	8	13	0	213	55	16.38	-	2	7
1973-74	Lee / Comb Is	5	10	1	362	78	40.22	-	3	1
1974-75	Combined Is	4	7	0	363	112	51.85	2	2	5
1975-76	Combined Is & WI	5	7	1	583	177	97.16	3	1	5
1976-77	Combined Is & WI	7	13	0	520	124	40.00	1	3	3
1977-78	Combined Is & WI	3	4	0	113	51	28.25	-	1	7
1979-80	Combined Is	4	7	0	165	78	23.57	-	1	3
1980-81	Combined Is & WI	8	12	2	663	182*	66.30	4	-	5
1981-82	Leeward Is	4	7	0	433	167	61.85	1	3	12
1982-83	Leeward Is & WI	6	8	0	327	109	40.87	1	2	9
1983-84	Leeward Is & WI	6	6	0	307	178	51.66	1	1	4
1984-85	West Indies	4	6	1	310	105	62.00	1	2	2
1985-86	Leeward Is & WI	9	11	1	518	132	51.80	2	2	6
1986-87	Leeward Is	1	2	0	58	42	29.00	-	-	-
1987-88	Leeward Is & WI	4	6	0	467	123	77.83	2	2	7
1988-89	West Indies	4	5	0	135	110	27.00	1	-	10
1989-90	Leeward Is & WI	5	8	1	199	70	28.42	-	1	5

Bowling

Year	Team	Overs	Mdns	Runs	Wkts	Avge	Best	5wI	10wM
1971-72	Lee / Comb Is	1	0	9	0	-	-	-	-
1972-73	Lee / Comb Is	141	23	268	11	24.36	3-49	-	-
1973-74	Lee / Comb Is	54	10	125	2	62.50	1-0	-	-

1974-75	Combined Is	59	20	102	1	102.00	1-14	-	-
1975-76	Combined Is & WI	11	5	10	0	-	-	-	-
1976-77	Combined Is & WI	78.3	18	184	4	46.00	2-34	-	-
1977-78	Combined Is & WI	27	11	60	2	30.00	2-29	-	-
1979-80	Combined Is	84	23	210	8	26.25	3-30	-	-
1980-81	Combined Is & WI	150.1	51	322	7	46.00	2-4	-	-
1981-82	Leeward Is	42	8	103	1	103.00	1-11	-	-
1982-83	Leeward Is & WI	36	9	89	1	89.00	1-34	-	-
1983-84	Leeward Is & WI	77	20	160	4	40.00	2-65	-	-
1984-85	West Indies	39	7	89	1	89.00	1-34	-	-
1985-86	Leeward Is & WI	141	34	265	7	37.85	4-80	-	-
1986-87	Leeward Is	9	0	35	1	35.00	1-35	-	-
1987-88	Leeward Is & WI	32	8	64	4	16.00	2-17	-	-
1988-89	West Indies	36	5	94	1	94.00	1-28	-	-
1989-90	Leeward Is & WI	62	18	126	2	63.00	2-74	-	-

In England

Batting and Fielding

Year	Team	Mtchs	Inns	NO	Runs	HS	Avge	100	50	Ct
1974	Somerset	23	38	1	1223	107	33.05	2	6	18
1975	Somerset	19	34	1	1174	217 *	35.57	3	3	29
1976	West Indies	16	25	1	1724	291	71.83	6	7	17
										(& 1St)
1977	Somerset	20	35	2	2161	241 *	65.48	7	9	15
1978	Somerset	21	38	4	1558	118	45.82	2	10	22
1979	Somerset	16	26	0	1043	156	40.11	3	4	14
1980	Somerset & WI	17	25	1	1217	170	50.70	5	5	19
1981	Somerset	20	33	3	1718	196	57.26	7	5	17
1982	Somerset	20	31	2	1324	181 *	45.65	4	5	11
1983	Somerset	12	20	4	1204	216	75.25	5	3	6
1984	West Indies	12	15	1	625	170	44.64	2	3	12
1985	Somerset	19	24	0	1836	322	76.50	9	6	9
1986	Somerset	18	28	1	1174	136	43.48	4	5	19
1988	West Indies	13	16	1	624	128	41.60	1	5	9
1990	Glamorgan	18	28	5	1425	164 *	61.95	7	3	8

Bowling

Year	Team	Overs	Mdns	Runs	Wkts	Avge	Best	5wI	10wM
1974	Somerset	95	33	273	8	34.12	2-53	-	-
1975	Somerset	132	34	364	11	33.09	2-10	-	-
1976	West Indies	31	12	56	1	56.00	1-11	-	-
1977	Somerset	89.5	24	248	7	35.42	3-15	-	-
1978	Somerset	89.5	16	268	8	33.50	2-11	-	-
1979	Somerset	77.3	11	270	5	54.00	2-47	-	-
1980	Somerset & WI	98	23	287	4	71.75	3-12	-	-
1981	Somerset	185.5	38	595	13	45.76	4-55	-	-
1982	Somerset	265.3	75	671	16	41.93	3-6	-	-
1983	Somerset	188	61	462	12	38.50	3-56	-	-
1984	West Indies	74	20	185	3	61.66	2-60	-	-

1985	Somerset	183	48	494	7	70.57	2-55	-	-
1986	Somerset	161	32	500	9	55.55	4-36	-	-
1988	West Indies	45.4	10	122	3	40.66	2-1	-	-
1990	Glamorgan	137	26	426	5	85.20	2-27	-	-

In Australia

Batting and Fielding

Year	Team	Mtchs	Inns	NO	Runs	HS	Avge	100	50	Ct
1975-76	West Indies	12	21	2	1107	175	58.26	4	4	11
1976-77	Queensland	5	8	0	349	143	43.62	1	2	4
1979-80	West Indies	5	6	0	592	140	98.66	2	4	6
1981-82	West Indies	7	11	1	436	121	43.60	1	3	4
1984-85	West Indies	10	17	1	606	208	37.87	2	2	9
1988-89	West Indies	7	11	1	683	146	68.30	3	4	5

Bowling

Year	Team	Overs	Mdns	Runs	Wkts	Avge	Best	5wI	10wM
1975-76	West Indies	30.4	2	143	2	71.50	2-42	-	-
1976-77	Queensland	4	0	40	0	-	-	-	-
1979-80	West Indies	5	1	9	0	-	-	-	-
1981-82	West Indies	120.5	28	304	6	50.66	5-88	1	-
1984-85	West Indies	94	26	175	7	25.00	4-18	-	-
1988-89	West Indies	168.1	20	440	8	55.00	3-78	-	-

In New Zealand

Batting and Fielding

Year	Team	Mtchs	Inns	NO	Runs	HS	Avge	100	50	Ct
1986-87	West Indies	4	5	1	194	117*	48.50	1	-	5

Bowling

Year	Team	Overs	Mdns	Runs	Wkts	Avge	Best	5wI	10wM
1986-87	West Indies	67	19	147	2	73.50	1-32	-	-

In India

Batting and Fielding

Year	Team	Mtchs	Inns	NO	Runs	HS	Avge	100	50	Ct
1974-75	West Indies	12	20	7	897	192*	69.00	3	4	11
1983-84	West Indies	10	14	0	527	120	37.64	2	2	10
1987-88	West Indies	6	8	2	439	138*	73.16	2	2	5

Bowling

Year	Team	Overs	Mdns	Runs	Wkts	Avge	Best	5wI	10wM
1974-75	West Indies	34	10	98	4	24.50	2-25	-	-
1983-84	West Indies	21.3	5	88	3	29.33	2-25	-	-
1987-88	West Indies	59	16	131	5	26.20	1-8	-	-

In Pakistan

Batting and Fielding

Year	Team	Mtchs	Inns	NO	Runs	HS	Avge	100	50	Ct
1974-75	West Indies	3	5	0	139	79	27.80	-	1	4
1980-81	West Indies	8	11	1	443	120*	44.30	1	3	13
1986-87	West Indies	6	8	0	276	70	34.50	-	2	4

Bowling

Year	Team	Overs	Mdns	Runs	Wkts	Avge	Best	5wI	10wM
1974-75	West Indies	9	2	17	0	-	-	-	-
1980-81	West Indies	26.2	5	61	4	15.25	2-20	-	-
1986-87	West Indies	14	3	35	1	35.00	1-9	-	-

In Sri Lanka

Batting and Fielding

Year	Team	Mtchs	Inns	NO	Runs	HS	Avge	100	50	Ct
1974-75	West Indies	2	3	0	231	151	77.00	1	1	1

Bowling

Year	Team	Overs	Mdns	Runs	Wkts	Avge	Best	5wI	10wM
1974-75	West Indies	-	-	-	-	-	-	-	-

DOMESTIC COMPETITIONS

In West Indies (Shell Shield & Red Stripe Cup)

Batting and Fielding

Year	Team	Mtchs	Inns	NO	Runs	HS	Avge	100	50	Ct
1971-72	Combined Is	4	8	0	217	58	27.12	-	2	-
1972-73	Combined Is	4	8	0	102	52	12.66	-	1	2
1973-74	Combined Is	4	8	1	270	78	38.57	-	2	1
1974-75	Combined Is	4	7	0	363	112	51.85	2	2	5
1976-77	Combined Is	1	2	0	169	124	84.50	1	-	-
1977-78	Combined Is	1	2	0	51	51	25.50	-	1	4
1979-80	Combined Is	4	7	0	165	78	23.57	-	1	3
1980-81	Combined Is	4	7	1	323	168*	53.83	2	-	2
1981-82	Leeward Is	4	7	0	433	167	61.85	1	3	12
1982-83	Leeward Is	1	2	0	45	45	22.50	-	-	2
1983-84	Leeward Is	1	1	0	37	37	37.00	-	-	2
1985-86	Leeward Is	4	5	0	187	132	37.40	1	-	4
1986-87	Leeward Is	1	2	0	58	42	29.00	-	-	-
1987-88	Leeward Is	2	2	0	189	119	94.50	1	1	2
1989-90	Leeward Is	2	3	1	58	25*	29.00	-	-	1
1990-91	Leeward Is	5	7	1	231	112	38.50	1	1	6

Bowling

Year	Team	Overs	Mdns	Runs	Wkts	Avge	Best	5wI	10wM
1971-72	Combined Is	-	-	-	-	-	-	-	-
1972-73	Combined Is	64	18	160	6	26.66	3-49	-	-
1973-74	Combined Is	38	7	85	1	85.00	1-0	-	-
1974-75	Combined Is	59	20	102	1	102.00	1-14	-	-
1976-77	Combined Is	9	2	31	0	-	-	-	-
1977-78	Combined Is	27	11	60	2	30.00	2-29	-	-
1979-80	Combined Is	84	23	210	8	26.25	3-30	-	-
1980-81	Combined Is	50.1	16	116	2	58.00	2-4	-	-
1981-82	Leeward Is	42	8	103	1	103.00	1-11	-	-
1982-83	Leeward Is	-	-	-	-	-	-	-	-
1983-84	Leeward Is	24	7	58	1	58.00	1-31	-	-
1985-86	Leeward Is	121	28	236	7	33.71	4-80	-	-
1986-87	Leeward Is	9	0	35	1	35.00	1-35	-	-
1987-88	Leeward Is	15	4	20	1	20.00	1-18	-	-
1989-90	Leeward Is	34	8	79	2	39.50	2-74	-	-
1990-91	Leeward Is	76.2	23	189	7	27.00	4-55		

In England (County Championship)

Batting and Fielding

Year	Team	Mtchs	Inns	NO	Runs	HS	Avge	100	50	Ct
1974	Somerset	20	34	1	1154	107	34.96	2	6	17
1975	Somerset	16	28	1	1096	217*	40.59	3	3	27
1977	Somerset	19	33	2	2090	241*	67.41	7	8	14
1978	Somerset	21	38	4	1558	118	45.82	2	10	22
1979	Somerset	15	24	0	996	156	41.50	3	4	13
1980	Somerset	4	8	0	306	170	38.25	1	1	6
1981	Somerset	19	33	3	1718	196	57.26	7	5	16
1982	Somerset	19	30	1	1143	178	39.41	3	5	11
1983	Somerset	12	20	4	1204	216	75.25	5	3	6
1985	Somerset	19	24	0	1836	322	76.50	9	6	9
1986	Somerset	18	28	1	1174	136	43.48	4	5	19
1990	Glamorgan	18	28	5	1425	164*	61.95	7	3	8

Bowling

Year	Team	Overs	Mdns	Runs	Wkts	Avge	Best	5wI	10wM
1974	Somerset	70	23	190	5	38.00	2-53	-	-
1975	Somerset	123	32	332	9	36.88	2-10	-	-
1977	Somerset	89.5	24	248	7	35.42	3-15	-	-
1978	Somerset	89.5	16	268	8	33.50	2-11	-	-
1979	Somerset	57	4	208	3	69.33	2-47	-	-
1980	Somerset	30	2	110	3	36.66	3-12	-	-
1981	Somerset	183.5	38	578	13	44.46	4-55	-	-
1982	Somerset	251.3	72	623	16	38.93	3-6	-	-
1983	Somerset	188	61	462	12	38.50	3-56	-	-
1985	Somerset	183	48	494	7	70.57	2-55	-	-
1986	Somerset	161	32	500	9	55.55	4-36	-	-
1990	Glamorgan	137	26	426	5	85.20	2-27	-	-

In Australia (Sheffield Shield)

Batting and Fielding

Year	Team	Mtchs	Inns	NO	Runs	HS	Avge	100	50	Ct
1976-77	Queensland	4	6	0	181	73	30.16	-	2	2

Bowling

Year	Team	Overs	Mdns	Runs	Wkts	Avge	Best	5wI	10wM
1976-77	Queensland	-	-	-	-	-	-	-	-

TOTAL FIRST-CLASS AVERAGES

Batting and Fielding

	Mtchs	Inns	NO	Runs	HS	Avge	100	50	Ct
as at 6.3.91	460	717	52	33327	322	50.11	110	145	419

Bowling

	Balls	Runs	Wkts	Avge	Best	5wI	10wM
as at 6.3.91	22242	9539	217	43.95	5-88	1	-

RUNS SCORED AGAINST INDIVIDUAL TEAMS

In West Indies (for Leeward Islands & Combined Islands)

Against	Runs	Avge
Trinidad & Tobago	813	54.20
Jamaica	661	34.78
Guyana	657	43.80
Barbados	601	27.31
Windward Islands	295	42.14

In England (for Somerset, West Indies & International XI)

Against	Runs	Avge
Warwickshire	1678	69.91
Worcestershire	1415	44.21
Sussex	1384	62.90
Glamorgan	1335	55.62
Gloucestershire	1322	44.00
Hampshire	1318	50.69
Leicestershire	1316	69.26
Yorkshire	1192	62.73
Northamptonshire	1072	44.66
Lancashire	937	52.05
Kent	912	57.00
Surrey	850	47.22
Essex	818	38.95
Middlesex	740	38.94
Nottinghamshire	726	42.70
Derbyshire	438	36.50
Somerset	207	41.40

HUNDREDS IN FIRST-CLASS CRICKET

1974 - in England

102	Somerset v Gloucestershire	Bristol
107	Somerset v Yorkshire	Bath

1974-75 - in India, Pakistan & Sri Lanka

102*	West Indians v West Zone	Puna
103*	West Indians v North Zone	Jullundur
192*	West Indies v India	Delhi
151	West Indians v Sri Lanka XI	Colombo

1974-75 - in West Indies

112	Combined Islands v Guyana	St George's
101	Combined Islands v Jamaica	St John's

1975 - in England

217*	Somerset v Yorkshire	Harrogate
128	Somerset v Gloucestershire	Taunton
122	Somerset v Kent	Folkestone

1975-76 - in Australia

175	West Indians v Western Australia	Perth
160 & 107*	West Indians v Tasmania	Hobart
101	West Indies v Australia	Adelaide

1975-76 - in West Indies

142	West Indies v India	Bridgetown
130	West Indies v India	Port of Spain
177	West Indies v India	Port of Spain

1976 - in England

176	West Indians v Hampshire	Southampton
113	West Indians v MCC	Lord's
232	West Indies v India	Trent Bridge
135	West Indies v England	Old Trafford
121	West Indians v Glamorgan	Swansea
291	West Indies v England	The Oval

1976-77 - in Australia

143	Queensland v Pakistanis	Brisbane

1976-77 - in West Indies

124	Combined Islands v Barbados	Bridgetown

1977 - in England

118	Somerset v Warwickshire	Taunton
241*	Somerset v Gloucestershire	Bristol
104	Somerset v Leicestershire	Leicester
204	Somerset v Sussex	Hove
101	Somerset v Warwickshire	Edgbaston
189	Somerset v Lancashire	Southport
204	Somerset v Surrey	Weston-super-Mare

1978 - in England

118	Somerset v Sussex	Hove
110	Somerset v Leicestershire	Taunton

1979 - in England

116	Somerset v Yorkshire	Harrogate
106	Somerset v Leicestershire	Leicester
156	Somerset v Middlesex	Lord's

1979-80 - in Australia

127	West Indians v Tasmania Invitation XI	Devonport
140	West Indies v Australia	Brisbane

1980 - in England

131	West Indians v Northamptonshire	Milton Keynes
145	West Indies v England	Lord's
160	West Indians v Glamorgan	Swansea
103	West Indians v Somerset	Taunton
170	Somerset v Gloucestershire	Bristol

1980-81 - in Pakistan

120*	West Indies v Pakistan	Multan

1980-81 - in West Indies

168*	Combined Islands v Trinidad & Tobago	Port of Spain
106	Combined Islands v Jamaica	St Kitts
182*	West Indies v England	Bridgetown
114	West Indies v England	St John's

1981 - in England

106	Somerset v Nottinghamshire	Bath
118	Somerset v Worcestershire	Worcester
196	Somerset v Leicestershire	Leicester
130	Somerset v Derbyshire	Taunton
153	Somerset v Yorkshire	Sheffield
150	Somerset v Worcestershire	Weston-super-Mare
128	Somerset v Essex	Taunton

1981-82 - in Australia

121	West Indians v Quaeensland	Brisbane

1981-82 - in West Indies

167	Leeward Islands v Trinidad & Tobago	St John's

1982 - in England

146	Somerset v Kent	Taunton
135	Somerset v Warwickshire	Edgbaston
181*	Somerset v Pakistanis	Taunton
178	Somerset v Lancashire	Taunton

1982-83 - in West Indies

109	West Indies v India	Georgetown

1983 - in England

216	Somerset v Leicestershire	Leicester
142*	Somerset v Surrey	Taunton
117*	Somerset v Northamptonshire	Northampton
128*	Somerset v Northamptonshire	Weston-super-Mare

1983-84 - in India

109	West Indians v South Zone	Hyderabad
120	West Indies v India	Bombay

1983-84 - in West Indies

178	West Indies v Australia	St John's

1984 - in England

170	West Indians v Glamorgan	Swansea
117	West Indies v England	Edgbaston

1984-85 - in Australia

102	West Indians v South Australia	Adelaide
208	West Indies v Australia	Melbourne

1984-85 - in West Indies

105	West Indies v New Zealand	Bridgetown

1985 - in England

186	Somerset v Hampshire	Taunton
105	Somerset v Yorkshire	Headingley
322	Somerset v Warwickshire	Taunton
100	Somerset v Glamorgan	Cardiff
135	Somerset v Middlesex	Lord's
120	Somerset v Lancashire	Old Trafford
123	Somerset v Derbyshire	Derby
112	Somerset v Sussex	Taunton
125	Somerset v Worcestershire	Taunton

1985-86 - in West Indies

132	Leeward Islands v Trinidad & Tobago	Basseterre
110*	West Indies v England	St John's

1986 - in England

102	Somerset v Glamorgan	Taunton
136	Somerset v Glamorgan	Cardiff
128	Somerset v Kent	Bath
115	Somerset v Warwickshire	Weston-super-Mare

1986-87 - in New Zealand

117*	West Indians v Shell XI	Napier

1987-88 - in India

138	West Indians v India Under 25 XI	Chandigarh
109*	West Indies v India	Delhi

1987-88 - in West Indies

119	Leeward Islands v Guyana	St John's
123	West Indies v Paksitan	Port of Spain

1988 - in England

128	West Indians v Sussex	Hove

1988-89 - in Australia

136	West Indians v South Australia	Adelaide
101	West Indians v New South Wales	Sydney
146	West Indies v Australia	Perth

1988-89 - in West Indies

| 110 | West Indies v India | Kingston |

1990 - in England

119	Glamorgan v Leicestershire	Cardiff
118*	Glamorgan v Sussex	Hove
109	Glamorgan v Northamptonshire	Northampton
164*	Glamorgan v Hampshire	Southampton
111 & 118*	Glamorgan v Essex	Southend
127	Glamorgan v Nottinghamshire	Worksop

1990-91 - in West Indies

| 112 | Leeward Islands v Jamaica | Bassterre |

FIRST-CLASS HUNDREDS ANALYSED

For each team

Somerset	47
West Indies (Tests)	24
West Indies (1st-class)	22
Leeward Is / Combined Is	9
Glamorgan	7
Queensland	1

In each country

England	67
West Indies	20
Australia	13
India	7
New Zealand	1
Pakistan	1
Sri Lanka	1

Against Test opposition

England	8
Australia	5
India	8
Pakistan	2
New Zealand	1

Against English counties

Glamorgan	6
Leicestershire	6
Sussex	5
Warwickshire	5
Yorkshire	5
Gloucestershire	4
Kent	4
Northamptonshire	4
Essex	3
Hampshire	3
Lancashire	3
Worcestershire	3
Derbyshire	2
Middlesex	2
Nottinghamshire	2
Surrey	2
Somerset	1

Against W. I. domestic opponents

Jamiaca	3
Trinidad & Tobago	3
Guyana	2
Barbados	1
Windward Islands	-

273

ONE-DAY INTERNATIONALS

MATCH BY MATCH

1975 - in England (World Cup)

Opposition	Venue	Date	Batting	Bowling	Ct
Sri Lanka	Old Trafford	7 June			
Pakistan	Edgbaston	11 June	13	1-21	
Australia	The Oval	14 June	15 *	2-18	
New Zealand	The Oval	18 June	5		
Australia	Lord's	21 June	5		

1975-76 - in Australia

Australia	Adelaide	20 Dec	74	0-10	

1976 - in England

England	Scarborough	26 Aug	119 *		
England	Lord's	28 Aug	97		1
England	Edgbaston	31 Aug	0	1-4	

1976-77 - in West Indies

Pakistan	Berbice	19 March	20		

1977-78 - in West Indies

Australia	St John's	22 Feb	9	0-12	1

1979 - in England (World Cup)

India	Edgbaston	9 June	28 *		
New Zealand	Trent Bridge	16 June	9		1
Pakistan	The Oval	20 June	42	3-52	1
England	Lord's	23 June	138 *	0-35	1

1979-80 - in Australia (World Series Cup)

Australia	Sydney	27 Nov	9	2-47	
Australia	Melbourne	9 Dec	153 *		1
Australia	Sydney	21 Dec	62	1-35	
England	Brisbane	23 Dec	85 *	0-44	
England	Adelaide	16 Jan	88	0-46	
England	Melbourne	20 Jan	23	0-34	
England	Sydney	22 Jan	65	0-19	

1980 - in England

England	Headingley	28 May	7	1-50	1
England	Lord's	30 May	26	0-28	

1980-81 - in Pakistan

Pakistan	Karachi	21 Nov	36	2-24	
Pakistan	Sialkot	5 Dec	83	2-53	
Pakistan	Lahore	19 Dec	0	0-18	

1980-81 - in West Indies

England	Berbice	26 Feb	3	1-26

1981-82 - in Australia (World Series Cup)

Pakistan	Melbourne	21 Nov	17	0-52	
Australia	Sydney	24 Nov	47		
Pakistan	Adelaide	5 Dec	9	1-35	
Pakistan	Perth	19 Dec	8	3-52	1
Australia	Perth	20 Dec	72 *	1-43	
Australia	Melbourne	10 Jan	32	0-31	
Pakistan	Sydney	12 Jan	41	0-41	
Pakistan	Brisbane	16 Jan	0	1-52	
Australia	Brisbane	17 Jan	34	2-36	
Australia	Sydney	19 Jan	64		
Australia	Melbourne	23 Jan	78	1-29	
Australia	Melbourne	24 Jan	60		
Australia	Sydney	26 Jan	4		1
Australia	Sydney	27 Jan	70	2-48	1

1982-83 - in West Indies

India	Port of Spain	9 March	32		
India	Berbice	29 March	64	1-44	
India	St George's	7 April	28		3

1983 - in England (World Cup)

India	Old Trafford	9 June	17	0-13	1
Australia	Headingley	11 June	7		
Zimbabwe	Worcester	13 June	16	0-13	
India	The Oval	15 June	119		
Australia	Lord's	18 June	95 *		
Zimbabwe	Edgbaston	20 June		3-41	2
Pakistan	The Oval	22 June	80 *	0-18	1
India	Lord's	25 June	33	0-8	

1983-84 - in India

India	Srinagar	13 Oct			2
India	Baroda	9 Nov	18		1
India	Indore	1 Dec	49 *		
India	Jamshedpur	7 Dec	149	0-8	
India	Gauhati	17 Dec	23	2-33	

1983-84 - in Australia (World Series Cup)

Australia	Melbourne	8 Jan	53	1-24	
Pakistan	Melbourne	12 Jan	7	0-26	1
Pakistan	Brisbane	14 Jan	37	2-37	1
Australia	Sydney	17 Jan	19	1-41	1
Pakistan	Sydney	19 Jan	2	0-24	
Australia	Melbourne	22 Jan	106	2-51	
Pakistan	Adelaide	28 Jan	18	0-30	1
Australia	Adelaide	29 Jan	0	2-28	
Pakistan	Perth	4 Feb	40	0-24	1
Australia	Perth	5 Feb	7	1-47	
Australia	Sydney	8 Feb		0-29	1
Australia	Melbourne	11 Feb	59	0-26	

1983-84 - in West Indies

Australia	Berbice	29 Feb	4 *	1-38	
Australia	Port of Spain	14 March	67		2
Australia	Kingston	26 April		0-24	

1984 - in England

England	Old Trafford	31 May	189 *	2-45
England	Trent Bridge	2 June	3	0-23
England	Lord's	4 June	84 *	

1984-85 - in Australia (World Series Cup)

Australia	Melbourne	6 Jan	47	0-37	
Sri Lanka	Hobart	10 Jan		2-47	1
Sri Lanka	Brisbane	12 Jan	98	2-45	1
Australia	Brisbane	13 Jan	49	3-38	
Australia	Sydney	15 Jan	103 *	1-41	
Sri Lanka	Sydney	17 Jan	30		
Australia	Melbourne	20 Jan	74	2-43	1
Sri Lanka	Adelaide	26 Jan		0-45	1
Australia	Adelaide	27 Jan	51	0-39	
Sri Lanka	Perth	2 Feb	46	2-47	
Australia	Sydney	6 Feb	68	0-58	1
Australia	Melbourne	10 Feb	9	0-51	1
Australia	Sydney	12 Feb	76	1-52	3

1984-85 - in Australia (World Championship of Cricket)

New Zealand	Sydney	19 Feb			
Sri Lanka	Melbourne	27 Feb	12	3-27	2
Pakistan	Melbourne	6 March	1	0-14	
New Zealand	Sydney	9 March	51		

1984-85 - in West Indies

New Zealand	St John's	20 March	70		1
New Zealand	Port of Spain	27 March	27		1
New Zealand	Berbice	14 April	51	0-23	1
New Zealand	Port of Spain	17 April		1-20	1
New Zealand	Bridgetown	23 April	33 *	0-31	1

1985-86 - in Sharjah (Sharjah Cup)

Pakistan	Sharjah	15 Nov	51	0-25	1
India	Sharjah	22 Nov	24 *		1

1985-86 - in Pakistan

Pakistan	Gujranwala	27 Nov	80 *	0-16	
Pakistan	Lahore	29 Nov	53		
Pakistan	Peshawar	2 Dec	66		
Pakistan	Rawalpindi	4 Dec	21	1-6	1
Pakistan	Karachi	6 Dec	40 *	0-9	

1985-86 - in West Indies

England	Kingston	18 Feb			1
England	Port of Spain	4 March	82		2
England	Bridgetown	19 March	62		1
England	Port of Spain	31 March	50 *		1

1986-87 - in Pakistan

Pakistan	Peshawar	17 Oct	7		
Pakistan	Gujranwala	4 Nov	17		1
Pakistan	Sialkot	14 Nov	0		
Pakistan	Multan	17 Nov	4	0-3	2
Pakistan	Hyderabad	18 Nov	0	1-24	1

1986-87 - in Sharjah

Pakistan	Sharjah	28 Nov	
India	Sharjah	30 Nov	62
Sri Lanka	Sharjah	3 Dec	39

1986-87 - in Australia (Perth Challenge)

Pakistan	Perth	30 Dec	10		2
England	Perth	3 Jan	45	0-5	
Australia	Perth	4 Jan	13		1

1986-87 - in Australia (World Series Cup)

England	Brisbane	17 Jan	0	1-27	
Australia	Melbourne	20 Jan		0-7	
England	Adelaide	24 Jan	43	1-21	
Australia	Adelaide	25 Jan	69		1
Australia	Sydney	28 Jan	70		1
England	Melbourne	30 Jan	58	0-16	
England	Devonport	3 Feb	1		
Australia	Sydney	6 Feb	25	3-29	1

1986-87 - in New Zealand

New Zealand	Dunedin	18 March	119	5-41	
New Zealand	Auckland	21 March	14 *	3-34	
New Zealand	Christchurch	28 March		0-37	

1987-88 - in India & Pakistan (World Cup)

England	Gujranwala	9 Oct	27		
Sri Lanka	Karachi	13 Oct	181	0-22	
Pakistan	Lahore	16 Oct	51	0-10	1
Sri Lanka	Kanpur	21 Oct	14	0-17	
England	Jaipur	26 Oct	51	1-32	
Pakistan	Karachi	30 Oct	67	0-45	1

1987-88 - in India

India	Nagpur	8 Dec	1	1-39	2
India	Gauhati	23 Dec	41	1-37	
India	Calcutta	2 Jan	3	2-48	
India	Rajkot	5 Jan	110 *	3-42	1
India	Ahmedabad	7 Jan	17	1-43	1
India	Faridabad	19 Jan	9	0-31	
India	Gwalior	22 Jan	33	2-34	
India	Trivandrum	25 Jan		2-40	1

1987-88 - in West Indies

Pakistan	Kingston	12 March	15	0-30	1

1988 - in England

England	Edgbaston	19 May	13	0-29	
England	Headingley	21 May	31	0-33	1

England	Lord's	23 May	9		

1988-89 - in Australia (World Series Cup)

Pakistan	Adelaide	10 Dec	1	0-43	2
Australia	Sydney	13 Dec	12	0-46	1
Australia	Melbourne	15 Dec	58	1-55	
Pakistan	Hobart	17 Dec	10	2-48	
Pakistan	Perth	1 Jan		0-21	1
Australia	Melbourne	5 Jan	48	1-29	
Pakistan	Brisbane	7 Jan	18	0-21	2
Australia	Sydney	12 Jan	3	0-6	
Australia	Melbourne	14 Jan	14	0-48	
Australia	Sydney	16 Jan	53		
Australia	Sydney	18 Jan	60 *	1-12	

1988-89 - in West Indies

India	Bridgetown	7 March	40	3-47	3
India	Port of Spain	9 March	11 *	4-45	2
India	Port of Spain	11 March	3	2-47	2
India	St John's	18 March		1-49	1
India	Georgetown	21 March		3-43	

1989-90 - in Sharjah (Champions Trophy)

India	Sharjah	13 Oct	34	2-44	
Pakistan	Sharjah	14 Oct	46	1-48	1
India	Sharjah	16 Oct	5	0-40	1

1989-90 - in India (Nehru Cup)

Sri Lanka	Rajkot	19 Oct	24	1-23	3
Australia	Madras	21 Oct	5	0-36	
India	Delhi	23 Oct	44	6-41	1
Pakistan	Jullundur	25 Oct	47 *	0-38	2
England	Gwalior	27 Oct	16	0-44	
India	Bombay	30 Oct		0-21	3
Pakistan	Calcutta	1 Nov	21	0-42	1

1989-90 - in West Indies

England	Port of Spain	14 Feb	32		
England	Port of Spain	16 Feb			
England	Kingston	3 March	25	0-32	
England	Georgetown	7 March	2		1

1990-91 - in West Indies

Australia	Kingston	26 Feb	18	0-37	
Australia	Port of Spain	9 March	27	0-4	

Australia	Port of Spain	10 March		1
Australia	Bridgetown	13 March	20	0-29
Australia	Georgetown	20 March	10	0-14

ONE-DAY INTERNATIONAL AVERAGES

SERIES BY SERIES

Batting and Fielding

Year	Opposition	Mtchs	Inns	NO	Runs	HS	Avge	100	50	Ct
1975	World Cup	5	4	1	38	15 *	12.66	-	-	-
1975-76	Australia	1	1	0	74	74	74.00	-	1	-
1976	England	3	3	1	216	119 *	108.00	1	1	1
1976-77	Pakistan	1	1	0	20	20	20.00	-	-	-
1977-78	Australia	1	1	0	9	9	9.00	-	-	1
1979	World Cup	4	4	2	217	138 *	108.50	1	-	3
1979-80	World Series Cup	7	7	2	485	153 *	97.00	1	4	1
1980	England	2	2	0	35	26	16.50	-	-	1
1980-81	Pakistan	3	3	0	119	83	39.66	-	1	-
1980-81	England	1	1	0	3	3	3.00	-	-	-
1981-82	World Series Cup	14	14	1	536	78	41.23	-	5	3
1982-83	India	3	3	0	124	64	41.33	-	1	3
1983	World Cup	8	7	2	367	119	73.40	1	2	4
1983-84	India	5	4	1	239	149	79.66	1	-	3
1983-84	World Series Cup	12	11	0	348	106	31.63	1	2	6
1983-84	Australia	3	2	1	71	67	71.00	-	1	2
1984	England	3	3	2	276	189 *	276.00	1	1	-
1984-85	World Series Cup	13	11	1	651	103 *	65.10	1	5	9
1984-85	W. Champ. Cricket	4	3	0	64	51	21.33	-	1	2
1984-85	New Zealand	5	4	1	181	70	60.33	-	2	5
1985-86	Sharjah Cup	2	2	1	75	51	75.00	-	1	2
1985-86	Pakistan	5	5	2	260	80 *	86.66	-	3	1
1985-86	England	4	3	1	194	82	97.00	-	3	5
1986-87	Pakistan	5	5	0	28	17	5.60	-	-	4
1986-87	Champions Trophy	3	2	0	101	62	50.50	-	1	-
1986-87	Perth Challenge	3	3	0	68	45	22.66	-	-	3
1986-87	World Series Cup	8	7	0	266	70	38.00	-	3	3
1986-87	New Zealand	3	2	1	133	119	133.00	1	-	-
1987-88	World Cup	6	6	0	391	181	65.16	1	3	2
1987-88	India	8	7	1	214	110 *	35.66	1	-	5
1987-88	Pakistan	1	1	0	15	15	15.00	-	-	1
1988	England	3	3	0	53	31	17.66	-	-	1
1988-89	World Series Cup	11	10	1	277	60 *	30.77	-	3	6
1988-89	India	5	3	1	54	40	27.00	-	-	8
1989-90	Champions Trophy	3	3	0	85	46	28.33	-	-	2
1989-90	Nehru Cup	7	6	1	157	47 *	31.40	-	-	10
1989-90	England	4	3	0	59	32	19.66	-	-	1
1990-91	Australia	5	4	0	75	27	18.75	-	-	1

Bowling

Year	Opposition	Overs	Mdns	Runs	Wkts	Avge	Best	5wI
1975	World Cup	10	0	39	3	13.00	2-19	-
1975-76	Australia	2	0	10	0	-	-	-
1976	England	1	0	4	1	4.00	1-4	-
1976-77	Pakistan	-	-	-	-	-	-	-
1978-79	Australia	1	0	12	0	-	-	-
1979	World Cup	18	0	87	3	29.00	3-52	-
1979-80	World Series Cup	44	1	225	3	75.00	2-47	-
1980	England	12	0	78	1	78.00	1-50	-
1980-81	Pakistan	19	0	95	4	23.75	2-24	-
1980-81	England	10	0	26	1	26.00	1-26	-
1981-82	World Series Cup	92	3	419	11	38.09	3-52	-
1982-83	India	6	0	44	1	44.00	1-44	-
1983	World Cup	24	2	93	3	31.00	3-41	-
1983-84	India	9	0	41	2	20.50	2-33	-
1983-84	World Series Cup	86	1	387	9	43.00	2-28	-
1983-84	Australia	17	0	62	1	62.00	1-38	-
1984	England	16	1	68	2	34.00	2-45	-
1984-85	World Series Cup	120	3	543	13	41.76	3-38	-
1984-85	W. Champ. Cricket	13	0	41	3	13.66	3-27	-
1984-85	New Zealand	26	5	74	1	74.00	1-20	-
1985-86	Sharjah Cup	6	0	25	0	-	-	-
1985-86	Pakistan	6	0	31	1	31.00	1-6	-
1985-86	England	-	-	-	-	-	-	-
1986-87	Pakistan	10	1	27	1	27.00	1-24	-
1986-87	Champions Trophy	-	-	-	-	-	-	-
1986-87	Perth Challenge	1	0	5	0	-	-	-
1986-87	World Series Cup	28.3	1	100	5	20.00	3-29	-
1986-87	New Zealand	28	0	112	8	14.00	5-41	1
1987-88	World Cup	31	0	126	1	126.00	1-32	-
1987-88	India	69	3	314	12	26.16	3-42	-
1987-88	Pakistan	5	1	30	0	-	-	-
1988	England	15	1	62	0	-	-	-
1988-89	World Series Cup	64	0	329	5	65.80	2-48	-
1988-89	India	50	2	231	13	17.76	4-45	-
1989-90	Champions Trophy	30	0	132	3	44.00	2-44	-
1989-90	Nehru Cup	44.3	0	245	7	35.00	6-41	1
1989-90	England	9	0	32	0	-	-	-
1990-91	Australia	17	0	84	0	-	-	-

AGAINST EACH OPPOSITION

Batting and Fielding

Opposition	Mtchs	Inns	NO	Runs	HS	Avge	100	50	Ct
England	33	31	6	1474	189*	58.96	3	10	10
Australia	54	50	7	2187	153*	50.86	3	20	20
New Zealand	12	9	2	379	119	54.14	1	3	6
India	31	26	5	997	149	47.47	3	2	26
Pakistan	41	39	4	1079	83	30.82	-	8	26
Sri Lanka	11	8	0	444	181	55.50	1	1	8
Zimbabwe	2	1	0	16	16	16.00	-	-	2

Bowling

Opposition	Overs	Mdns	Runs	Wkts	Avge	Best	5wI
England	132.3	4	593	8	74.12	2-45	-
Australia	282	4	1328	32	41.50	3-29	-
New Zealand	54	5	186	9	20.66	5-41	1
India	170.4	4	797	36	22.13	6-41	1
Pakistan	204.5	3	984	20	49.20	3-52	-
Sri Lanka	66	2	273	10	27.30	3-27	-
Zimbabwe	16	2	54	3	18.00	3-41	-

TOTAL ONE-DAY INTERNATIONAL AVERAGES

Batting and Fielding

	Mtchs	Inns	NO	Runs	HS	Avge	100	50	Ct
as at 6.3.91	180	161	23	6381	189*	46.24	11	41	97

Bowling

	Overs	Mdns	Runs	Wkts	Avge	Best	5wI
as at 6.3.91	921	24	4191	117	35.83	6-41	2

DOMESTIC ONE-DAY CRICKET

CAREER RECORD

In England

Batting and Fielding

Competition	Mtchs	Inns	NO	Runs	HS	Avge	100	50	Ct
Gillette Cup /									
NatWest Trophy	34	34	4	1410	139 *	47.00	4	7	16
Benson & Hedges Cup	48	44	6	1499	132 *	39.44	1	10	21
John Player League /									
Refuge Assurance League	158	153	17	5235	126 *	38.49	7	35	70

Bowling

Competition	Balls	Runs	Wkts	Avge	Best	5wI
Gillette Cup /						
NatWest Trophy	967	592	20	29.60	3-15	-
Benson & Hedges Cup	712	425	12	35.41	3-38	-
John Player League /						
Refuge Assurance League	2741	2189	84	26.06	6-24	1

In West Indies

Batting and Fielding

Competition	Mtchs	Inns	NO	Runs	HS	Avge	100	50	Ct
Geddes Grant Trophy	17	15	0	470	77	31.33	-	4	10

Bowling

Competition	Balls	Runs	Wkts	Avge	Best	5wI
Geddes Grant Trophy	630	430	12	35.83	4-18	-

In Australia

Batting and Fielding

Competition	Mtchs	Inns	NO	Runs	HS	Avge	100	50	Ct
Gillette Cup	2	2	0	50	50	25.00	-	1	1

Bowling

Competition	Balls	Runs	Wkts	Avge	Best	5wI
Gillette Cup	-	-	-	-	-	-

HUNDREDS

In England

Gillette Cup

139*	Somerset v Warwickshire	Taunton	1977
116	Somerset v Essex	Taunton	1977
117	Somerset v Northamptonshire	Lord's (final)	1979

NatWest Trophy

118	Glamorgan v Dorset	Swansea	1990

Benson & Hedges Cup

132*	Somerset v Surrey	Lord's (final)	1981

John Player League

108*	Somerset v Nottinghamshire	Trent Bridge	1974
126*	Somerset v Gloucestershire	Bristol	1975
119	Somerset v Warwickshire	Edgbaston	1975
104	Somerset v Derbyshire	Taunton	1977
101	Somerset v Warwickshire	Taunton	1981
117*	Somerset v Nottinghamshire	Trent Bridge	1983

WORLD SERIES CRICKET AVERAGES - 1977-78 & 1978-79

FIVE-DAY MATCHES (not first class)

1977-78 - in Australia (for World XI & West Indies XI)
1978-79 - in Australia (for West Indies XI)
1978-79 - in West Indies (for West Indies XI)

Batting and Fielding

	Mtchs	Inns	NO	Runs	HS	Avge	100	50	Ct
World Series Cricket	14	25	2	1281	177	55.69	4	4	19

Bowling

	Overs	Mdns	Runs	Wkts	Avge	Best	5wI	10wM
World Series Cricket	20	1	40	0	-	-	-	-

HUNDREDS

123	West Indies XI v Australia XI	Adelaide	1977-78
119	World XI v Australia XI	Sydney	1977-78
177	World XI v Australia XI	Perth	1977-78
170	World XI v Australia	Melbourne	1977-78

VIV RICHARDS'S CAREER IN CONTEXT

BATSMEN WITH 100 FIRST-CLASS HUNDREDS

J.B.Hobbs	197
E.H.Hendren	170
W.R.Hammond	167
C.P.Mead	153
G.Boycott	151
H.Sutcliffe	149
F.E.Woolley	145
L.Hutton	129
W.G.Grace	126
D.C.S.Compton	123
T.W.Graveney	122
D.G.Bradman	117
I.V.A.Richards	112
Zaheer Abbas	108
M.C.Cowdrey	107
A.Sandham	107
T.W.Hayward	104
J.H.Edrich	103
G.M.Turner	103
L.E.G.Ames	102
D.L.Amiss	102
E.Tydesley	102

LEADING RUN-SCORES IN TEST CRICKET

	Mtchs	Inss	NO	Runs	HS	Avge	100	50
S.M. Gavaskar	125	214	16	10122	236 *	51.12	34	45
A.R. Border	121	207	37	9013	205	53.01	23	51
G. Boycott	108	193	23	8114	246 *	47.72	22	42
D.I. Gower	114	199	16	8081	215	44.15	18	38
Javed Miandad	109	165	18	8064	280 *	54.85	22	39
I.V.A. Richards	112	168	11	8053	291	51.29	24	39
G.St.A. Sobers	93	160	21	8032	365 *	57.78	26	30

VIV RICHARDS
STATISTICAL HIGHLIGHTS

1952 9th March - born in St John's, Antigua
1972 first-class début for Leeward Islands v Windward Islands at Roseau
      first first-class 50 for Combined Islands v Trinidad & Tobago at Basseterre
1974 first-class début for Somerset v Indians at Taunton, scoring 7
      maiden first-class 100 for Somerset v Gloucestershire at Bristol
      102* in his first innings on tour with the West Indies against North Zone at Pune
      Test début against India at Bangalore, scoring 4 and 3
      192* in his second Test match, v India at Delhi
1975 hit his first 100 in West Indies for Combined Islands v Guyana at St George's
      first doulbe century – 217* for Somerset v Yorkshire at Harrogate
      played in the first World Cup final as West Indies beat Australia
1976 hit 100s in three consecutive Tests v India
      his first Test double century, v England at Trent Bridge – his score of 232 was then his
      highest in first-class cricket
      improved his highest Test & first-class scores with 291 v England at The Oval.
      It was his seventh 100 of 1976 and gave him a new world record aggregate of 1710 Test
      runs in a calendar year
      scored his first 100 in a one-day international v England at Scarborough
      played for Queensland in the Sheffield Shield
1977 improved his highest score for Somerset with 241* v Gloucestershire at Bristol
      2161 runs in 1977 was his best aggregate in an English season
      joined Kerry Packer's World Series Cricket
1979 scored 138* in the World Cup final as West Indies beat England to retain their title. It
      remains the highest score made in a World Cup final
      scored 117 and was Man of the Match in Somerset's Gillette Cup win
1981 hit a century in the first Test to be played in Antigua – 114 v England at St John's
      best first-class bowling figures – 5 for 88 for West Indies v Queensland at Brisbane
1984 made the highest score in one-day international cricket – 189* v England at Old Trafford
1985 appointed West Indies captain on retirement of Clive Lloyd
      scored his highest score in first-class cricket – 322 for Somerset v Warwickshire at
      Taunton. It was also the highest individual score ever made for Somerset
1986 led West Indies to 5-0 success over England
      hit the fastest 100 in a Test match, in terms of balls faced, v England at St John's
      released by Somerset at the end of the 1986 English season
1987 played for Rishton in the Lancashire League
      hit 181 v Sri Lanka at Karachi, the highest score ever made in the World Cup
1988 first West Indian to hit 100 first-class 100s with his 101 v New South Wales at Sydney
      played in his 100th Test match v Australia at Brisbane
1990 scored 119 on his first-class début for Glamorgan v Leicestershire at Cardiff
      hit 100s in both innings of a match in English cricket for the first time – v Essex at
      Southend – and made another 100 in his next innings v Notts at Worksop
1991 became the seventh batsman to score 8000 runs in Test cricket during the first Test v
      Australia at Kingston
      in the same match, he became the leading run-scorer for West Indies, overtaking Sir Gary
      Sobers's aggregate of 8032